CAMBRIDGE SERIES ON HUMAN–COMPUTER INTERACTION 2

Formal Methods in
Human–Computer Interaction

Cambridge Series on Human–Computer Interaction

Managing Editor: Professor J. Long,
Ergonomics Unit, University College, London.

Editorial Board
Dr P. Barnard, Medical Research Council,
Applied Psychology Unit, Cambridge, UK
Professor H. Thimbleby, Department of Computing Science,
University of Stirling, UK
Professor T. Winograd, Department of Computer Science,
Stanford University, USA
Professor W. Buxton, Rank Xerox Ltd, Cambridge EuroPARC, UK
Dr T. Landauer, Bellcore, Morristow, New Jersey, USA
Professor J. Lansdown, CASCAAD, Middlesex Polytechnic, UK
Professor T. W. Malone, MIT, Cambridge, Massachusetts, USA
Dr J. Grudin, MCC, Austin, Texas, USA

Formal Methods in Human–Computer Interaction

Edited by Michael Harrison
University of York
and
Harold Thimbleby
University of Stirling

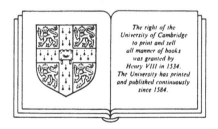

The right of the
University of Cambridge
to print and sell
all manner of books
was granted by
Henry VIII in 1534.
The University has printed
and published continuously
since 1584.

CAMBRIDGE UNIVERSITY PRESS

Cambridge
New York   Port Chester
Melbourne   Sydney

CAMBRIDGE UNIVERSITY PRESS
Cambridge, New York, Melbourne, Madrid, Cape Town, Singapore, São Paulo, Delhi

Cambridge University Press
The Edinburgh Building, Cambridge CB2 8RU, UK

Published in the United States of America by Cambridge University Press, New York

www.cambridge.org
Information on this title: www.cambridge.org/9780521448673

First published 1990
This digitally printed version 2009

A catalogue record for this publication is available from the British Library

ISBN 978-0-521-37202-2 hardback
ISBN 978-0-521-44867-3 paperback

CONTENTS

3   Putting design into practice: formal specification and the user interface   **63**
Roger Took

Bernard Sufrin and Jifeng He

9 Structuring dialogues using CSP   273

Heather Alexander

Bibliography   297

Index   317

PREFACE

This is the first book specifically to relate modern, formal, ideas in Software Engineering to Human Computer Interaction. The book is intended to be read by software engineers, HCI researchers, and postgraduate students working in or with HCI and Software Engineering.

By collecting and representing the state of the art in relevant HCI research, this book addresses the question of how software systems can be designed and built that incorporate a full consideration of the user. Formal design methods should capture the perspective of the user within a software engineering framework.

Our aim is to contribute to both HCI and formal methods by applying one to the other, in particular, by showing how formal methods may be used to model and implement prototypes of interactive systems. The material, then, is of advantage to people working in conventional HCI— we expose them to the power and relevance of formal methods—and conversely, to people working in formal methods—we expose them to the applications and potential in HCI.

Chapters 2 and 3 illustrate the gulf between software engineering and HCI. Subsequent chapters first show how formal modelling techniques may be used to describe interactive behaviour, and discuss how these models may be used to assist the design process (chapters 4, 5 and 6) and then discuss the relationship between models and implementations:

rapidly developed prototypes on the one hand; and system architectures on the other (chapters 7, 8 and 9).

A note on producing this book

This book was produced using LaTeX, a system that enabled us to collate and edit the contributions and work at two distant sites in the UK, exchanging manuscripts and corresponding by email. LaTeX produces very good results when it works; for our purposes, it was better than alternatives—but it would have been *much* better for want of a formal model!

Acknowledgements

The work collected here represents an outgrowth of the activities of the Human Computer Interaction Group at York, both through research carried out there since 1983 and workshops, colloquia and conferences organised by the editors. We are particularly grateful to members of our research groups for providing stimulating working environments— particularly Chris Roast who helped with the diagrams and Chris Johnson who read the penultimate version.

MacDraw and MacWrite are registered trademarks of Claris Corporation. MacIntosh is a registered trademark of Apple Computer Inc. Multiplan is a registered trademark of Microsoft Corporation. UNIX is a registered trademark of AT & T Bell Laboratories.

CONTRIBUTORS

Heather Alexander   British Telecom PLC,
Exchange House,
229, George Street,
Glasgow, G1 1B2,
Scotland.

Gilbert Cockton   Department of Computer Science,
University of Glasgow,
17, Lilybank Gardens,
Glasgow, G12 8QQ,
Scotland.

Alan Dix   Human Computer Interaction Group,
Department of Computer Science,
University of York,
Heslington,
York, YO1 5DD,
England.

Thomas Green   MRC Applied Psychology Unit,
                            15, Chaucer Road,
                            Cambridge, CB2 2EF,
                            England.

Michael Harrison   Human Computer Interaction Group,
                            Department of Computer Science,
                            University of York,
                            Heslington,
                            York, YO1 5DD,
                            England.

Jifeng He   Programming Research Group,
                            Oxford University Computing Laboratory,
                            8–11, Keble Road,
                            Oxford, OX1 3QD,
                            England.

Colin Runciman   Department of Computer Science,
                            University of York,
                            Heslington,
                            York, YO1 5DD,
                            England.

Franz Schiele   GMD-IPSI,
                            Cognitive User Interface Group,
                            Dolivostr. 15,
                            D-6100, Darmstadt,
                            West Germany.

Bernard Sufrin   Programming Research Group,
                            Oxford University Computing Laboratory,
                            8–11, Keble Road,
                            Oxford, OX1 3QD,
                            England.

Harold Thimbleby   Department of Computing Science,
                            University of Stirling,
                            Stirling, FK9 4LA,
                            Scotland.

Roger Took   Human Computer Interaction Group,
Department of Computer Science,
University of York,
Heslington,
York, YO1 5DD,
England.

CHAPTER ONE

THE ROLE OF FORMAL METHODS IN HUMAN-COMPUTER INTERACTION

MICHAEL HARRISON AND HAROLD THIMBLEBY

1.1   Introduction

In many respects Human-Computer Interaction, HCI, is a discipline
that is still in its infancy; its growth to maturity is stunted because it
is the child of the marriage of two rather disparate subjects, psychology
and computing. This book contains a collection of contributions that
have in common the belief that the subject's multidisciplinary nature,
which at the moment polarises and hampers its development, will eventually lead to a rich and significant body of knowledge. Uncertainty
about HCI's parentage, whether psychological or computational, tends
to lead to work which is adopted by one heritage to such an extent that
it is not easily recognised by the other. Such rather biased genealogies
in practice do little to aid understanding of *what* makes an effective
human-computer system and *how* to systematically design, implement,
evaluate, improve and maintain one.

We believe that much of the early work in HCI has been encumbered
by a lack of appropriate abstractness or applicability to the design
process; so research results are too specific to be generally applicable,

or perhaps too abstract to be applicable at all, or relate to aspects of user behaviour without providing information that can be used in design (before the user can use the system). There is a dilemma that design comes 'first' and use 'last,' and the effectivness of a working system depends on many criteria that cannot be anticipated at the early stages of design—for instance, how introduction of a computer system changes a user's error rate, productivity or job satisfaction. On the one hand, such details quickly overwhelm designers and are likely to be ignored; on the other hand, though abstraction promises a way out of this complexity, so far HCI as a discipline has not progressed sufficiently for a designer to know what to abstract and what to represent—nor how to reason about the design in abstract form.

Why *formal methods* in HCI? HCI is a multidisciplinary activity. It is difficult to express the contributions of psychology, sociology, software engineering and so on, in forms that are understood properly and contextually by all parties to the design process. In order to understand the contributions of the different approaches and their proper bearing on design we need to be precise about scope and role. The challenge of formal methods (precise notations and mathematical models) in interactive system design and human computer interaction is to produce a precise framework in which the role and scope of these models may be clearly understood. It is possible for people to make accidental or deliberately outrageous claims that in fact have little substance; indeed, this happens rather too often. It is difficult to assess such claims. Any system is 'easy to use' under the right circumstances (say, when it is used by its designer!)—and other workers interested in achieving the same effects probably do not have the resources to check out the claim *unless* it can be expressed formally.

1.2   Some examples

Formal methods first specify *what* we are talking about and lay down precise rules about *how* one is allowed to reason about those things. Three examples will illustrate these ideas (the last two are also to be found elsewhere in this book). They are intended to demonstrate how formal methods are to be developed to describe different aspects of the HCI problem and demonstrate strengths and weaknesses of current approaches.

Time

Perhaps an extreme example will initially illustrate the idea: suppose we decide to formalise the notion of **response time**. How fast does and how fast should, the computer respond to the user's actions?

A decision to formalise issues of time naturally restricts us; we cannot make claims about noise, or colour, or command syntax being relevant. On the other hand, we gain a whole body of mathematics, for instance we know how to add, average, and perform all sorts of reliable, standard statistical operations on response times. So long as we are happy being restricted to such an abstract level of discussion, and very carefully circumscribe our claims, then our results are quite certain. Furthermore, the formal process can be written down, and communicated precisely (possibly after training) to other workers, designers or evaluators. Anything written as a formal statement can be, and is *intended* to be, criticised.

As a research issue: if we find some factor of response time that is essential for usability (in terms of response times) but which we cannot formalise as a measure of time, then we have discovered something very important that will impinge on the whole programme of formalising HCI and the design of interactive systems. This situation is analogous to the hypothetical discovery in physics that, say, the gravitational attraction of two bodies depends not just on their mass but also on their flavour. It is curious that we can obtain *general* abstract notions such as force in the natural world, but we have, so far, sought vainly for them in HCI.

Competence

As a contrast with the precise framework described in the previous subsection, a formalisation of the **competence** of the user is certainly more difficult to be precise about. We can formalise the notion of task, the actions that the user must carry out in order to complete the task, and perhaps observe that the nature of consistency in understanding the functionality of a system corresponds to regularities in action sequences. So-called Task Action Grammar (TAG, described in Chapter 2) thereby provides a structure for a notion of competence. However it is not clear how such a structure and analysis could be used prescriptively to produce acceptable consistency. Despite these reservations, TAG provides a clarity in the design process that aids an understanding of the concepts involved, and may provide a means for preventing the familiar *ad hoc* accretion of features in interactive systems.

Determinism

A third example of models that bridge the gulf between user and system is discussed in Chapter 4, where it is shown that **determinism** is a phenomenon that occurs at several levels in interaction. A deterministic system may *appear* non-deterministic to a user because the user has incomplete information about how the system works. Formal descriptions of the system to reason about real and apparent non-determinism in the design of the system are relatively easy to formulate, and highlight and inter-relate many interesting issues.

1.3   The scope of formal methods

Formal methods, then, provide a clarity which is much needed in HCI. With some mathematical training, one can enter into *rigorous* debates about design issues. It is not necessary to have a certain sort of system, nor is it necessary to take experimental steps to control for interpersonal variation (differences between users) or subjective opinions.

The main difficulty of formal methods in HCI, which this book starts to address, is the limitation in their scope. If discussion about interactive systems is restricted sufficiently to be able to talk about them formally, then many important features that *may* affect the user are lost. For example, response time can be talked about formally, but this discussion does not include the effect, for instance, of the hourly-rate wages on the user's strategy for delaying the system. This is a fundamental tradeoff: the balance between being precise and being able to be precise about aspects of interaction that are truly significant.

But the effort to develop formal methods is worth making, as may be highlighted by viewing, say, typical high volume commercial software products such as spreadsheets. It is clear that visible features sell systems and that, currently, usability features (or, rather, usability *claims*) are in vogue. This notion of usability is often communicated to a potential buyer by stressing design features and styles such as WYSIWYG, direct manipulation, the use of windows etc. These blanket notions are currently only loosely understood—or, at least, we do understand some aspects of the ideas, but are not yet agreed what the essence of the notions really are or when these notions will produce improvement in usability. Formal methods should cut to the essence.

We should start asking, not what can we formalise, but what is worth formalising? And thereby expose and clarify what the essence of such interactive styles really is. Generally, more precision is required in the description of styles, direct manipulation and so on, and many other features of interactive systems. We need to explain to designers and implementers what they must or could do in order to make their interactive system adequately directly manipulable, or whatever. We also need to understand what makes a certain style (e.g., direct manipulation) applied in a particular system and context, more truly usable. We believe that a more precise understanding of these issues will not only improve future generations of design but will also give precise shape to features of design that may be used to control evaluation of the usability of interactive systems incorporating these styles.

There are many technical approaches to formal methods; the choice of approach is tailored to the design context and the sort of design decisions that are required. Perhaps one of the most exciting aspects of formal methods is that of *insight*: suddenly, precise reasoning is not so much onerous as creative. A formal model may suggest new ways of looking at a system design, new ways of evaluating it, new ways of inventing features and new ways of improving human computer interaction.

1.4   Book structure

This book aims to contribute to HCI by exposing a range of formal methods. We discuss ways of improving our understanding of both the concepts of interaction and the process of design of interactive systems. Hence, formal methods provide a framework within which the concepts of user, system and their interaction may be made precise. Our purpose in providing this framework is to underpin the design and implementation process. A conceptual framework without predictive or evaluative functions and which cannot eventually be transferred to the everyday domains of application design is of no value. Hence this framework should be sufficiently tractable to make it possible to reason about design; and sufficiently pragmatic to guide the design process. Several of the chapters illustrate this point in more detail:

INSIGHT: *the gulf between software engineering and human computer interaction.*

The two initial chapters in this section take two standpoints. Schiele and Green's chapter takes a "psychological engineering" perspective of *consistency* in interactive systems. They are concerned with psychological structures; whether a psychologically valid notion of consistency may be used to analyse or predict the structure of user interfaces for commercial scale interactive systems. Took on the other hand is rooted in the traditions of software engineering. He is concerned principally with functionality and computational issues such as *completeness* and *consistency*. The fact that he is developing an interactive system leads him to propose constraints that are not only *hard* (i.e., based on implementation) but also *soft* (i.e., dependent on more normative concerns). He develops extensions to the notions of completeness and consistency within the Z specification method that encompass intuitive ideas of usefulness or usability. Such notions include *power* or *equippedness* of the interface. Z is particularly interesting because it is a method that has been finding increased industrial acceptance in the UK over the last few years.

Bridging the gulf then involves recognising the software engineering implications of a psychologically derived notion of consistency based in a notation such as Task Action Grammar, and the psychological implications of the soft constraints based on consistency and completeness contained in Took's Chapter 3. These two chapters establish the agenda for the rest of the book.

MODELLING: *interactive behaviour and applications to the design activity.*

The middle chapters of the book develop various models of interactive behaviour that allow designers to reason about the interactive behaviour of the system from the user's point of view. Many representations exist that describe the *user computer system* from different perspectives, but here the authors are concerned with abstract models of interactive behaviour of the system and their relation to the design process. These models may be used by the designer as early descriptions of the emerging design. The three chapters have strong similarities. One of them (Sufrin and He, Chapter 6) describes the trace behaviour of an interactive system using Z. This model is interesting both because it demonstrates the possibility of formulating user-engineering principles within an accepted engineering framework, and because it demonstrates that notations like Z may be used as a basis for reasoning.

The other two chapters use mathematical frameworks to provide models of important issues in the design of *user computer systems*. Dix, Chapter 4, tackles the problem of non-determinism. It notes that different notions are relevant to actual non-determinism in the system and perceived non-determinism in the user. Harrison & Dix, Chapter 5, develops a state-display model of interactive behaviour that is appropriate for the modelling of direct manipulation characteristics of interactive systems.

REFINEMENT: *models to prototypes.*

The later chapters either describe the transition from abstract models to rapidly developed prototypes, or from abstract models to production systems. A model of interactive behaviour provides a designer of interactive systems with an uncluttered description to be used as a framework for discussing design alternatives; furthermore, a mathematical model may also be used as a means of constraining implementation to be consistent with respect to stated design concepts or principles. Such analysis and discussion is useful in helping the designer to reflect on design from a more user-orientated perspective. However, ultimately the final arbiter of a successful design is the user in the context of actual use of the system.

Methods are therefore required to produce executable representations of models that clearly reflect the principles used in design. This part of the book contains three chapters. Runciman and Alexander, Chapters 7 and 9, address directly the problems of rapid prototyping of interactive systems; the Cockton, Chapter 8, considers issues related to the structure of an architecture for interactive systems based on formal models. These chapters point to a number of problems that must be solved before an effective methodology for the rapid development of interactive systems may be derived from models.

1.5   The future

It is tempting to assess the future possibilities of a synthesis of Formal Methods and HCI. With increasing appreciation of the benefits of formal methods in HCI, the two subjects will develop symbiotically. Formal methods will become easier to use and therefore more widely relevant outside the academic community; and HCI will become better, more coherent and easier to apply in the critical early stages of design. We hope that this collection of research contributions will positively support this symbiosis.

CHAPTER TWO

HCI FORMALISMS AND COGNITIVE PSYCHOLOGY: THE CASE OF TASK-ACTION GRAMMAR

FRANZ SCHIELE AND THOMAS GREEN

2.1   Introduction

Formal methods already have a recognised place in software engineering. The arguments for using formal descriptions and specifications in that context are familiar and are frequently rehearsed again for the benefit of apprentices: they bring precision of meaning, and they allow quasi-algebraic techniques of manipulation, verification, etc. Bringing them into the realm of Human-Computer Interaction (HCI) can contribute similar benefits.

However, bringing formal methods into HCI can do more than just extend their domain. When an interface has been formally described, we can potentially apply metrics to that description and *predict* whether the interface will be easy to use. An interface whose description is more complex, according to some criterion, will be harder to use. This formalist approach might well turn out to be helpful in design and evaluation. Particularly appealing is the fact that formal descriptions might *reveal the inner workings* of the systems they describe rather than the surface characteristics, since it is the inner workings that are hardest to evaluate by traditional human factors approaches. But to achieve this ambition, the formal description and the metrics of complexity must be based on psychologically valid principles.

The authors now regard that platform with some scepticism. In the first place, we believe that very few methods for the formal description of interfaces even attempt to describe things from the user's point of view. Second, even where such attempts have been made, we believe they do not possess adequate structural power to describe the user's conceptualisations. This point has been developed in a review of formalisable models of user knowledge [77] where we discuss a number of such methods, including GOMS [33] and 'Cognitive Complexity Theory' [113], and illustrate some of their shortcomings. And third, we now believe that formal methods must either accept sharply-defined boundaries of applicability, or else be replaced by conceptual modelling techniques.

We shall consider in detail the case of Task-Action Grammar (TAG) [149], a formalism which presents a psychologically-grounded analysis of the property of *consistency*. In Green et al. [77] we show that TAG has greater structural power, and is better able than earlier formalisms to describe those properties of the user's conceptualisation which make an interface appear consistent or inconsistent. Because it has greater expressive power, and because this power is based on known phenomena of cognitive psychology, it has succeeded in making correct predictions of performance in some contexts; it has also been the starting-point for some spin-off developments. On the other hand, when applied to real applications programs, we have found ourselves juggling with the constraints of the formalism and being forced to invent ingenious solutions to local difficulties, rather than, as we would ideally have found ourselves, restfully choosing from alternative representations the one that most clearly fitted our intuitions.

This case study illustrates several propositions. On the plus side, formal methods can yield successful performance predictions and reveal flaws in the design of a user interface, as long as they are psychologically-grounded and possess adequate descriptive power. They can also lead to interesting spin-off developments such as described below (see §2.4). On the minus side, formal methods can lead to preoccupation with detail, and in the end they are ineffective unless they are rich enough to become conceptual models of the user.

2.2   The notion of consistency

Consistency has become a very prominent issue in user interface design. There is a general view that consistent interfaces allow users to make generalizations on the basis of their current knowledge thus facilitating the learning process, improving retention, and preventing negative transfer. The increased interest in consistency as a quality of user interfaces (e.g., Reisner [157]; Robert [160]; Polson, Muncher and Engelbeck [155]; Kellogg [112]) may be due to practical concerns: with application programs becoming more widely used and also increasingly powerful, the amount of training required to use them becomes a critical factor. Consistency appears to be a major vehicle for keeping the inherent complexity of functionally rich systems within reasonable limits.

But just which properties of an interface make for its consistency, is less clear. While the term has been referred to (e.g., in design guidelines) as a desirable quality of user interfaces for some time, it was largely used on an intuitive basis, usually illustrated with some examples. Attempts to define it are rare. However, if designers are to be aware of and employ consistency as a means for reducing interface complexity in a methodical way, an intuitive grasp will not do. A more formal and theoretical account of consistency is needed. Moreover, the account must be capable of matching human performance.

We do not intend to present a comprehensive and conclusive definition here of what it means for an interface to be consistent, but rather want to make a few general points which we regard as being central to the notion of consistency—leaving a more detailed account of the concept as it is construed within the TAG framework to a later section.

Consistency is a multi-faceted concept. This becomes evident from the diversity of examples that have been used for illustrating its manifestation in the design of interfaces. It obviously can refer to regularities in various aspects of the interface: the actions the user has to perform in order to achieve his tasks, the feedback the system provides, the spatial layout of the screen, etc. While this suggests that consistency is a quality of the system, it is nonetheless difficult to operationalize it in terms of directly observable and measurable properties of the interface, as is indeed the case with many other usability criteria that have been put forward for interface design.

The important thing about consistency is that users can make use of regularities they perceive in an interface, e.g., to infer new procedures, or, more generally, that they can make valid generalisations from partial knowledge of the system. This points to the fact that, whatever the specific properties of an interface are that make for its consistency, they ultimately do so via *the user's mental representation* of these properties. An obvious corollary of this view is that there may well be some kinds of regularities in an interface (e.g., menu items having the same number of characters) which the user cannot make use of in learning and using the system and which will consequently not contribute to the consistency of the interface and not figure in the users' mental representation of the system. Therefore attempts to capture consistency by comparing sets of interface elements (e.g., commands) with respect to all possible kinds of (ir)regularities without considering how these kinds of regularities might be related to the knowledge the user has to acquire in order to perform his tasks [160, 159], are in our view mistaken.

Our first point, then, is that if consistency is taken to be those properties of an interface which foster the generalization of device-related user knowledge, then any account of consistency should be related to the content and structure of that knowledge, rather than based on mere descriptions of the device itself.[1]

This leads to another important point about the concept of consistency: consistency must be viewed as *relative to a given basis of user knowledge*. This has implications for both the perception of consistency by the user and the measurement of consistency. In the first place, the amount and kind of perceived consistency will often change as the user acquires additional knowledge about a system. Also prior knowledge the user brings to bear upon his learning of the system may well influence what kinds of consistencies he will initially perceive. In the second place, any measure of consistency of an interface only describes the consistency of whatever sub-part of the system is analysed. One might for instance analyse the drawing functions of a graphics program but not take into consideration the file-handling functions, or one might anal-

---

[1] The recent interest in models of user knowledge as potential methods to be used for improving interface design may actually be seen as an explicit acknowledgement that most aspects of usability are not just a quality of the device per se, but rather a consequence of the users' mental representation of the device.

yse a graphics program without analysing the packages for textual and numerical work in use at the same time. While this implicit 'closed world' assumption or rather, 'closed knowledge' assumption of measures of consistency is inevitable if one wants to assess the consistency of (parts of) interfaces, rather than explore the mass of idiosyncratic consistencies that might be conceivable, it should be clear that the individual user's view may not be blinkered in the same way.

A final and more specific point we want to emphasize concerns the role of semantics in identifying consistency: we consider it essential for any analysis or measure of user interface consistency to take into account the *semantics* of the interface aspects analysed.

These have been largely neglected in most formal accounts of consistency presented so far. For instance, Reisner's [157] attempt to measure interface complexity focussed on the identification of common syntactic structures in task-related sequences of user input. Also in Polson and Kieras' [154] definition of consistency which is based on identifying common production rules in the user's how-to-do-it knowledge, semantic knowledge is, if anything, reflected only implicitly in the goals stated in the if-part of rules. However the semantic relationship between the task at hand and the individual actions required to perform it, and, in particular, the alignment of syntactic and semantic structure of task-related user actions is an important determinant of perceived consistency [149].

The failure to consider semantics is even more apparent in Robert's [160, 159] approach to consistency, which is built on a description of the system rather than on a description of the user's knowledge of the system. Clearly, addressing e.g., the number of characters of menu items as an issue of (in)consistency would make sense only, if differences in the length of menu items convey some *meaning* to the user that is of relevance to his use of the system. Likewise, the notion of inconsistencies that "could be desirable to draw the user attention on some special operations" (Robert [160, p. 517]) seems due to a disregard for semantic aspects; if these were taken into account, such cases would not figure as inconsistencies in the first place—for the very reason that they pinpoint a semantic difference ('special operation') and thus prevent undue generalization.

It is the capability of expressing semantic knowledge involved in the

perception of consistency that we regard as one of the major virtues of
the TAG approach, which will be briefly described in the next section.

2.3   Task-Action Grammar to analyse consistency

TAG was developed to describe the consistency of an interface, more
precisely, the consistency of an interface's input language. In this section we shall introduce the type of analysis afforded by TAG.

2.3.1   *An informal account*

TAG is a formalism in which to describe the users' knowledge of how
to perform simple tasks in an application, such as creating a rectangle
in a drawing package. A simple task (see §2.3.3), for present purposes,
is a task that requires no control structure—whether drawing a rectangle qualifies as a simple task depends upon the application program.
TAG is not limited to computer applications, and could also be used
to describe a user's how-to-do-it knowledge of other artefacts, but in
the present chapter we shall draw all our examples from applications
programs.

   We shall start with informal representations of how-to-do-it knowledge. In MacDraw, an applications program for the Apple Macintosh
which forms one of the examples we shall investigate closely in this
chapter, it is possible to draw both rectangles and ellipses. We can
express the user's knowledge in the form of two simple rules, as follows.

> *How to draw a rectangle*: select rectangle tool, place mouse
> at one corner of the desired rectangle, depress button, drag
> to opposite corner, release button.

> *How to draw an ellipse*: select ellipse tool, place mouse at one
> corner of the desired ellipse, depress button, drag to opposite
> corner, release button.

   As it stands, this is not particularly exciting. What TAG adds is a
formalism that will express family resemblance. When several tasks are
similar, in a well-defined sense, and are achieved by actions which are
similar, also in a well-defined sense, the how-to-do-it knowledge can be
expressed by a *schema* which encapsulates several individual rules of
the type above. The schema might read:

> *How to draw things like rectangles and ellipses*: select appro-
> priate tool, place mouse at one corner of the desired shape,
> depress button, drag to opposite corner, release button.

It is the notion of expressing several rules as a single schema that
underlies TAG. This is only possible in the example because rectangles
and ellipses are drawn in essentially the same way in MacDraw. In a
different program (the Sketch package in the Xerox Interlisp-D environment) rectangles are drawn in much the same way as in MacDraw,
but ellipses are drawn in a quite different way, by marking the centre
and two points on the circumference. Because the individual rules for
ellipses and rectangles are so different, they cannot be encapsulated in a
single schema. So a TAG for Sketch would need two different schemas,
one for rectangles and one for ellipses, and indeed there would be no
difference between expressing the user's knowledge in terms of schemas
and expressing it in terms of individual how-to-do-it rules. There is
a strong claim implicit in that fact: any regularities that Sketch may
in fact possess with respect to these tasks is not helpful to the user,
however experienced. (Sketch might exhibit some forms of regularities;
for example, every task might demand the same number of actions,
although the actions themselves were different. This form of regularity
could not be expressed in TAG. To the degree that there exist forms
of regularities that are helpful to users but which cannot be expressed
in TAG, the formalism is imperfect.)

In the MacDraw case, where only a single schema was needed, the
actions for drawing an ellipse could easily be generated from a knowledge of how to draw a rectangle, but in the Sketch program knowing
how to do one task will not help greatly with finding out how to do the
other. The intention of TAG is that the *number of schemas* should give
an indication of the consistency or the quirkiness of the interface language. We earlier interpreted consistency in terms of using perceived
regularities to infer new procedures, and TAG's claim is that the fewer
the schemas, the more likely it is that the user can generalise from
partial knowledge.

It is vital, however, that the grammar that is constructed should
model the tasks as the user sees them, not as the designer finds it
convenient to see them. We can illustrate that by extending our example to deal with squares and circles. The MacDraw program treats
squares as special cases of rectangles and circles as special cases of el-

lipses; moreover, both special cases are handled the same way by the program:

> *How to draw a square*: select rectangle tool, hold the SHIFT key down and proceed as though drawing a rectangle.

> *How to draw a circle*: select ellipse tool, hold the SHIFT key down and proceed as though drawing an ellipse.

This leads to a simple schema:

> *How to draw special cases of things*: select appropriate tool, hold the SHIFT key down and proceed as usual.

This is all very well, but is it reasonable to suppose that users perceive circles as special cases of ellipses? We have no direct data, but we believe that many children become familiar at an early stage with squares, rectangles, and circles, all of which are quite easy to construct by standard geometric means using ruler, setsquare, and compass. Ellipses are different, since they need special drawing apparatus; if anything, an ellipse is seen as a special case of a circle. Thus the MacDraw design would not be immediately comprehensible to children until they had altered their mental representation of the structure of the four tasks.

2.3.2   *A formalisable account*

A truly formal model is accompanied by the proper and rigorous apparatus of set theory, algebra, or whatever is appropriate. The account we shall present is not truly formal, but is sufficiently developed to be capable of rigorous presentation.

TAG uses a grammatical notation to model the relationships between the tasks, as seen by the user, and the actions required to accomplish those tasks. Tasks are regarded as concepts defined by *features*, more accurately, by 'semantic components', which are the values of particular features. Continuing to use MacDraw as our example, typical features and their possible values include:

```
Effect:          add, remove, move
Type of object: rectangle, ellipse,
                 line, freehand-shape
Constraint:      yes, no
```

Thus the task 'draw a square' (conceptualised as a special or constrained case of a rectangle) is defined by the semantic components:

```
Effect           = add
Type of object = rectangle
Constraint       = yes
```

Every task is defined by a distinct set of semantic components. The reverse is not always true: some combinations of semantic components may in practice be semantically meaningless, e.g., `Type of object = freehand-shape` and `Constraint = yes`. The 'current task' is the task the user wishes to perform at a given moment.

The actions to perform tasks are described by means of a 'feature grammar', a conventional rewriting system in which non-terminal symbols may be associated with particular semantic components. A rewriting rule for a non-terminal symbol may be applied only if the features associated with that symbol match the features of the current task. For drawing a square, the features are those just listed above:

```
Draw a square:
task [Effect = add,
      Type of object = rectangle,
      Constraint = yes
     ] := select-tool [Type of object = rectangle]
            + press SHIFT + place mouse ...
```

This rule will be invoked when and only when the current task is to draw a square. The rule invokes a sub-rule, `select-tool`, which is not stated here but which can be assumed to describe the actions of choosing the appropriate drawing tool, and calls for a direct action, `press SHIFT`, which in turn is followed by further direct actions to mark the location and size of the desired square. The hierarchical composition of rules and sub-rules corresponds to the hierarchical composition of methods and sub-methods in GOMS and similar systems.

Potentially we also represent the rule for drawing a rectangle in a very similar way:

```
Draw a rectangle:
task [Effect = add, Type of object = rectangle,
      Constraint = no
```

```
] := select-tool [Type of object = rectangle]
    + place mouse ...
```

We can now generalise these two rules to a single rule-schema that
will handle both cases by introducing a sub-rule **draw**:

Draw a rectangle or square:
```
task [Effect = add, Type of object = rectangle,
    Constraint = any
    ] := select-tool [Type of object = rectangle]
        + draw [Constraint]
draw [Constraint = yes] := press SHIFT +
                              place mouse ...
draw [Constraint = no] := place mouse ...
```

Note that when this task rule is invoked, the feature `Constraint`,
which is unbound on the left-hand side, is given the value of that feature
in the current task so that it can be transmitted to the right-hand side,
where it is used to determine which version of the two **draw** rules shall
be performed.

The rule schema can be further generalised within the existing notational framework. As we saw above, drawing ellipses and circles in
MacDraw is very similar to drawing rectangles and squares. This consistency will be readily apparent to most users, or so it is presumed;
this statement is readily testable, since it predicts that most users, once
shown how to draw a rectangle and a square, will be able to generalise
to drawing ellipses and circles, as long as they conceptualise a circle as
a special case of an ellipse. TAG describes this consistency by allowing
a single generalised rule which draws many kinds of graphic objects:

Draw a graphic object:
```
task [Effect = add, Type of object = any,
    Constraint = any
    ] := select-tool[Type of object] +
        draw [Constraint]
```

In this manner, a single expression becomes a generalised statement
applying to several types of action sequence.

Rules may not be context-sensitive in any other way than through
the use of the features. The number of distinct features must be finite

and the number of distinct values of each feature must also be finite; these restrictions ensure that for each TAG there is a weakly equivalent context-free phrase-structure grammar, constructed by replacing the unbound features of rules with each of their possible feature values in all possible ways.

It is useful to extend the formalism in several ways which seem innocuous. The rule schemas for MacDraw include boolean combinations of feature values; e.g., Rule T1 (see Appendix, §2.9) has the feature value `Object-class = NOT-text` (read as "any object-class except text"), and Rule T3 invokes the sub-rule `edit-text` with the feature `Unit = char/word` (read as "character or word"). Some less innocuous extensions will be described below.

2.3.3   *TAG as a psychological theory*

The most important aspects of TAG are its fundamental construct, the simple task, and its use of feature-tagged rule-schemas. It is important to relate these to existing cognitive science.

The notion of simple tasks describes the grain size of the task analysis underlying TAG representations. Simple tasks are tasks without internal control structure, for which distinct action sequences have to be learned, and which roughly correspond, at least for the novice, to the application of individual functions or commands in a given system. They can be seen as system-specific operators (in the 'internal' task space defined by the functionality of a system) onto which the user has to break down whatever complex higher-level tasks he or she wants to perform. Thus, while experienced users may soon develop routines comprising several simple tasks, at least in the initial learning phase they will have to acquire a knowledge of these basic tasks afforded by the system. Choosing simple tasks as the unit of analysis seems particularly appropriate in view of TAG's concern with learnability and consistency of user interfaces. Also by focussing on such 'internal' tasks, the problem of sampling the open-ended 'external' task space, which arises if higher-level tasks are analysed, is circumvented.

TAG treats simple tasks as concepts defined by values of features. This is a classical view in cognitive psychology (Bruner, Goodnow and Austin [29]). More recent views have espoused schematic prototypes (Rosch and Mervis [161]) and networks of exemplars (Medin and Schaffer [122]); the present literature (Smith and Medin [176]) suggests that no single view of the structure of concept representations is correct, but that it is extremely rich and that its apparent structure is greatly influenced by various factors such as pragmatics, task or problem characteristics, and by properties of the concept domain itself. While, for instance, in the domain of natural objects the classical feature approach faces problems because it cannot cope with phenomena such as typicality effects, it is more successful with well-defined artificial concepts. We would argue that simple tasks come close to the latter. Typicality, for example, is not an issue with simple task concepts such as 'delete a word'. Likewise, many of the other criticisms brought forward against the classical view do not apply to the domain of simple tasks. Thus while TAG's view is certainly an over-simplification, and its effectiveness might be limited in some contexts, it seems a reasonable view given the domain it deals with.

The use of semantic features in syntactic rules is a departure from conventional practice in the computer science literature, where formal languages are usually defined by unadorned BNF or some closely related notation. In linguistics, however, there has been much interest both in developing the notion of feature sets (e.g., Gazdar, Klein, Pullum and Sag [72]) and in bringing semantics and syntax into closer correspondence. Particularly relevant is the use of semantic devices to filter the applicability of rules in grammars which otherwise would generate large numbers of anomalous sentences (see Winograd [209], for a brief review of some developments). Thus TAG presents no claims that exceed the power of mechanisms proposed for the handling of English. The status of linguistic theories of grammar as models of human performance is very unclear, but what TAG proposes is a model of knowledge rather than a model of performance. What becomes evident from comparing TAG to linguistic grammar theories is that people's knowledge about the structure of natural language is much more complex than what is being proposed by TAG as the users' knowledge about the structure of artificial languages for using a system. Thus the claims do not seem excessive, more likely, over-modest.

2.3.4   *TAG as a predictive tool*

To some degree TAG is sufficiently motivated merely by the goal of making explicit that which was implicit, namely, the user-perceptible family resemblances within the interface language. But the real goal of

TAG is predictive. The predictive power rests, obviously, on the fidelity of the formalisms' representation of user knowledge: the TAG formalism, like other formalisms claiming psychological validity, is bound to be a drastic over-simplification, but we claim that it is less over-simple than current alternatives.

A number of metrics can be defined over the grammars created by TAG analysis, but the only metric that has received any empirical investigation is the simplest, the number of rule schemas, which has been shown to have some power in predicting ease of learning a system. We do not suggest that this metric should be used to predict absolute learnability, because interfaces to application programs differ in many ways that affect learnability, which do not come within the purview of TAG (e.g., the kind of feedback provided by the system). As mentioned above, TAG is concerned only with some aspects of learnability, albeit important ones: the complexity, and in particular, the consistency of input languages. We therefore suggest that the use of TAG as a predictive tool should be restricted to comparing alternative designs that differ in their interface language but which are otherwise relatively similar.

Another constraint on the use of TAG, or, in fact, of any other HCI formalisms that have been presented as predictive tools, lies in the extent to which they lend themselves to provide predictive measures for learning and using whole systems, rather than fragments. Formal methods are laborious to use, and to give complete representations of reasonably powerful systems is beyond the resources most people would be prepared to commit. The full scale use of formal methods demands tools to assist their efficient application, and, as for TAG, there are none available yet (but see §2.4.1). On the other hand, the TAG formalism affords comparatively concise and compact representations of substantial parts of interface languages (see below).

Besides the general aspect of formal methods being hard to use, it is doubtful whether TAG representations of complete systems, even if they were possible, would serve a useful purpose: comparative evaluations are more difficult to make the more comprehensive and varied the things to be compared. Since hardly any two systems will be equivalent with respect to the overall functionality offered, there will almost certainly arise questions of trade-off between the cognitive complexity of an interface and its functionality.[2] These, however, cannot be answered by formal models of user knowledge.

Thus, whether the focus is on evaluating extant systems or on supporting design decisions, the prime use of TAG should be for analysing design alternatives for *parts* of interfaces where the functionality (or the 'internal' task space) is at least roughly equivalent but where there is a choice as to the details of the pertinent interface language. In these terms, TAG has shown that it can predict the results of a number of laboratory studies more successfully than other formalisms [147, 150]. Further investigations by Cramer [48] sound a cautionary note, though, since some of the consistency effects previously reported appear to be weaker than had been believed.

TAG has limited aspirations. It only attempts to display the expert user's how-to-do-it knowledge, hoping thereby to reveal something about the cognitive demands of the interface language. To avoid misconception, let's also look at what TAG does not do. First, it does not describe the cognitive or motor processes by which tasks are accomplished. This is why TAG does not make quantitative predictions about the time to learn or perform given tasks. Second, it does not describe the processes of planning complex action sequences. It has no representation of preconditions, for instance. The simple tasks TAG focusses on are assumed to require no planning effort. Third, it does not describe the interpretation side of the action cycle.[3] And fourth, it does not sufficiently describe the conceptual entities in the user's mind. For instance, there is no adequate description of the user's mental representation of the system.

To summarise, TAG describes neither the full range of knowledge and external information involved in task performance nor the processes by which these are put to use. What it does describe is some aspects of user knowledge which appear to be particularly relevant in determining the perceived consistency, and thus the learnability of a system's interface language.

---

[2] Trade-off between functionality and consistency is illustrated in our example by the difference between Sketch and MacDraw: MacDraw is more consistent than Sketch partly because MacDraw's ellipses must always have horizontal axes (a reduction in functionality), whereas Sketch can cope with any orientation.
[3] Norman [139] gives a good account of the need to include what he calls 'the gulf of evaluation': perceiving, interpreting, and evaluating the system's response, the result of one's actions.

2.4   Related research using rule-schemas

A number of previous attempts have been made to represent the users'
knowledge of the interface language, among them the grammar-based
model of Reisner [157] and the production-system model of Kieras &
Polson [113] which, in its turn, was based on the GOMS formalism.
Green et al. [77] review these representations, comparing the roles of
performance models (such as GOMS) and competence models (such as
TAG). One of their major criticisms of earlier work, such as GOMS, is
that it lacks explanatory adequacy, because it contains no representation of the family resemblances that are the foundation of consistency
as perceived by the user.

Family resemblances are, of course, modelled by TAG as rule-schemas.
In this section we shall briefly report recent developments which make
use of the TAG idea of rule schemas to address other issues beyond
the original topic of consistency of interface languages. In the following
section we shall return to issues of consistency.

2.4.1   *An executable Task-Action Grammar*

Green has developed an interpreter written in Prolog that accepts a
version of TAG. Given a task, characterised by its features, it uses
the grammar rules to discover how to perform the task, if that is possible. The interpreter not only handles the basic formalism described
above, but also some convenient extensions, such as tasks defined by
the absence of particular feature values ('How to create anything except text: . . . '). The interpreter also provides for a limited number of
mental functions, such as 'Look up a word whose lexical entry includes
the following features: . . . ' and 'Take the first letter of the given word'.
By this means, the method given by Payne and Green [149] for representing simple mnemonics, such as H for Hot or B for Backwards, can
be handled in the interpreter.

The value of executable specifications to designers is, of course, well
known, since they provide a method to develop a prototype directly
from the requirements rather than by translating those requirements
into another formalism first. The value of executable representations
of user knowledge is rather less immediate. It seems unlikely that an
interface would be designed in that way.

The real advantage of executable TAGs is that, once the grammar is

in machine-readable form and its correctness has been verified by exploration, various analytic techniques can be applied to it. One of the
most intriguing possibilities is that the effects of users' slips of action
can be explored. Slips were characterised by Norman [138] into description errors, capture errors, mode errors, etc; several of these classes can
be analysed in this system. For instance, it is easy to compute the
space of off-by-one errors, in which the user proceeds as though one
feature had a different value. This class, which corresponds to Norman's description errors, gives rise to some unexpected behaviours in
daily life, such as filling the washing machine with porridge oats instead
of washing powder. At the present moment, however, there has been
no attempt to compare the pattern of slips which can be obtained from
static analysis of a TAG with a corpus of actual slips recorded from
practised users of a system.

2.4.2   *Recognition of users' plans*

The development of active help systems (Fischer, Lemke and Schwab
[68]) has shown the potential value of understanding users' intentions.
An active help system is one which volunteers useful information, to
help users find more efficient ways to work: if a user starts to delete a
long passage by repeatedly pressing the Delete key to rub out a single
character each time, the system might after a while suggest that alternative means exist. Active help systems are highly desirable, but only
if they make more-or-less correct guesses about what the user really
wants to do; which requires understanding users' plans.

Hoppe [98] extended the ideas of TAG by creating a 'Task-Oriented
Parser' (TOP) based on attribute grammars (which could then be expressed in Prolog). Like TAG, TOP defines action sequences to accomplish simple tasks, and uses a feature-based grammar for this purpose;
but TOP introduces a representation of task composition allowing the
elementary unit, the 'simple task', to be built up into more complex
tasks, and also a symbolic representation of the system state. Using this
richer representation Hoppe was able to demonstrate that sequences of
user actions could successfully be 'parsed' with respect to the TOP
grammar, so that the program could infer what plan the user was following. When the parsing process could not be continued or the user
requested help, it was possible to offer guidance based on what the
program thought the user was trying to do.

While formal models of user knowledge in HCI are typically thought of as analytical tools that could help in the evaluation of interface usability, Hoppe's research illustrates another area of application: such models could also serve to represent task-related knowledge in knowledge based user interfaces.

2.4.3   *Inclusion of system responses*

The original conception of TAG, as a representation of users how-to-do-it knowledge, has proved somewhat limiting. It is clear that users of modern interfaces rely extensively on system prompts and indicators, and that a more truthful description of their how-to-do-it knowledge might be on the lines of "If I do such-and-such, I'll get a prompt telling me what to do next", rather than a complete account of the action sequence required.

Some developments have taken place on these lines. Howes and Payne [99] have applied TAG to the problem of understanding users' interactions with systems where tasks can be achieved in many ways and starting from many points. Menu-based systems often have this property, since users can perform in 'multi-tasking' ways, pursuing several goals in an interleaved fashion. For this purpose they have extended TAG to include a representation of the system state as indicated by the visual display or other means of feedback. Thus the task rule for pasting a string may only be invoked if the feature "The Clipboard contains the desired string" is true. System states, including the state of the displayed information, are thereby treated as features on the same footing as the semantic features defining the task space. It is too soon to anticipate how this line of enquiry will work out.

2.4.4   *Formalising the underlying semantics*

The tasks, as represented in TAG, are expressed in a 'language' that is intuitively reasonable but has no firm foundation. Tauber [189] has attempted to find a more rigorous representation, adopting an analysis of conceptual structure proposed by Jackendoff [103] to create a new system called Extended Task-Action Grammar (ETAG).

Jackendoff argues that the 'basic spatial ontological category' is the concept THING or OBJECT; other ontological categories, such as EVENT, PLACE, and PATH, are based on OBJECTS and their PROPERTIES. Tauber's work has been to express the idea of a 'user's virtual machine' in terms of Jackendoff's semantics, to create a moderately formal conceptual language in which to represent the user's model of the system. For instance, the user's model of the event "a string is moved to the clipboard" is an EVENT that may be expressed in terms of OBJECTS, PLACES, and PATHS. All the entities and operations of the virtual machine may be expressed in this way.

In Tauber's ETAG, task rules, at the level used by TAG, must be expressed as manipulations on the user's virtual machine. Thus no untoward happenings may be smuggled in. The paper cited gives a representation of part of the MacWrite 'machine' in terms of Jackendoff semantics, followed by examples of some typical task rules.

The choice of Jackendoff semantics was motivated partly by psychological considerations, but no empirical work on ETAG has been reported yet.

2.5   Applying TAG to life-size examples

The task languages that have been analyzed in earlier work on TAG were largely toy systems or small subsets of extant systems. While these served well to test the basic assumptions of the model and to demonstrate the mechanism of the formalism, any cognitive modelling technique, in order to be useful in the design, analysis, or evaluation of real systems, must be capable of representing coherently a substantial part of the user's knowledge.

To illustrate TAG's capability of doing so, we will give a revised version of a spreadsheet analysis (first presented in Green et al. [77]) and also analyze two other types of application in this section. At the same time, these representations will serve to show how TAG may be used for capturing consistencies across different application programs (see §2.6).

The task of accounting for three different life-size application programs is a considerable challenge to any formalism, and in this case it proved necessary to extend the formalism somewhat. We will therefore present a brief account of the results of applying TAG to the three programs in question: Claris's MacWrite word processor; Microsoft's Multiplan spreadsheet for the Macintosh; Claris's MacDraw graphics program.

The appendix contains TAG representations of these application programs for different domains. They express users' mental representations of the systems' task languages for sets of core tasks in each system. These core tasks are create, delete, replace, copy, and move. Some of these tasks may involve the use of the Macintosh clipboard, a buffer for temporary storage during operations such as cut-and-paste.

It is not necessary to discuss each of these grammars in detail. In the first grammar, which describes MacWrite, the core tasks are applied to the entities char (character) and word, since these are the only entities known by MacWrite. To simplify the grammar we have introduced a *co-occurrence restriction* that if the value of the feature Effect is copy, the value of the feature Clipboard must be yes. The force of this restriction is felt in task rule T3, where the rule will operate with any value for Clipboard but would subsume a semantically meaningless task if the restriction were removed. The raised index R in the expression any^R signifies that the restriction must not be overlooked. If the co-occurrence mechanism were not used, a separate rule would be required for the task of copying text in order to rule out the meaningless combination of Effect = copy, Clipboard= no.

Another addition to the notation in this grammar is the use of *imported variables*, %location, %unit, and %char, distinguished by a percent sign. These variables can be regarded as arguments, denoting quantities that the user brings to the action sequence, such as, in the case of task 1 ('insert new text') the actual text to be inserted. There are no other innovations.

The grammar specifies three task rules and seven subtask rules which allow a mapping from tasks listed in the 'dictionary of simple tasks' onto their pertinent action sequences.[4]

The subtask rules deal with two types of subtasks which frequently occur in using MacWrite, selection and editing. As can be seen, the overall structure of MacWrite is very simple.

The Multiplan spreadsheet program features a more complex task domain than the MacWrite text editor. Apart from basic text editing facilities for creating and manipulating cell-entries or parts thereof, such as characters and words, Multiplan provides a range of functions to manipulate the typical structural units of a spreadsheet document, i.e., cells, rows and columns.

---

[4] In fact, there are quite a few more tasks that are covered by these rules (e.g., 'remove a string to clipboard'), but which have not been listed due to space restrictions.

As compared to MacWrite, the Multiplan representation contains one further feature co-occurrence restriction, which expresses the fact that cells, rows, and columns can be replaced only by pasting from the clipboard (as opposed to text which can also be replaced by over-typing). This restriction was necessary in order to be able to subsume these tasks under rule schema T3, and thus to capture their similarity to the simple tasks T7, T8, and T9.

Task rules T1 and T2 show a deviation from the general mechanism of uniform replacement of feature values throughout a rule: the values of the features Unit and Extent are temporarily changed, which is indicated in our notation by a back-arrow indicating *temporary re-assignment*. In a procedural programming language, that would be equivalent to temporarily storing the current value of the feature and assigning it a new one, with the old value being recovered as soon as the sub-rule had completed. The need for this extension of the formalism is due to the structural relations between entities of a spreadsheet document: since text is encapsulated in cells, any manipulation of text requires the respective cell to be selected first. It seems likely, though, that other applications with a rich internal structure of domain entities may also require such a mechanism.

Another notational device often used in grammar formalisms has been introduced in task rule T2 to handle *optional iteration* of sub-tasks: The asterisk after the non-terminal symbol edit-entry signifies that the overall task of editing a cell-entry may involve several editing operations before it is terminated by pressing the ENTER key.

Finally, in task rules T3 and T4 the non-terminal confirmation has been enclosed in question marks (?confirmation?). This is to indicate that execution of the pertinent subtask is both contingent and prompted by a *system query*. In Multiplan, if the user wants to remove cells to, or paste cells from, the clipboard, he or she may be prompted to specify how adjoining cells should be shifted, depending on where cells are to be removed or pasted. This is clearly a case of the phenomenon mentioned earlier (see §2.4.3), that users will not always need to memorize the complete action sequence for a task but will be able to rely on system prompts telling them what to do next. Our notational device merely signifies such subtasks, but says nothing on how they should be treated in the derivation of complexity measures from a TAG representation. Obviously, they should not be regarded as contributing to the complexity of an interface language in the same way as subtasks that are not prompted.

The TAG for Multiplan specifies five task rules each of which covers groups of similar tasks. Again, not all these tasks have been listed in the dictionary (e.g., 'insert columns from clipboard' or 'insert new columns', for which rules T4 and T5 would apply, respectively). The 15 subtask rules specified in the grammar refer to groups of subtasks which, as in MacWrite, deal with general selection (S1–S3) and editing operations (S7–S12), plus a group of subtasks for editing parts of a cell-entry (S4–S6), which in turn make use of the former ones. The latter are actually identical with the task rules in the MacWrite TAG, thus indicating that, within a cell, editing in Multiplan works just as in MacWrite. The final three rules (S13–S15) prescribe the expansion of the non-terminal symbol `?confirmation?` the special status of which has been mentioned above.

The MacDraw graphics program is quite different from both MacWrite and Multiplan. In the MacDraw domain, the user operates essentially in a world of 'objects' (either graphic objects of some sort or text objects), which he can create and manipulate in various ways. The ontology of objects is quite rich, hence the need to distinguish different classes. Also, with some graphic object-classes special or constrained versions are possible, such as `square` in the case of object-class `rectangle`. While text objects are, obviously, composed of text units (characters and words) which the user can manipulate individually, graphic objects are unitary objects and thus can be manipulated only as a whole.

In the MacDraw representation, a new feature co-occurrence restriction was introduced because certain types of graphic objects (perpendicular or horizontal lines and freehand shapes) are not subject to constraint. This restriction is effective in task rule T1 which expresses the general procedure for drawing any graphic object. In the same rule, rather than describing the set of values for the feature `Object-class` by enlisting each possible type of graphic object, we used the term `NOT-text` (meaning 'any object-class but text') as a shorthand.

Two notational devices introduced in the Multiplan representation have been used here as well, the asterisk and the back-arrow. In the procedures for adding new graphic or new text objects, respectively, MacDraw treats tool selection inconsistently: a graphic tool is de-selected once an object has been drawn thus allowing only one object to be added at a time. On the other hand, after selecting the text tool, the user can add however many text objects are desired. This is indicated in rule T2 by the asterisk expressing "repeat this action any number of times". Likewise, the user can perform any number of editing operations on parts of text objects without having to re-select the text tool (see rule T3). For similar reasons as in Multiplan, the back-arrow, indicating temporary change of a feature value, was necessary in the MacDraw grammar too: the task of adding new text objects implies, of course, adding characters as a subtask and thus a temporary change of the value of the feature Unit (see rule T2).

Five task rules have been listed in the grammar, which capture the procedures for performing the tasks listed in the dictionary (and several more). Rather more subtask rules were required for MacDraw than for MacWrite or Multiplan, which is partially due to its comparatively rich structure of domain entities. Nineteen distinct subtask rules were defined, although some of them are trivial (S4, select tool) and none are deeply complex. As in the previous two applications, there are groups of rules dealing with general selection (S1–S3) and general editing operations (S13–S19). S19 in fact is a rather specific rule in that it is applicable only with Unit=object. Moreover, being subsumed by rule S16, the pertinent command provides no additional functionality and thus could be dispensed with. With rules S10–S12 we are already familiar from the MacWrite and Multiplan grammars: they prescribe the expansion of subtasks which occur in creating and in editing text objects. Finally, rules S5–S9 refer to subtasks involved in drawing graphic objects.

The rule for drawing polygons with arbitrary numbers of points, rule S7, is somewhat problematic. The asterisk is used to indicate that the subtask rule for marking corners can be repeatedly invoked. Ideally, this rule would express the fact that each individual edge of the polygon can independently be constrained (to be vertical, horizontal, or at 45 degrees), which would require that the feature for constraint could be given a new value each time the subtask rule is invoked. At present, TAG has no convenient way to express that. One possibility to cope with this problem would be to allow lists of feature values. The appropriate solution depends on the intended use of a TAG. While its use as a generative grammar would require such an extension of the formalism, the present specification of rule S7 is sufficient for parsing purposes.

What should become evident from the representations discussed in this section is that the TAG formalism is indeed capable of expressing the complexity of large parts of task languages found in commercially used systems. In fact, compared with the production systems used in Kieras and Polson's model [113], the representations are much more compact, while reflecting more of the consistency of a system's input language due to their richer expressive power. On the other hand, this analysis of three different life-size application programs revealed some aspects of interface languages which could not easily be expressed in the original TAG formalism but required a few notational extensions the psychological status of which is not always clear. We will come back to that problem in §2.7, but will now discuss how TAG could be used to capture consistencies that may exist between different application programs.

2.6   Using TAG to capture cross-applicational consistency

Our case for consistency is that it reduces interface complexity. This case holds just as strongly where users have to perform tasks in various domains using different applications, such as a word-processor, a spreadsheet, and a graphics package. Obviously, learning to use different systems poses higher demands upon users, retention is more difficult, and additional problems arise due to negative transfer. Consistency across the interfaces would alleviate the situation: in learning and using one system the user could capitalize on his or her knowledge of another system.

In this section we shall explore to what extent the TAG model can be used to express the consistency of interface languages not only within a single system but also across different application programs. For this purpose we shall draw on the three Macintosh applications discussed in the previous section.

It is well-recognized that the Apple Corporation has successfully created a Macintosh style, by a combination of convenient facilities (the ROM toolkit) and advice to developers. Style, in this sense, has many of the qualities of the notion of consistency: a user who is familiar with several Macintosh applications can probably quickly understand and learn to use a new application. To what degree can a TAG analysis reveal this effect?

It should come as no surprise that the TAG representations of the three Macintosh applications in the appendix show a good deal of overlap.[5] The problem, then, is to find a way to express this overlap. One way to achieve this would simply be to identify those rules that appear in all three TAGs. An example would be, for instance, the rule for selecting a word, a subtask which occurs and is executed in the same way in each of the three applications. Such an approach would be very much along the lines of the 'common elements' theory used in Kieras and Polson's production system model to account for transfer of learning [113]—although the 'common elements' would still be of a different kind.

However, looking for identical task-action mappings would be not quite in the spirit of TAG which asserts that users perceive family resemblances amongst similar (if different) tasks. Any TAG analysis aims at specifying a set of rules that express not only the mapping of tasks occurring in a given task space (which is defined by the chosen scope of the analysis) onto the pertinent action sequences but also the semantic and syntactic similarities among those task-action mappings. There may well be such family resemblances between tasks occuring in different applications which are not captured by rules specified for a single application.

It would therefore be more in the spirit of TAG to consider the union of task spaces represented in the three applications as one single task space for which to establish a TAG, which consequently would also take account of similarities between task-action mappings that belong to different applications. Thus, the way to capture cross-applicational consistency by means of a TAG would be essentially the same as if only one application were to be analysed: i.e., to compare tasks with respect to their semantics, their syntactic structure and their action sequences and to describe meta-rules for those task-action mappings that have a common semantic and syntactic structure. Cross-applicational con-

---

[5] Of course, since TAG focusses on the input language of interfaces, not every aspect that may contribute to the overall consistency of these applications (e.g., the file menu being the leftmost on the screen, etc.) is reflected in the TAG representations.

sistency would then be expressed by those rules that are applicable to tasks or subtasks from different applications.

There are several ways to compare tasks in different applications. Firstly, one can look for 'conceptual entities' (Greeno [78]) in the respective application domains which are shared by tasks in several programs. In our case, a candidate area to look for such common entities would certainly be the text domain which is shared by all three Macintosh applications. Secondly, one can look for operations which are common to tasks in various applications, regardless of the specific entities they are applied to. These would by definition be generic operations such as deletion. And thirdly, one would try to abstract from the specific entities and operations involved in individual tasks and task-action mappings, in order to seek common structures of task-action mappings that apply to tasks from all three applications.

In the case at hand, with the TAGs for each application already available, this analysis is much facilitated. Rather than doing it from scratch, we can simply look for rule schemas that either appear in different TAGs or else for rule schemas that can be modified or merged to more comprehensive ones which then express task-action mappings for tasks or subtasks from different applications.

The appendix contains a list of such 'Common Rules' which reflect the result of our analysis of cross-applicational consistency in the three Macintosh programs. Some of these rule schemas (e.g., R1–R3) appear identically in all three TAGs, but most of them are new rules that subsume similar rules from the individual TAGs. While the Common Rules R1–R11 capture commonalities between all three programs, R12–R15 are applicable to tasks/subtasks from Multiplan and MacDraw only.[6] Note that these rules do not form a TAG in the usual sense. Firstly, since in Multiplan and particularly in MacDraw there are several task-action mappings which are specific to the respective application (e.g., the rules for inserting new rows or for creating graphic objects), the Common Rules cover only part of the combined task space of all three applications. Secondly, the Common Rules do not distinguish between tasks and subtasks.

Focussing on tasks with common entities, we find that treatment of text is highly consistent across the different applications. The text en-

---

[6] §2.9.13 in the appendix to this chapter shows which of the rules in the TAGs for MacWrite, Multiplan, and MacDraw are covered by each Common Rule.

tities of MacWrite (char, word) are present in the other applications as well, wherever text can be edited, i.e., within cells in Multiplan and within text objects in MacDraw. Not only do these entities occur in all three programs, which as such does not yet establish consistent task-action mappings; also, the method for selecting these entities is the same. Moreover in all three applications the core editing functions insert, delete, replace, copy, and move are applicable to these text entities and are executed in the same way, respectively.

These commonalities are expressed in the Common Rules R1–R11. Note that they subsume the complete set of rules specified in the MacWrite TAG. MacWrite is in a sense embedded in the other two applications: its core text-editing facilities are available for editing text encapsulated in cells (Multiplan) or text-objects (MacDraw). This is why MacWrite task rules figure as subtask rules in the other TAGs.

Multiplan and MacDraw both have richer sets of domain entities than MacWrite, the text entities being only a subset of these. This, however, does not mean that commonalities of the three task languages are restricted to the text domain. For instance, selecting a number of cells or objects works much the same as selecting a string of characters (see rule R4). Also, almost all the core editing functions of the text domain are generic functions that can in principle be applied equally well to other domain entities (e.g., cells or objects). Again, the question is not only if this is possible but also if it is done in the same fashion. This has indeed largely been realised in the applications under consideration: deleting 'things' by removing them to the clipboard, copying 'things' to the clipboard, inserting the contents of the clipboard into the document, or (with one exception) replacing 'things' with the contents of the clipboard, is done the same way in each of the applications—no matter what the 'things' are, be it characters or words in any of the applications, cells, rows, or columns in Multiplan, or any type of object in MacDraw. This can be seen from the Common Rules R10, R11, R7, and R8. They refer to the 'Cut', 'Copy', and 'Paste' operations which are so ubiquitous in Macintosh applications. The one exception with respect to the generic function replacing 'things' with the contents of the clipboard is objects in MacDraw. These cannot be replaced by pasting other objects onto them. While this does not severely decrease MacDraw's utility, it is an inconsistency due to a lack of 'semantic completeness' (cf. Payne and Green [149]).

Deleting 'things' for good is also a generic function shared by all three applications. And indeed, this is done in almost every case by pressing the 'backspace' key. But again, there is one exception to this rule: in Multiplan, to erase a cell-range (i.e., to delete its entries), a different command is required (`Edit-Clear`, from a pull-down menu). Here, the inconsistency is due to the fact that the same generic function (deleting something) requires a different user action. It is not quite obvious why the designers deviated here from the general method used elsewhere. While MacDraw also offers the `Edit-Clear` command for deleting something, namely objects, the general method of pressing the 'backspace' key can be used there as well.

The just-mentioned `Edit-Clear` command is an example of commonalities between Multiplan and MacDraw only. These are expressed by Common Rules R12–R15 in the appendix. Rules R12 and R13, which capture similarities between tasks such as, e.g., removing cell-ranges and removing objects to the clipboard, are problematic: Their RHS contains the contingent non-terminal symbol ?confirmation? which represents a subtask that may occur in Multiplan but not in Mac-Draw. There is a conflict here between TAG's aim to express similarities among tasks and its aim to completely prescribe the mapping of tasks onto actions. It would seem unduly pedantic to ignore the similarity expressed in Rules R12 and R13 merely because of an application-specific subtask which is prompted anyway and, moreover, is contingent on the task context. On the other hand, without an additional (but psychologically implausible) rule ?confirmation? [Unit=object, ...] := NULL, the rules are not quite in accordance with the re-write mechanisms employed in TAG. The formalism seems to permit no convincing solution to this problem.[7]

Having represented consistency across applications by means of Common Rules, how would we go about assessing transfer of learning, its prime correlate in terms of user performance? TAG does not lend itself to quantitative predictions of learning times. Based on the number of rule schemas, it rather makes comparative assessments on an

---

[7] There is another example which illustrates that the two aims of a TAG may potentially be in conflict. Due to the task-action-mapping function there is no straightforward way to express in a TAG similarities that may exist between tasks and subtasks in an application. In Multiplan between the task of copying a cell-range to clipboard and the subtask of copying a string to clipboard (while editing a cell-entry).

ordinal scale, e.g., 'system *A* should be faster to learn than system *B*'. In the case of cross-applicational consistency it seems appropriate to base predictions of transfer between two applications on the ratio of tasks/subtasks for which Common Rules can be described to tasks/subtask for which application-specific rules are required. As for the task spaces modelled in the three TAGs, transfer from Multiplan or from MacDraw to MacWrite should be considerably greater than the other way round, since the latter is completely subsumed in the Common Rules that can be established for either pair of applications. Likewise, transfer from MacDraw to Multiplan should be greater than vice versa, since there are fewer application-specific rules in Multiplan.

Certainly, the relatively high proportion of Common Rules we were able to establish for the three applications is partially owed to the particular range of tasks we analysed. Nevertheless, we think that our formal representation captures much of the consistency that makes for the typical 'style' of Macintosh user interfaces.

The preceding analysis of how TAG could be used to capture cross-applicational consistency is of course somewhat sketchy and speculative. As yet no empirical work has been done on this and there remain questions concerning both the formal representation as well as the derivation of metrics for predicting transfer of learning. However, from a theoretical point of view there is no reason why TAG's assumptions concerning the users' perception of family resemblances among tasks should hold with respect to single applications only. The thrust of this analysis was to point out that the TAG model can in principle be applied to capturing cross-applicational consistency in much the same way as to capturing consistency in a single application.

2.7   The psychological credibility of lifesize TAG

The analysis of consistency within and across real-life applications, has brought a number of problems to light, which we shall now briefly review. Although these problems are, of course, specific to TAG, we believe that they are likely to be typical of difficulties experienced with other formalisms for modelling user knowledge.

In its original conception, TAG was seen as a system with an explicit psychological grounding (Payne [147]; Payne and Green [149]). It is this grounding which gives TAG its superior psychological credibility when compared to armchair creations. Unfortunately some of the credibility was necessarily sacrificed when TAG was applied to real-life applications.

2.7.1   *TAG representations are fragile*

The first credibility problem is that the TAG representations turn out to be fragile. It has always been the intention that TAG, like its predecessor set grammar (Payne and Green [148]), should capture configural properties, applying to the interface language as a whole. Family resemblances between parts of the interface language cannot be captured by atomistic approaches such as GOMS. However, the representation of configural properties adopted in TAG, being highly detailed, is easily upset by small changes in the interface language. Suppose, for instance, that operations A, B, and C are all very similar except that C has one slight difference. That one slight difference could force TAG to create a new rule-schema for C, just as though C were wildly different from A and B; whereas to a user the mental representation might very well be of the form "C is just like A and B except that ..." In consequence, introducing one extra feature to an interface language may have the effect of changing the overall consistency by what seems an unreasonably large amount. Human perceptions seem to be more resilient than that, and we feel that a formalism intended to capture human psychology should also be resilient rather than fragile.

The difficulties we mentioned above concerning the Common Rules R12 and R13 illustrate this kind of problem (but it may occur in TAG analyses of single applications as well): 'Removing cells to clipboard' in Multiplan, for instance, is just like 'removing objects to clipboard' in MacDraw, except that the first task may sometimes require an additional 'confirmation' action. There, we observed a conflict between TAG's aim to capture similarities among tasks and its aim to completely and unequivocally prescribe the mapping of these tasks onto actions. Of course, strictly speaking, these aims as such are not in conflict, since it is above all the similarities among task-action-mappings which underly TAG's notion of 'similar tasks', and which are to be captured by a TAG. If conflicts arise, they are rather due to the formal machinery employed by TAG, which in some cases may be too weak to fully achieve both aims without sacrificing psychological plausibility.

TAG representations may be fragile in another sense which rather bears on the reliability of TAG as a predictive tool than on its psychological adequacy: often different TAG representations are possible for an interface language. From a psychological point of view, this does not discredit the TAG model, because inter- as well as intra-individual differences in the mental representation of an interface language are likely to occur and TAG analyses may reveal alternative structurings. It may pose problems, however, when deriving metrics from TAGs for assessing the relative complexity of interface languages. If alternative representations are possible, there should be clear criteria that reflect the intrinsic or objective complexity of an interface language rather than some other conceivable representations that may apply to individual users. It has been suggested that comparative assessments of interface languages should be based on TAGs that minimize the number of task rules (Payne and Green [149]). However, it may be possible to reduce the number of task rules by making them more abstract and introducing additional subtask rules instead (and vice versa). This certainly casts doubt on the number of task rules as being the prime indicator of complexity. In contrast, the total number of rules seems to remain relatively stable across alternative representations. But, as yet there have been no sensitivity analyses that could tell how robust various possible complexity metrics are when derived from alternative TAG representations of the same interface language.

2.7.2   *Restrictions of features*

The second problem is the co-occurrence restrictions of features. Feature co-occurrence is, of course, a central representational device in TAG; it is used to unequivocally describe simple tasks and the LHS of rules. By introducing additional co-occurrence restrictions on top of the feature lists in the LHS of rules we were able to obtain more compact TAG representations. Convenience is obviously not a sufficient ground for introducing a new mechanism into the formalism, since it must be shown that the new feature does not imply psychological mechanisms that are implausible. As justification for the psychological plausibility of co-occurrence restrictions, we can cite their widespread use in formal grammars. Generalized Phrase Structure Grammar (Gazdar et al. [72]), for example, makes free use of restrictions on the co-occurrence of features, and also structures the features that it uses in interesting and powerful ways.

We think that co-occurrence restrictions are too powerful. We used them when we felt that the additional rules we would otherwise have had to introduce would unduly increase the complexity of the TAG representation. Take, for instance, the restriction: IF Effect=copy THEN Clipboard=yes. While experienced Macintosh users will certainly know about this peculiarity of the copy operation, it is very unlikely that this knowledge will cause them to develop a distinct representation of how to perform the task of copying something, since in procedural terms a copy operation works just like a delete operation (which may or may not use the clipboard). Introducing the feature co-occurrence restriction allowed us to express this procedural similarity by a single rule schema. However, by using feature co-occurrence restrictions extensively, the number of rules required for a TAG could be reduced almost ad lib. Thus, while we had good reason for extending the formalism, the extension may well be too powerful. Free use of this device could 'explain' far too much.

2.7.3 *Alteration of task features*

Thirdly, we consider the introduction of the operation for temporary alteration of task features, shown by a back-arrow symbol ('<-') in the TAGs (e.g., rule T2 of the Multiplan TAG given in the Appendix). This operation allows non-terminal rules, such as select in the Multiplan example, to be used as though they were subroutines being passed arguments. The idea is very convenient and has a degree of plausibility. The caveat, however, is that arguments to subroutines demand working memory capacity. By introducing this symbol with no restrictions on its use, we have furtively smuggled in a push-down stack as part of the interpretation system for TAG rules and we know that humans do not have push-down storage capacity. The symbol could be restricted, by saying that no TAG derivation could employ it more than a small number of times to restrict the demands on working memory. The use of the back-arrow symbol constitutes a large and at present ungrounded postulate about the operations of the TAG interpreter, which may weaken TAG's claim to model the users' how-to-do-it knowledge.

As in the previous case, we introduced this extension to the TAG formalism because we found that TAG's limited view of user knowledge would otherwise have led to implausible results. In richly structured domains, uniform replacement of feature values will often be too strong a constraint on the re-writing of simple tasks, since it cannot cope with relationships between domain entities that may impinge on the way a task is performed. In the Multiplan example, it would have precluded representing the task of editing a 'cell-entry' as a simple task at all, just because it entails the subtask of selecting a 'cell'.

We had to extend the formalism in order to take account of knowledge about the device which experienced users indubitably have and bring to bear upon their performance of tasks, but which is not represented in the TAG formalism. Users of Multiplan, or any other spreadsheet, for that matter, will surely know that cell-entries are encapsulated in cells (which therefore have to be accessed before entries can be manipulated), that the clipboard can hold only one item, etc. In other words, users will know about conceptual entities of the device and their various properties—and they are likely to take account of that knowledge in their representations of how to perform tasks; in this light, the common distinction between declarative and procedural knowledge seems by no means clear cut.

But TAG has very limited means, if any, to represent conceptual entity knowledge and TAG's rewrite mechanism does not allow for its impact on the mapping of tasks onto actions. Even if TAG representations could be enriched with descriptions of the device, uniform replacement of feature values might not suffice to warrant psychologically adequate representations of task-action mappings.

Our solution to the problem, the 'backarrow', is in a sense elliptic: its use is based on assumptions about the knowledge that users have which is not expressed in TAG itself and is therefore not strictly controlled by the formalism.

2.7.4   *Unrepresented knowledge*

As is indicated already by the preceding remarks, there are clearly some aspects of knowledge that go unrepresented in TAG descriptions. By starting out with the feature-based concept as the unit of knowledge, which is then mapped onto action sequences, TAG has adopted a position in which there is little room to express knowledge of control of action sequences (e.g., conditionality), the conceptual entities in the user's mental representation of the system, or the response given by the system. These have already been alluded to above.

There are several kinds of control information that may influence task execution, even at the level of simple tasks. For instance, depending on the *current state of the system*, performing a simple task may require certain 'dialogue control' actions. A typical example, occurring in many text editors, is the need to enter the appropriate mode for replacing rather than inserting text and vice versa. TAG's feature-based representation scheme seems to be versatile enough though to cope with such context dependencies, e.g., by introducing an additional feature like `Current-mode=add/replace` into the descriptions of the respective tasks and re-write rules.

Information about the *current task environment* is another type of control information that may affect the way a simple task is performed. This is illustrated by the `?confirmation?` operation which may be required in Multiplan when cells are to be inserted or replaced—depending on whether adjoining cells are empty. While the question marks signify such operations as being contingent on the task context they do not make explicit the kind of contingency, as is the case in the example above, where it is incorporated into the feature description of tasks.

Obviously, the *user's goals* will also determine how simple tasks are performed, although usually not on a level that affects the structure of task-action mappings which TAG is primarily concerned with. To a large extent, such control information can be incorporated in TAG representations by means of variables, such as `%location`, `%char`, etc. or notational devices such as the asterisk for optional repetition of subtasks. There may be simple tasks with more complex control components which are difficult to express in TAG—as demonstrated by the MacDraw procedure for drawing arbitrary polygons, which says: "Point to where the polygon is to begin and click the mouse, then point to each vertex in turn and click the mouse there (using SHIFT if a particular segment is to be constrained to be vertical/horizontal/45 degrees), ending with an additional click at the same location". The asterisk, used to denote optional repetition, is as near as we could come to expressing the control component of this procedure in subtask rule 7 of the MacDraw TAG, which clearly misses the fact that each segment can be constrained individually.

Note that neither repetition of subtasks nor a change of feature values during such repetitions could be derived from the feature descriptions of simple tasks unless they contain e.g., lists of feature values, which limits the status of a TAG as a generative grammar.

The absence of conceptual entities describing the device from TAG grammars means that there is no way to represent the *user's mental model of the device*. While some features do refer to entities of the system (e.g., `Clipboard`), they are used only for the description of task-action mappings and do not form an adequate description of the device. As Howes and Payne [99] have pointed out, novices learning a new system frequently have a choice. They can use a simplified mental model of the device, for which many of the actions are essentially meaningless operations performed by rote; or they can develop a more elaborate device model, and reconstrue those same actions as performing subtasks which change the state of the device. TAG descriptions need to be enriched to be able to describe both possibilities.

Finally, we have already mentioned the absence of any way in which TAG representations are 'aware' of the *system's response* to the user's actions. The main reason for this is that TAG is primarily concerned with the configural properties of input languages of user interfaces, which are independent of the system's response; in this sense, TAG is a 'limited theory' (see below). However, it is obvious that system feedback may have a considerable effect on the learnability of a user interface. The work of Howes and Payne [99] is aimed at taking account of system response in the TAG framework.

As is evident from this discussion, the extensions we introduced are largely motivated by the need to take account of user knowledge which impinges on the execution of tasks (even simple tasks), but which is not represented in the TAG formalism. Although TAG started out with limited aims, focussing on particular aspects of user knowledge, it turns out that even those limited aims cannot always be achieved without reference to other kinds of knowledge. Obviously, the users' knowledge is not as nicely partitioned as the TAG formalism would have it. While the notational extensions which were meant to take account of that fact rely on tacit assumptions about knowledge not expressed in TAG, they allowed us to keep the formalism simple. The coherent representation of the diverse knowledge involved in the users' representation of simple tasks is likely to be beyond the power of the TAG formalism and possibly of any single formalism.

Thus, TAG clearly is a limited theory, not only with respect to the phenomena it addresses and the questions it tries to answer but also with respect to the accuracy it is likely to achieve in doing so. But then, this is the case with most theoretical models in cognitive psychology, and in an applied field like HCI, approximative theories will often do [135].

2.8   Formalisms in HCI: some evaluative remarks

The research reviewed in this chapter has shown

- That descriptions of substantial fragments of lifesize application programs can be achieved in a compact representation;

- That the approach has been fruitful in suggesting new lines of research;

- That a degree of predictiveness can be achieved in laboratory experimentation, although we have not reported on that in detail since it is fully reported elsewhere;

- Perhaps most importantly, that rich descriptions of user knowledge are important, and that formalisms should describe what is important, not what is convenient, to describe.

What have we learnt from our detailed and candid case study? Formalisms in HCI should *reveal* and *predict*. Both demand adequate descriptive power and we consider each in turn.

2.8.1   *Revelation*

This case study has demonstrated, we believe, that formal approaches do have the power to reveal psychologically important aspects of interface designs. The original work on TAG showed that TAG descriptions could express aspects of internal consistency that were not included in other formalisms at that time. Our analyses of the three applications and their consistency across applications have led us into problems. Partly this is due to TAG's failure to describe some important aspects of user knowledge; partly it has been because, even in its own terms, the TAG formalism turned out to be too weak. To restate one of the premises of our introduction (§2.1), *preoccupation with formal detail should be resisted, if the aim is to capture psychological insights.*

We would suggest—rather tentatively, for the case study of one formalism does not entitle us to more—that when a formalism is intended to make psychological claims, one of two courses should be adopted. Either the formalism should be developed as a 'limited theory' and kept strictly within bounds, or else a rich (and probably messy) representation of user knowledge and behaviour should be adopted, a 'cognitive architecture'.

The 'limited theory' argument has been developed elsewhere by Green [76]. Briefly, the suggestion is that all theories in HCI should be regarded as limited theories of particular aspects of human performance, because the only alternative is to solve the whole of cognitive psychology before we start doing HCI, which is clearly a counsel of perfection. If we adopt this limited-theory view, however, it is necessary to associate with each theory a clear statement of what problem it was attempting to solve. Green's paper suggests that HCI topics should be linked by a 'requirements structure' describing what attributes are required of an interface in order to permit a certain type of interaction. The example taken is opportunistic, or serendipitous, planning, which seems to be a preferred mode of interaction in many contexts containing a large element of design (e.g., CAD, designing a large program, designing a graphic system). Opportunistic planning requires that the final construction can be built incrementally, that each state of the design be evaluable, and that the design is easily modifiable. These requirements in turn generate other requirements. In the present context, incremental construction requires that the user can have random access to required operations, which means that the operations required to achieve any goal must be 'findable'; one solution is to use a consistent interface structure. The purpose of a TAG-type theory, seen in this way, is strictly to tell us about whether an interface structure allowed the user to find ways to achieve arbitrary goals. Every theory, on this argument, is built with a question it can solve, and should not be pressed to answer other questions.

Limiting the theory does not solve all problems, as our previous section showed. There are no clear limitations in the user's head, and thus limited theories are artificial constructions. Nevertheless, they can have profound heuristic value.

The alternative approach is to build a much richer representation of the user. A relatively modest move in that direction might be to adopt conceptual modelling languages, rather than grammatical formalisms (Brodie et al. [27]; Borgida [22]); these languages would allow the user's conceptual entities to be described, as well as tackling other limitations we have identified above. A much more ambitious move would be to apply a 'cognitive architecture', one that modelled not only the user's knowledge but also the processes of figuring out how to do things. Among various interesting approaches we can highlight the idea of a 'programmable user model' (Young, Green and Simon [212]), in which "an interface designer is invited to simulate a user performing a range of tasks"; the hope is that the designer would receive insight into the usability of the interface by vicariously experiencing the user's difficulties and successes.

2.8.2   *Prediction*

The effectiveness of HCI formalisms as predictive tools still needs to be convincingly demonstrated outside the laboratory. In saying this, one should distinguish between formalisms for design, formalisms for evaluation, etc. All, in a sense, are intended to be predictive, but we will confine ourselves to evaluative formalisms, including TAG.

Formalisms with limited aims have an easier target. They can be used to compare and evaluate systems which differ in appropriately limited respects. In the present case study, TAG, being limited to the analysis of consistency, can be used to compare designs which are broadly similar but have different degrees of internal consistency. While the evidence indicates that useful predictions can be drawn from limited theories, the literature does not so far contain any insights that can be attributed solely to the use of a formalism.

Limited formalisms by their nature only allow expression of certain kinds of knowledge. What is not expressed in a formalism is the 'interconnections' of the knowledge which is represented with other relevant knowledge the user has which is not represented (the 'non-ideal' knowledge of Wilson et al. [208]). An unresolved problem is that limited formalisms seem to be bound to make tacit assumptions about user knowledge that is not represented in the formalism itself. These assumptions should be made explicit.

If, on the other hand, we regard formalisms as potentially unlimited, able to predict or evaluate designs with no holds barred, the evidence is at present discouraging. One reason for the difficulty is that most formalisms to date either have limited expressive power, and furthermore concentrate upon the generation of user actions; little attention is paid to the input and evaluation of evidence from the system and the construction of a mental or conceptual model by the user. As Briggs [26] shows, doing it that way simply does not predict the real-world difficulties of novices.

2.9 Appendix: Task-Action Grammars

2.9.1 *How to read a TAG*

- The 'List of Features' and their 'Possible Values' list the semantic features and feature values that are used in the TAG for describing simple tasks and feature lists in re-write rules.

- The 'Dictionary of Simple Tasks' describes the simple tasks, for which the TAG is specified, in terms of semantic components.

- The 'Task Rules' prescribe the expansion of simple tasks into 'Primitives' and/or subtasks, the expansion of which is in turn prescribed by 'Subtask Rules'.

- The 'Primitives' (the terminal symbols of a TAG) represent user actions.

The task-action mapping process is guided by two mechanisms: matching of semantic components and uniform replacement of feature values throughout a rule (exceptions where the latter are denoted by a back-arrow, '<-').

	Notation
"AB"	Literal string AB
T [...]	Start-symbol (LHS of task rules)
xyz [...]	Non-terminal symbol (LHS of subtask rules)
XYZ	Primitive or terminal symbol (action specification)
XYZ (p)	Primitive with argument p
|	Alternative primitives (functionally equivalent)
/	Exclusive disjunction of feature values
any^R	Any value (subject to co-occurrence restriction)
+	'Followed by' (task concatenation)
*	Optional repetition
,	Separator in feature lists
%variable	'Imported' variable, not part of the defining features of task
::	Simple task is defined by the following features
:=	Task is rewritten as concatenation of subtasks or primitives
NOT-xyz	Any feature value except XYZ
<-	Temporary re-assignment of feature value
?confirmation?	Non-terminal prompted by system query

2.9.2   *MacWrite*
          Imported variables
          %location, %unit, %char

Feature	*Value*
Unit	char/word
Extent	number of units involved in action
Effect	add/remove/replace/copy
Clipboard	yes/no

Feature co-occurrence restrictions
IF Effect=copy THEN Clipboard=yes

Primitives

MOUSE-point (%)	point to appropriate unit or location
MOUSE-drag (%)	press mouse-button, drag pointer to appropriate unit or location, release mouse-button
MOUSE-click	click mouse-button
MOUSE-double-click	click mouse-button twice
TYPE (%char)	perform typing
MENU (Edit-item)	point to 'Edit' on menu bar, drag to item on pulldown menu
"key"	press specified keys

2.9.3   *Dictionary of simple tasks in MacWrite*
   (1) INSERT NEW TEXT::
            Unit=char, Extent=any, Effect=add, Clipboard=no

   (2) INSERT TEXT FROM CLIPBOARD::
            Unit=char, Extent=any, Effect=add, Clipboard=yes

   (3) DELETE CHARACTER::
            Unit=char, Extent=1, Effect=remove, Clipboard=no

   (4) DELETE TEXT::
            Unit=char, Extent=any, Effect=remove, Clipboard=no

   (5) DELETE WORD::
            Unit=word, Extent=1, Effect=remove, Clipboard=no

(6) REMOVE WORD TO CLIPBOARD::
   Unit=word, Extent=1, Effect=remove, Clipboard=yes

(7) COPY TEXT TO CLIPBOARD::
   Unit=char, Extent=any, Effect=copy, Clipboard=yes

(8) OVER-WRITE TEXT::
   Unit=char, Extent=any, Effect=replace,
   Clipboard=no

(9) REPLACE TEXT WITH TEXT FROM CLIPBOARD::
   Unit=char, Extent=any, Effect=replace,
   Clipboard=yes

2.9.4   *Rule schemas in MacWrite: task rules*

T1 (1,2) 'INSERT NEW TEXT', 'INSERT TEXT FROM CLIPBOARD'

```
T [Unit=char/word, Extent=any, Effect=add,
   Clipboard=any] :=
MOUSE-point (%location) + MOUSE-click +
edit [Effect=add, Clipboard=any]
```

T2 (3) 'DELETE CHARACTER'

```
T [Unit=char, Extent=1, Effect=remove,
   Clipboard=no] :=
MOUSE-point (%location) + MOUSE-click +
edit [Effect=remove, Clipboard=no]
```

T3 (4,5,6,7,8,9) 'DELETE TEXT', 'DELETE WORD', 'REMOVE WORD
      TO CLIPBOARD', 'COPY TEXT TO CLIPBOARD', 'OVERWRITE
      TEXT', 'REPLACE TEXT WITH TEXT FROM CLIPBOARD'

```
T [Unit=char/word, Extent=any,
   Effect=remove/copy/replace, Clipboard=anyR] :=
select [Unit=char/word, Extent=any] +
edit [Effect=remove/copy/replace, Clipboard=anyR]
```

2.9.5   *Rule schemas in MacWrite: subtask rules*
S1   select [Unit=char, Extent=any]
         := MOUSE-point (%unit) + MOUSE-drag (%unit)

S2   select [Unit=word, Extent=1]
         := MOUSE-point (%unit) + MOUSE-double-click

S3   edit [Effect=add/replace, Clipboard=no]
         := TYPE (%char)

S4   edit [Effect=add/replace, Clipboard=yes]
         := MENU (Edit-Paste) | "CTRL-V"

S5   edit [Effect=remove, Clipboard=no]
         := "BKSP"

S6   edit [Effect=remove, Clipboard=yes]
         := MENU (Edit-Cut) | "CTRL-X"

S7   edit [Effect=copy, Clipboard=yes]
         := MENU (Edit-Copy) | "CTRL-C"

2.9.6   *Multiplan*
         Imported variables
         %location, %unit, %char

Feature	Value
Unit	char/word/cell-entry/cell/row/column
Extent	number of Units involved in action
Effect	add/remove/replace/copy
Clipboard	yes/no

Feature co-occurrence restrictions
IF Effect=copy THEN Clipboard=yes
IF Unit=cell/row/column AND
   Effect=replace THEN Clipboard=yes

Primitives

MOUSE-point (%)	point to appropriate unit or location
MOUSE-drag (%)	press mouse-button, drag pointer to appropriate unit or location, release mouse-button
MOUSE-click	click mouse-button
MOUSE-double-click	click mouse-button twice
TYPE (%char)	perform typing
MENU (Edit-item)	point to 'Edit' on menu bar, drag to item on pulldown menu
"key"	press specified keys
CLICK-DIALOGUE-BUTTONS	point to appropriate dialogue buttons, click mouse-button

2.9.7   *Dictionary of simple tasks in Multiplan*

(1) CREATE CELL-ENTRY::
      Unit=cell-entry, Extent=1, Effect=add, Clipboard=no

(2) DELETE CELL-ENTRY::
      Unit=cell-entry, Extent=1, Effect=remove,
      Clipboard=no

(3) OVER-WRITE CELL-ENTRY::
      Unit=cell-entry, Extent=1, Effect=replace,
      Clipboard=no

(4) INSERT NEW TEXT INTO A CELL-ENTRY::
      Unit=char, Extent=any, Effect=add, Clipboard=no

(5) DELETE A CHAR IN A CELL-ENTRY::
      Unit=char, Extent=1, Effect=remove, Clipboard=no

(6) OVER-WRITE A WORD IN A CELL-ENTRY::
      Unit=word, Extent=1, Effect=replace, Clipboard=no

(7) ERASE COLUMN::
      Unit=column, Extent=1, Effect=remove, Clipboard=no

(8) REMOVE ROWS TO CLIPBOARD::
      Unit=row, Extent=any, Effect=remove, Clipboard=yes

(9) COPY CELL-RANGE TO CLIPBOARD::
    Unit=cell, Extent=any, Effect=copy, Clipboard=yes

(10) REPLACE CELL-RANGE WITH CELL-RANGE FROM CLIPBOARD::
    Unit=cell, Extent=any, Effect=replace,
    Clipboard=yes

(11) INSERT ROWS FROM CLIPBOARD::
    Unit=row, Extent=any, Effect=add, Clipboard=yes

(12) INSERT NEW ROW::
    Unit=row, Extent=1, Effect=add, Clipboard=no

Rule schemas in Multiplan: task rules

T1 (1,2,3) 'CREATE CELL-ENTRY', 'DELETE CELL-ENTRY', 'OVER-WRITE CELL-ENTRY'

```
T [Unit=cell-entry, Extent=1,
   Effect=add/remove/replace, Clipboard=no] :=
select [Unit <- cell, Extent=1] +
edit [Unit=cell-entry, Effect=add/remove/replace,
      Clipboard=no] + "ENTER"
```

T2 (4,5,6) 'INSERT, DELETE, OVER-WRITE PART OF CELL-ENTRY'

```
T [Unit=char/word, Extent=any,
   Effect=add/remove/replace, Clipboard=any] :=
select [Unit <- cell, Extent <- 1] +
edit-entry [Unit=char/word, Extent=any,
            Effect=add/remove/replace,
            Clipboard=any] * + "ENTER"
```

T3 (7,8,9,10) 'ERASE COLUMN', 'REMOVE ROWS TO CLIPBOARD', 'COPY CELL-RANGE TO CLIPBOARD', 'REPLACE CELL-RANGE WITH CELL-RANGE FROM CLIPBOARD'

```
T [Unit=cell/row/column, Extent=any,
   Effect=remove/copy/replace, Clipboard=any^R] :=
select [Unit=cell/row/column, Extent=any] +
```

```
        edit [Unit=cell/row/column,
            Effect=remove/copy/replace, Clipboard=any^R]
        + ?confirmation? [Effect=remove/copy/replace,
                          Clipboard=any^R]
```

T4 (11) 'INSERT ROWS FROM CLIPBOARD'

```
        T [Unit=cell/row/column, Extent=any, Effect=add,
            Clipboard=yes] :=
        MOUSE-point (%location) + MOUSE-click +
        edit [Unit=cell/row/column, Effect=add,
            Clipboard=yes] +
        ?confirmation? [Effect=add, Clipboard=yes]
```

T5 (12) 'INSERT NEW ROW'

```
        T [Unit=row/column, Extent=any, Effect=add,
            Clipboard=no] :=
        "SHIFT" + select [Unit=row/column, Extent=any]
```

Rule schemas in Multiplan: subtask rules

```
S1      select [Unit=char/cell/row/column, Extent=any]
        := MOUSE-point (%unit) + MOUSE-drag (%unit)

S2      select [Unit=word, Extent=1]
        := MOUSE-point (%unit) + MOUSE-double-click

S3      select [Unit=cell/row/column, Extent=1]
        := MOUSE-point (%unit) + MOUSE-click

S4      edit-entry [Unit=char/word, Extent=any, Effect=add,
                    Clipboard=any]
        := MOUSE-point (%location) + MOUSE-click +
            edit [Unit=char/word, Effect=add, Clipboard=any]

S5      edit-entry [Unit=char, Extent=1, Effect=remove,
                    Clipboard=no]
        := MOUSE-point (%location) + MOUSE-click +
            edit [Unit=char, Effect=remove, Clipboard=no]
```

S6   edit-entry [Unit=char/word, Extent=any,
                    Effect=remove/copy/replace,
                    Clipboard=any^R]
        := select [Unit=char/word, Extent=any] +
           edit [Unit=char/word, Effect=remove/copy/replace,
                 Clipboard=any^R]

S7   edit [Unit=char/word/cell-entry,
              Effect=add/replace, Clipboard=no]
        := TYPE (%char)

S8   edit [Unit=any, Effect=add/replace, Clipboard=yes]
        := MENU (Edit-Paste) | "CTRL-V"

S9   edit [Unit=char/word/cell-entry,
              Effect=remove, Clipboard=no]
        := "BKSP"

S10   edit [Unit=any, Effect=remove, Clipboard=yes]
        := MENU (Edit-Cut) | "CTRL-X"

S11   edit [Unit=any, Effect=copy, Clipboard=yes]
        := MENU (Edit-Copy) | "CTRL-C"

S12   edit [Unit=cell/row/column, Effect=remove,
              Clipboard=no]
        := MENU (Edit-Clear) | "CTRL-B"

S13   ?confirmation? [Effect=add/remove/replace,
                        Clipboard=yes]
        := CLICK-DIALOGUE-BUTTONS

S14   ?confirmation? [Effect=copy, Clipboard=yes]
        := NULL

S15   ?confirmation? [Effect=any, Clipboard=no]
        := NULL

2.9.8   *MacDraw*
        Imported variables
        %location, %unit, %char, %tool-icon

Feature	Value
Object-class	text/rectangle/ellipse/polygon...
Constraint	yes/no
Unit	object/char/word
Extent	number of units involved in action
Effect	add/remove/replace/copy
Clipboard	yes/no

Feature co-occurrence restrictions

IF Effect=copy THEN Clipboard=yes

IF Object-class=perpendicular-line OR
    Object-class=freehand-shape THEN Constraint=no

Primitives

MOUSE-point (%)	point to appropriate unit or location
MOUSE-drag (%)	press mouse-button, drag pointer to appropriate unit or location, release mouse-button
MOUSE-click	click mouse-button
MOUSE-double-click	click mouse-button twice
TYPE (%char)	perform typing
MENU (Edit-item)	point to 'Edit' on menu bar, drag to item on pulldown menu
"key"	press specified keys

2.9.9   *Dictionary of simple tasks in MacDraw*

(1) DRAW A RECTANGLE::
        Unit=object, Extent=1, Effect=add, Clipboard=no,
        Object-class=rectangle, Constraint=no

(2) DRAW A CIRCLE::
        Unit=object, Extent=1, Effect=add, Clipboard=no,
        Object-class=ellipse, Constraint=yes

(3) CREATE A TEXT-OBJECT (CAPTION-TEXT)::
    Unit=object, Extent=1, Effect=add, Clipboard=no,
    Object-class=text

(4) INSERT INTO A TEXT-OBJECT::
    Unit=char, Extent=any, Effect=add, Clipboard=any,
    Object-class=text

(5) DELETE A CHAR IN A TEXT-OBJECT::
    Unit=char, Extent=1, Effect=remove, Clipboard=no,
    Object-class=text

(6) OVER-WRITE A WORD IN A TEXT-OBJECT::
    Unit=word, Extent=1, Effect=replace, Clipboard=no,
    Object-class=text

(7) DELETE OBJECT::
    Unit=object, Extent=any, Effect=remove,
    Clipboard=no

(8) REMOVE OBJECTS TO CLIPBOARD::
    Unit=object, Extent=any, Effect=remove,
    Clipboard=yes

(9) COPY OBJECTS TO CLIPBOARD::
    Unit=object, Extent=any, Effect=copy, Clipboard=yes

(10) ADD OBJECTS FROM CLIPBOARD::
    Unit=object, Extent=any, Effect=add, Clipboard=yes

Rule schemas in MacDraw: task rules

(T1) (1,2) 'DRAW A GRAPHIC OBJECT'

    T [Unit=object, Extent=1, Effect=add, Clipboard=no,
       Object-class=NOT-text, Constraint=any^R] :=
    select-tool [Object-class=NOT-text] +
    draw [Object-class=NOT-text, Constraint=any^R]

(T2) (3) 'CREATE TEXT-OBJECTS (CAPTION-TEXT)'

```
        T [Unit=object, Extent=any, Effect=add,
           Clipboard=no, Object-class=text]  :=
        select-tool [Object-class=text] +
        edit-text [Unit <- char, Extent=any,
                   Effect=add, Clipboard=no] * + "ENTER"
```

(**T3**) (4,5,6) 'INSERT INTO, DELETE, REPLACE PARTS OF TEXT OB-
    JECTS'

```
        T [Unit=char/word, Extent=any,
           Effect=add/remove/replace,
           Clipboard=any, Object-class=text]  :=
        select-tool [Object-class=text] +
        edit-text [Unit=char/word, Extent=any,
                   Effect=add/remove/replace,
                   Clipboard=any] * + "ENTER"
```

(**T4**) (7,8,9) 'DELETE OBJECTS, REMOVE OBJECTS TO CLIPBOARD,
    COPY OBJECTS TO CLIPBOARD'

```
        T [Unit=object, Extent=any,
           Effect=remove/copy, Clipboard=any$^R$]  :=
        select [Unit=object, Extent=any] +
        edit [Unit=object, Effect=remove/copy,
              Clipboard=any$^R$]
```

(**T5**) (10) 'ADD OBJECTS FROM CLIPBOARD'

```
        T [Unit=object, Extent=any,
           Effect=add, Clipboard=yes]  :=
        MOUSE-point (%location) + MOUSE-click +
        edit [Unit=object, Effect=add, Clipboard=yes]
```

Rule schemas in MacDraw: subtask rules

```
S1    select [Unit=char/object, Extent=any]
      := MOUSE-point (%unit) + MOUSE-drag (%unit)

S2    select [Unit=word, Extent=1]
      := MOUSE-point (%unit) + MOUSE-double-click
```

S3   select [Unit=object, Extent=1]
        := MOUSE-point (%unit) + MOUSE-click

S4   select-tool [Object-class=any]
        := MOUSE-point (%tool-icon) + MOUSE-click

S5   draw [Object-class=NOT-polygon, Constraint=no]
        := MOUSE-point (%location) + MOUSE-drag (%location)

S6   draw [Object-class=NOT-polygon, Constraint=yes]
        := MOUSE-point (%location) +
           "SHIFT" + MOUSE-drag (%location)

S7   draw [Object-class=polygon, Constraint=any]
        := MOUSE-point (%location) + MOUSE-click +
           mark-corner [Constraint=any] * + MOUSE-click

S8   mark-corner [Constraint=no]
        := MOUSE-point (%location) + MOUSE-click

S9   mark-corner [Constraint=yes]
        := "SHIFT" + MOUSE-point (%location) + MOUSE-click

S10   edit-text [Unit=char/word, Extent=any,
                   Effect=add, Clipboard=any]
        := MOUSE-point (%location) + MOUSE-click +
           edit [Unit=char/word, Effect=add, Clipboard=any]

S11   edit-text [Unit=char, Extent=1,
                   Effect=remove, Clipboard=no]
        := MOUSE-point (%location) + MOUSE-click +
           edit [Unit=char, Effect=remove, Clipboard=no]

S12   edit-text [Unit=char/word, Extent=any,
                   Effect=remove/copy/replace,
                   Clipboard=any^R]
        := select [Unit=char/word, Extent=any] +
           edit [Unit=char/word,
                 Effect=remove/copy/replace,
                 Clipboard=any^R]

S13   edit [Unit=char/word, Effect=add/replace,
              Clipboard=no]
         := TYPE (%char)

S14   edit [Unit=any, Effect=add, Clipboard=yes]
         := MENU (Edit-Paste) | "CTRL-V"

S15   edit [Unit=char/word, Effect=replace,
              Clipboard=yes]
         := MENU (Edit-Paste) | "CTRL-V"

S16   edit [Unit=any, Effect=remove, Clipboard=no]
         := "BKSP"

S17   edit [Unit=any, Effect=remove, Clipboard=yes]
         := MENU (Edit-Cut) | "CTRL-X"

S18   edit [Unit=any, Effect=copy, Clipboard=yes]
         := MENU (Edit-Copy) | "CTRL-C"

S19   edit [Unit=object, Effect=remove, Clipboard=no]
         := MENU (Edit-Clear) | "CTRL-B"

2.9.10   *Common rules ('MacGeneric')*
This section gives rule schemas that are applicable to tasks and/or
subtasks from all three Macintosh applications, MacWrite, Multiplan
and MacDraw.

         Imported variables
         %location, %unit, %char

         Feature co-occurrence restrictions
         IF Effect=copy THEN Clipboard=yes

2.9.11   *Rule schemas in MacGeneric: task rules*
R1 'INSERT NEW TEXT, INSERT TEXT FROM CLIPBOARD'

```
    T [Unit=char/word, Extent=any,
       Effect=add, Clipboard=any] :=
    MOUSE-point (%location) + MOUSE-click +
    edit [Unit=char/word, Effect=add, Clipboard=any]
```

R2 'DELETE A SINGLE CHARACTER'

```
    T [Unit=char, Extent=1,
       Effect=remove, Clipboard=no] :=
    MOUSE-point (%location) + MOUSE-click +
    edit [Unit=char, Effect=remove, Clipboard=no]
```

R3 'DELETE TEXT, REMOVE TEXT TO CLIPBOARD, COPY TEXT TO
    CLIPBOARD, OVER-WRITE TEXT, REPLACE TEXT WITH TEXT
    FROM CLIPBOARD'

```
    T [Unit=char/word, Extent=any,
       Effect=remove/copy/replace, Clipboard=any^R] :=
    select [Unit=char/word, Extent=any] +
    edit [Unit=char/word, Effect=remove/copy/replace,
          Clipboard=any^R]
```

2.9.12   *Rule schemas in MacGeneric: subtask rules*
  R4   select [Unit=char/cell/row/column/object,
                 Extent=any]
         := MOUSE-point (%unit) + MOUSE-drag (%unit)

  R5   select [Unit=word, Extent=1]
         := MOUSE-point (%unit) + MOUSE-double-click

  R6   edit [Unit=char/word/cell-entry,
               Effect=add/replace, Clipboard=no]
         := TYPE (%char)

  R7   edit [Unit=char/word/cell/row/column/object,
               Effect=add, Clipboard=yes]
         := MENU (Edit-Paste) | "CTRL-V"

  R8   edit [Unit=char/word/cell/row/column,
               Effect=replace, Clipboard=yes]
         := MENU (Edit-Paste) | "CTRL-V"

R9   edit [Unit=char/word/cell-entry/object,
          Effect=remove, Clipboard=no]
     := "BKSP"

R10 edit [Unit=any, Effect=remove, Clipboard=yes]
     := MENU (Edit-Cut) | "CTRL-X"

R11 edit [Unit=any, Effect=copy, Clipboard=yes]
     := MENU (Edit-Copy) | "CTRL-C"

2.9.13   *Common rules in Multiplan and MacDraw*
R12 'ERASE CELL-RANGE OR OBJECTS', 'REMOVE CELL-RANGE OR
     OBJECTS TO CLIPBOARD', 'COPY CELL-RANGE OR OBJECTS
     TO CLIPBOARD'

     T [Unit=cell/row/column/object, Extent=any,
        Effect=remove/copy, Clipboard=any^R] :=
     select [Unit=cell/row/column/object, Extent=any] +
     edit [Unit=cell/row/column/object,
          Effect=remove/copy, Clipboard=any^R] +
     ?confirmation? [Unit=cell/row/column/object,
                    Effect=remove/copy, Clipboard=any^R]

R13 'INSERT CELL-RANGE FROM CLIPBOARD', 'ADD OBJECTS FROM
     CLIPBOARD'

     T [Unit=cell/row/column/object, Extent=any,
        Effect=add, Clipboard=yes] :=
     MOUSE-point (%location) + MOUSE-click +
     edit [Unit=cell/row/column/object, Effect=add,
          Clipboard=yes] +
     ?confirmation? [Unit=cell/row/column/object,
                    Effect=add, Clipboard=yes]

R14 select [Unit=cell/row/column/object, Extent=1]
     := MOUSE-point (%unit) + MOUSE-click (%unit)

R15 edit [Unit=cell/row/column/object,
          Effect=remove, Clipboard=no]
     := MENU (Edit-Clear) | "CTRL-B"

The following table shows which rules in the TAGs for the three Macintosh applications are covered by the common rules.

Common Rules	MacWrite	Multiplan	MacDraw
R1	T1	S4	S10
R2	T2	S5	S11
R3	T3	S6	S12
R4	S1	S1	S1
R5	S2	S2	S2
R6	S3	S7	S13
R7	S4	S8	S14
R8	S4	S8	S15
R9	S5	S9	S16
R10	S6	S10	S17
R11	S7	S11	S18
R12		T3[8]	T4
R13		T4	T5
R14		S3	S3
R15		S12	S19

[8] T3 (Multiplan) is only partly subsumed by R12. T3 also applies to tasks of replacing cells, rows, etc.

CHAPTER THREE

PUTTING DESIGN INTO PRACTICE: FORMAL SPECIFICATION AND THE USER INTERFACE

ROGER TOOK

3.1 Introduction

The proportion of user interface code in interactive systems is variously reported: over 50% [186]; 80% [131]. Such a cost would not be tolerated in the case, for example, of software components that interfaced to storage devices: here we expect simple read and write calls on abstractions like files. As a justification of this cost, engineering the user interface can produce large performance gains — Bailey, Knox and Lynch [16] claim an end-user productivity gain of 77%. There may thus be a trade-off between end-user productivity and interface designer productivity: the more effort expended by the latter, the less by the former.

In window-managed and software engineering environments, however, user interface facilities are typically expected to be *common* to a range of applications. This reduces the possibility of fine-tuning the user interface for a particular application functionality. On the other hand, it promotes external consistency between application interfaces. The recent Open Look proposals [94] for a standard 'look and feel' across applications take this to the extreme. A common user interface also promotes interface designer productivity since interface constructs can be *factored out* from a range of applications. If suitably expressed, such constructs can also provide levels of *independence* from particular devices, interface styles, or interactive dialogues.

Current user interface design is thus predicated on the possibility of separating user interface concerns from application concerns. It also exploits formal notations for abstracting features of application functionality and thus providing levels of independence. An abstraction commonly performed is over interactive dialogue, using formal notations for syntax such as transition networks or grammars. This emphasis is typified by the Seeheim model [74, 75] for User Interface Management Systems (UIMS). However, as §3.3.4 argues, this approach has been less than successful. An alternative approach is represented by Presenter [200] and its paradigm of *surface interaction*. This seeks to provide a separation of interface and application based on an abstraction for presentation-level objects (graphics and text), their structure and behaviour. Presenter is unusual among presentation systems in having been formally specified (in Z [178]) prior to implementation.

This chapter is based on the experience of designing, specifying, and implementing Presenter. It makes two points:

- Design cannot be mechanised. While we may be able to make formal judgements about the internal consistency of the specification and the accuracy of an implementation with respect to it, we can only ever make qualitative judgements about the completeness and usefulness of the design with respect to the problem. This follows simply from the fact that as soon as the problem is expressed precisely enough to draw inferences, then design has already taken place. Therefore design is also influenced by the notation available to express it. This is true of the design of interface functionality as much as of any other (application) functionality.

- Design cannot be localised. This chapter argues that creative design is involved at all stages of development from specification to implementation, and that constraints arising during development can force a radical redesign. This chapter identifies four classes of constraint, which are here called *soft, firm, hard* and *environmental* constraints. In contrast to the first

point, these constraints apply particularly to user interface design, since the user interface is the most concrete and refined
(in the formal sense) component of a computer system.

This chapter is in two parts, corresponding to the above points. The
first part (§3.2) critically examines the contractual software engineering
development methodology, gives a brief overview of the styles of notation available to a software designer, and then attempts to reconstruct
the design process using the Z notation. The second part (§3.3) outlines the four constraints on design, and accounts for the discrepancies
between initial specifications and final implementations. These parts
are preceded by a brief introduction to Presenter.

3.1.1   *Presenter*

Presenter is the user interface component of the ASPECT IPSE (Integrated Project Support Environment) [7]. Presenter is a *screen operating system*, in the sense that it manages a limited resource (the screen)
via a virtual model (discrete coordinate areas called regions). Regions
may be composed hierarchically, but only leaf regions in the hierarchy
have displayable content, which may be text, graphics, or bitmapped
images. Regions have behaviour, principally geometric manipulability
and content editability (textual or graphical), which is controlled simply
by a set of attributes. These operate mainly by constraining the basic
behaviour (for instance so that a region is movable by the user only
horizontally, or only inside another region). Other attributes affect the
appearance of regions, for instance to make them transparent or high-
lit. Region identity and appearance persist over all operations offered
by Presenter, which include cutting and pasting the region tree, and
loading and saving subtrees to files. There is a rich set of input events
which can be filtered *via* each region individually. The application may
therefore vary its involvement in screen interaction.

Presenter has no knowledge of application semantics, and imposes
very little of its own: it has no built-in constructs like windows, icons,
or menus, for example. A fundamental principle in the design is that of
equal access: end-user and application perceive the same objects (although obviously through different representations) and have an equivalent set of operations on them. Equal access enables the user and
the application to communicate using the screen objects as a *medium*.
It also enables the interface designer to construct the interface inter-

actively, by direct manipulation of the objects. The intention in this design is to optimally *factor* the generation and maintenance of application screen interfaces: firstly by filling a perceived gap between screen handling systems that simply provide low level operations like RasterOps [137] on the one hand, and toolkits [143, 156, 185, 49] that provide ready-built components, on the other; secondly by abstracting and centralising generic functionality like textual and graphical editing and geometric manipulation. A more detailed informal description of the design can be found in [199], while the principles, context, and full formal specification can be found in [200].

It is interesting to look back on the development of this design. Certain features (like the hierarchical structure) are basic building blocks present from the beginning, and derive from work by Coutaz [44, 45] and Shaw [173]. Other features (like the notion of equal access) were inherent but unrecognised at the beginning, and have emerged (and been labelled) through experience and refinement. Yet other features expressed in early specifications have not survived the practicalities of implementation and use, and have been abandoned. Characters in text, for example, were originally modelled as individual regions: this proved impossibly slow in practice.

An important first application to run on Presenter was its interactive interface editor Doubleview [96]. As well as underlying the user interface to the ASPECT IPSE, Presenter is in use at a number of academic sites, in the development of graphical database and image processing applications. In addition two, more substantial, systems have been produced: a Mascot 3 Paintbox [207] and a CORE requirements method workstation [9]. The design is currently completing its second specify-implement-use cycle.

3.2   The design process

3.2.1   *Software engineering and formal methods*

The use of formal methods in software engineering is often presented as a panacea. Once the essence of a system is captured in a formal specification, the argument goes, the product follows automatically or at least deterministically by a process of transformation or refinement. Even if it is recognised that there must be a 'Eureka step', this is localised and minimised. The contractual software development methodology is structured along these lines, insulating the stages of development from each other by means of immutable, contractually binding documents. Since the production of large-scale software often involves a team of people, this structuring is commonly reflected not only in the stages of development but also in distinct developer roles. Guttag and Horning [81] reflect this attitude:

> "On large software projects those making the critical design decisions should be a small subset of those people involved in building the system. Significant design decisions should not be left to the 'programmers'."

Although the term does not suggest it, 'analysts' expect to have creative freedom in formulating specifications, insofar as the requirements are vague, while 'programmers' are expected to implement these specifications slavishly. Concealment and isolation are virtues: programmers are allowed 'views' of the system on a need-to-know basis; and an ideal specification insulates the analyst from involvement in 'productisation'. The formal specification is a costly, high-profile, possibly legally-binding document. Insights (and constraints) that may arise during implementation are therefore prevented from 'iterating' back into the specification. Swartout and Balzer [184] and Fischer [67] express a rare dissatisfaction with this approach.

3.2.2   *Formal notations and abstraction*

Apart from any imposed methodological structure, formal methods hold out the promise that, by means of abstraction, generic device-independent components can be identified and minimally specified. By the use of sound principles and rigorous reasoning, usable effective systems can be derived or evaluated. The implicit justification for the use of formal methods is that abstraction enables the essence of a system's functionality to be captured, without early commitment (see Thimbleby [197]) to particular, contingent representations.

A number of qualifications can be made to this ideal, however:

- Except in formal specifications which are determined entirely by an existing (manual or computer) system, the principles, operations, and fundamental objects and relations upon which a specification is based are necessarily products of creative design. They may be unaccountably influenced (for better or worse) by prejudice, breadth of insight into the problem, and even by the formal notation itself.

- A perfect specification may abstract away from, and take no account of, features which prove to be critical to the usability, or implementability, of the interface. That is, even apparently fundamental abstractions remain vulnerable to constraints arising throughout the development and use of a system.

- There is nothing special about a formal notation: a specification (and its refinement into executable code) is still subject to the full gamut of lexical, syntactic, semantic and conceptual errors — indeed, while automatic parsers and type checkers for formal notations remain relatively unavailable, possibly more so than a conventional program.

The bulk of formal methods literature is concerned with presenting new notations and system paradigms, or with case studies intended to illustrate these [85, 73]. Only a small proportion reports experience in putting formal methods to their intended use: the specification, implementation and subsequent use of large, industrial-strength systems. This chapter contends that it is only in these cases that the limitations and constraints on formal methods are revealed.

3.2.3   *Notation and design*
Two orthogonal axes in the use of formal notations can be distinguished:

- Along one axis, formal specification may be used at one extreme as a *description* of an existing manual or informally described system; at the other extreme as a *prescription* for a new system or class of systems.

- Along the other axis, formal specification may be analytic, or *convergent*, aiming for high levels of abstraction, and for concise, globally applicable properties; alternatively it may be synthetic, or *divergent*, expressing a constructive *design* for a particular system.

The earlier work of Dix, Harrison, Runciman and Thimbleby [61, 84], for example, can be characterised as convergent and prescriptive. The aim was to formalise *generative user engineering principles* (gueps), such as reachability and predictability, according to which systems could be built and evaluated. Later work [83] has recognised the intransigence of many features of systems which interface extensively with the real world (like user interfaces), and the intent has become more descriptive, whilst retaining the drive towards convergence. Divergent descriptive specifications include industrial examples where existing large-scale manual systems have been formalised with a view to computerisation [85], computer systems developed informally have been formalised for the sake of case study [25], or informal specifications have been re-expressed in a formal notation, as has been the case with GKS [63] and ODA [12]. In this scheme, the use of formal methods in Presenter can be seen as divergent and prescriptive: the intention is to produce a design for a generic component, rather than to analyse the nature of interaction in general.

There are essentially two subjects for a formal definition:

- the *functionality* of a system;

- the *behaviour* of a system.

There are two main classes of formal notation for defining functionality (see Cohen [43]): model-based (like VDM and Z), and algebraic or equational (like CLEAR and Larch). A model-based specification seems more suited to systems which have a complex data structure, but a relatively simple set of operations (like a structured text editor or a database), while the reverse is true of algebraic specifications (these might be more suited to a statistics or image processing package, for example). In a purely algebraic specification, the data type is implicit in the operations, while in a model-based specification it is expressed in the constructs of the model: sets, lists, etc. In both notations it is possible to argue how well, or to what extent, the operations generate, or provide access to, values of the data type. By expressing the data type explicitly, a model-based specification is often easier to assess against this criterion than an algebraic specification. It may also be easier to express limits, boundary conditions and other exceptions in a model-based specification.

On the other hand, the *behaviour* of a system is defined as possible sequences of its states. Model-based specifications, for example, express operations as mappings between states, with pre- and post-conditions (they are therefore also called state-based methods). In Chapter 6, Sufrin abstracts sequences of these states into *traces*, so that it is possible to make judgements about the behaviour of a system in abstraction from its functionality. A similar approach is taken by Bartussek and Parnas [18]. In user interface design, describing the behaviour of system separately from its functionality has been an important goal, and there is a wide literature on notations for such descriptions (see Green [75] and Farooq [66]). In this approach, system behaviour is regarded as having syntactic regularities, and typical notations for these can thus be placed at some point on the Chomsky hierarchy of expressive power. Least powerful are simple transition networks [204] where all possible arcs from each state are explicitly (possibly graphically) represented. Augmented Transition Networks [210] can model pushdown automata [140] by allowing manipulation of a stack on transitions. These are equivalent in power to context-free grammars in which the transitions can be modelled by the grammar's productions [170].

However, definitions of functionality and definitions of behaviour are theoretically equivalent, since, as Sufrin has shown, the functionality implies the possible behaviour. For example, operations in abstract data types, such as push and pop on an empty stack, are not in general commutative. Similarly, defining behaviour completely is a constructive way of defining functionality, since a semantic interpretation function can in theory be applied to the syntactic structures. Attempts in user interface design to abstract behaviour (dialogue) are based on the premise that it can be described *more* concisely through a syntactic notation than through a definition of functionality. This approach has suffered from the problems of *attaching* semantics to the syntax, and of expressing and parsing *interleaved* dialogues. These points are amplified in §3.3.4.

Alternative notations for specifying behaviour rely on the notion of *events* generated and accepted by processes (where the user also is regarded as a process). Process algebras (like CSP [93]) can thus model not only interleaved processes, but also *communicating* processes. Process algebras impose no syntactic structure, and thus in user interface terms allow the dialogue to be user-directed (that is data-driven as opposed to control-driven). However, some process algebras, for instance CSP, have no way of expressing functionality. Formalisms

combining events and functionality are only just beginning to appear
[104, 91, 34, 1].

The choice of notation for the designer is thus governed by whether
he or she wishes to put emphasis on system data structure, operations,
or behaviour. However, as Dijkstra [53] points out, although notations
may be equivalent, they may well differ in the ease with which they can
be manipulated. For example,

$$47 + 4 = 51$$

is easier to evaluate than

$$XLVII + IV = LI$$

By implying a methodology, the notation chosen may influence the
design expressed.

A Z specification, for example, by allowing the schematisation of
the data structures separately from their operations, encourages the
design of data before the design of operations on the data. An algebraic
specification, on the other hand, encourages a *task* abstraction, in which
tasks may be functionally decomposed into sub-tasks.

Because its data structure is explicit, and because of its inherent
notion of state, it is also easier to move to an imperative implementation of a model-based specification like Z. Z may therefore be most
suited to systems that require efficient implementation. Algebraic specifications, on the other hand, are more mathematically tractable, and
in some cases [3] are directly executable. Proponents (e.g., Henderson
and Minkowitz [88]) point to the usefulness of this in rapid prototyping.

3.2.4   A reflection on design in Z

This section attempts to reconstruct the design process using Z. Rather
than abstracting Presenter's specification, two small illustrative examples are given. Some familiarity with Z's schema language [178] is
assumed.

We define design as a transformation for which no algorithm exists.
Naur [133] quotes Popper: "there is no such thing as a logical method
of having new ideas". That is, design is a non-mechanisable process.
Certainly such processes exist, in the class of non-computable problems. We recognise, intuitively, when such a process has taken place,
although of course we cannot explain how. To the extent that system

requirements are specific or readily formalisable, then, in this definition, design has already taken place.

Is there anything positive we can say about design? In essence it is a process which increases the information content of a system. An empty system is informationally chaotic: it tells us nothing (or anything):

$$\begin{array}{|l}\hline \text{\_\_}SYSTEM\text{_____}\\ \hline \\ \hline\end{array}$$

From this point on we can distinguish two stages in the design of a system: differentiation and structuring.

3.2.5   *Differentiation*

A system becomes differentiated by making design choices about the state space (in programming terms, the environment — deciding on terms and their types):

$$\begin{array}{|l}\hline \text{\_\_}SYSTEM\text{_____}\\ x, y : \mathsf{N}\\ \hline \\ \hline\end{array}$$

In this way we stake out our problem area. Further differentiation comes with the introduction of relations assumed, hoped, or needed to hold between these terms:

$$\begin{array}{|l}\hline \text{\_\_}SYSTEM\text{_____}\\ x, y : \mathsf{N}\\ \hline y = x^2\\ \hline\end{array}$$

Unless there is an internal contradiction, we can make formal judgements about such a system by applying predicates to it:

$$P(2,4) = \textit{true}$$
$$P(3,4) = \textit{false}$$

Or we may derive theorems from the specification:

$$\vdash \forall x, y \bullet x \leq y$$

Such theorems may be useful in proving implementations against the specification [119].

State

Let us add another term to the environment:

```
┌─ GLOBAL_STATE ──────────────────────────────────────
│  s : N
│
└─────────────────────────────────────────────────────
```

The Z notation allows the designer to express a rudimentary change of state:

```
┌─ EFFECTIVE_SYSTEM ──────────────────────────────────
│  SYSTEM
│  ΔGLOBAL_STATE
│ ──────────────
│  s' = x
└─────────────────────────────────────────────────────
```

where the prime (′) expresses the state of the variable after the change.

Using this notation, we have defined an *operation* on the global state. That is, we have established some preconditions: in this case, the existence of variables s, x, and y, and the relationship $y = x^2$; and a postcondition: that the variable s should be updated to the value of x. That is, we have implicitly defined a sequence of updates of s where s takes on the value of x. It is therefore also necessary to define an initial state which specifies the starting value for s:

```
┌─ init_GLOBAL_STATE ─────────────────────────────────
│  ΔGLOBAL_STATE
│ ──────────────
│  s' = 0
│
└─────────────────────────────────────────────────────
```

Input and output

Although we can read and discuss the specification of EFFECTIVE_SYSTEM, such a system cannot be observed in any operational sense. What is needed are mechanisms for input and output. In Z, the suffixes ? and ! perform this designation. Let us rename x and y to denote output and input channels respectively:

OBSERVABLE_SYSTEM ≙ EFFECTIVE_SYSTEM[$x!/x, y?/y$]

Notice that we have now given the abstract relationship between the terms x and y a direction. OBSERVABLE_SYSTEM delivers the square root of its input; if we had reversed the ! and ?, it would have delivered the square of its input. Thus at this level we can abstract away from any procedural bias.

OBSERVABLE_SYSTEM is operational. We have defined what sorts of things go in, what sorts of things come out, what the relationship is between anything that does go in and the thing that comes out, and what things are saved between each operation. It may not be very useful, but it does meet the requirement that it should be illustrative of the process of design: it came out of chaos by a gradual differentiation of the problem space. Whereas in an algebraic or functional design the operations would express the data structures, in a model-based design the data structures typically come first, and, as in this simple example, may well *suggest* the possible operations.

Usability

The only overall formal judgement we can make about such a system as OBSERVABLE_SYSTEM is consistency: as a specification it is 'correct' only in this sense. If another term in the predicate had been

$$y < x$$

the specification would have been inconsistent and therefore incorrect: there are no values of x and y which would satisfy this predicate.

The judgement of consistency is, however, not entirely an internal concern. We import, and take on trust, some types from outside. A specification such as OBSERVABLE_SYSTEM can be thought of as an abstract data type, and Guttag and Horning [80] make the point that in a type defined solely in terms of itself no value could be distinguished from any other. Such a type would be meaningless. In the case of OBSERVABLE_SYSTEM, we import the type N, and on the basis of its algebra we judge

$$y = x^2$$
$$y < x$$

to be inconsistent, and (in the consistent version) we calculate the output values from the input values.

We should also like to make a formal judgement of *completeness* on the system as specified. This will depend critically on the designer's aspirations for the type he is defining. If the designer wished the user to be able to generate *all* values of the external type (in this case, all natural numbers) then there would be a burden of proof on him to show that the operations in fact did this. On the other hand, the designer might wish that the values of the type be restricted to precisely those generated by the operations (which may be a smaller set). In this second sense, all consistent abstract specifications are automatically complete.

Guttag and Horning [80] point out that the problem of completeness may be more severe than the problem of consistency. In the general case, it is impossible to give a formal judgement on completeness, since the formal specification itself may be the only formal definition of the domain available. The terms in the predicate may be regarded as a set of constraints. If the constraints are circular, then iterative rather than single-pass methods may have to be used in their resolution, and these may fail to converge. This is equivalent to an inconsistency (although it may not be easily detectable). However, if the constraints are simply weak and the results non-deterministic, or if the constraints are strong and the domain is limited, then in either case this may well be what the designer intended. At best the only judgement of completeness we can make is that the domain generated by the constraints is co-extensive with the set of values *intended* in the design.

OBSERVABLE_SYSTEM, for example, generates all natural numbers as values of $x!$, since every natural number is the square root of some natural number. However, it does not generate a value of $x!$ for all possible values of $y?$ since not every number has an integer square root. Whether this is complete or not is decidable only by inquiring the intentions of the designer. We can say that in order to be **usable**, a system must, at least, be consistent, meaningful, and (informally) complete with respect to its intended range.

Usefulness

In addition to usability, the *usefulness* of the operations for the user must be taken into account. Some systems may provide a consistent, meaningful, and complete set of operations to generate their domain, but may, like a Turing machine, be of limited practical use. A useful system, therefore, must be usable:

$$useful \Rightarrow usable$$

What qualities make a usable system useful? Consider, for example, the design of a text editor, and let us treat text, for simplicity, as a sequence of characters:

$$TEXT \triangleq SEQ[CHAR]$$

(we import the type CHAR). Let us also establish a target document in the environment:

```
┌─ EDITOR_STATE ─────────────────────────────
│ doc : TEXT
│
└───────────────────────────────────────────
```

and initialise it to be empty:

```
┌─ init_EDITOR_STATE ────────────────────────
│ ΔEDITOR_STATE
├───────────────────────────────────────────
│ doc' = ⟨⟩
└───────────────────────────────────────────
```

Then, for constructive completeness, all we need is an *append* operation:

```
┌─ APPEND ───────────────────────────────────
│ ΔEDITOR_STATE
│ key? : CHAR
├───────────────────────────────────────────
│ doc' = doc ⌢ ⟨key?⟩
└───────────────────────────────────────────
```

That is, any document can be created simply by appending the appropriate sequence of characters one to the next. In an abstract sense this is perfectly adequate, but it clearly doesn't take the existence of a human user into account, who may make mistakes and want to backtrack. We need to include a *truncate* operation to remove the last character:

```
┌─ TRUNCATE ─────────────────────────────────
│ ΔEDITOR_STATE
├───────────────────────────────────────────
│ doc' = #doc ◁ doc
└───────────────────────────────────────────
```

We would not normally include a *truncate* operation in a printer-driver protocol in case the *computer* made a mistake, for example. Now at least we not only can create any document, but we can create any document from any other (even though in the worst case we might

have repetitively to truncate the whole document and start again).
The system is now strongly reachable in the sense defined in [61, 84].

The human user is capable of interacting with two-dimensional objects (e.g., screens) as well as linear objects (e.g., strings), and we can exploit this capability by providing some mechanism whereby append and truncate could be generalised to take place at any position in the text sequence:

```
┌─ INSERT ──────────────────────────────────────
│ ΔEDITOR_STATE
│ key? : CHAR
│ pos? : N⁺
├────────────────────────────────────────────────
│ ∀ u, v : TEXT| doc = u ⌢ v ∧ #u = pos? − 1 •
│     doc' = u ⌢ ⟨key?⟩ ⌢ v
└────────────────────────────────────────────────
```

```
┌─ DELETE ──────────────────────────────────────
│ ΔEDITOR_STATE
│ pos? : N⁺
├────────────────────────────────────────────────
│ ∀ u, v : TEXT| doc = u ⌢ v ∧ #u = pos? − 1 •
│     doc' = u ⌢ tail v
└────────────────────────────────────────────────
```

That is, *pos?* indicates, in the case of *insert*, the position of the new character after insertion, or, in the case of *delete*, the old position of the deleted character.

If the user can designate one position in text then he can also designate two positions. That is, he may well be able to select a section of text. On this basis we can argue for the inclusion of *cut* and *paste* operations:

```
┌─ CUT ─────────────────────────────────────────
│ ΔEDITOR_STATE
│ pos1?, pos2? : N⁺
│ sel! : TEXT
├────────────────────────────────────────────────
│ ∀ u, v, o : TEXT| doc = u ⌢ o ⌢ v ∧ #u = pos1? − 1 ∧
│     #(u ⌢ o) = pos2? • doc' = u ⌢ v ∧ sel! = o
└────────────────────────────────────────────────
```

```
  ┌─ PASTE ─────────────────────────────────────────────
  │ ΔEDITOR_STATE
  │ pos? : N⁺
  │ sel? : TEXT
  ├──────────────────────────────────────────────────────
  │ ∀ u, v : TEXT| doc = u ⌢ v ∧
  │     #u = pos? − 1 • doc' = u ⌢ sel? ⌢ v
  └──────────────────────────────────────────────────────
```

By considering the needs and capabilities of the human user, and potential devices, a certain amount of redundancy has been introduced into the operations provided. In abstract data type terms, we have provided composite operations built from the basic constructors. It would be easy to go on adding operations. We could easily construct a *move* operation using *cut* and *paste*, for example:

$$MOVE \mathrel{\hat{=}} CUT \gg PASTE$$

Other operations might require further differentiation: *copy*, *wordcut*, *sentencepaste* etc.

Essentially we have provided operations which make it convenient for the eventual user to generate values of the type documents, in this case, and to get from one document (which might contain an error) to another (without the error). A convenient criterion for deciding on usefulness is Kapur and Srivas' notion of 'expressive richness' [111]. An expressively rich set of operations generates the domain by simple sequential applications without the need for recursion or iteration. However, there is a balance to be maintained: we could abstractly design a system with an infinite number of operations, each of which generated an entire document — if there was a correction to be made, then it would simply be a matter of pressing the button for the corrected document! In one sense maximally useful (one operation invocation per document), this system is obviously unworkable. Even if it could be implemented, there would be insurmountable problems in presenting and selecting the functionality. The tendency is real, however, and is sometimes called 'creeping featurism'. A rule of thumb might be that a new (redundant) operation should not be introduced if the time gained by using it is outweighed by the time lost finding and learning it. We develop the idea of expressive richness here by an appeal to (less rigorous) notions of *power* and *equipment*.

Composite systems consist of a set of operations closely related in the types of their operands: editing operations on text, or operating system functionality on files, for example. We can make at least informal judgements of usefulness on the extent of the set. Take the text editor we have constructed:

_EDITOR_____
| INSERT
| DELETE
| CUT
| PASTE
|_____

If our system were limited to inserting and deleting:

$$EDITOR \triangleright (INSERT, DELETE)$$

we would certainly be able to construct any document. Insertion and deletion (by single characters) are capable of all the effects of cutting and pasting, but at a considerable loss of usefulness. We can say the system is **under-powered**: we can go anywhere, but slowly. Real examples of this are interface systems which are programming language-driven (like Postscript in Sun's NeWS [8]). These expect the interface designer to build his own constructs, rather than providing them for him.

In contrast, a system limited to cutting and pasting:

$$EDITOR \triangleright (CUT, PASTE)$$

would be **over-powered**, in the sense that the system takes over power from the designer. That is, the basic operations of adding and removing data are there, but only on data already supplied by the system. The system constrains the designer to some arbitrarily limited domain of interaction. A real example of this is an interface system which restricts interaction to a particular style such as menus or command-line conversation, or provides a pre-packaged set of interactive objects in a toolkit.

An orthogonal axis can be distinguished. A system consisting only of delete and cut operations:

$$EDITOR \triangleright (DELETE, CUT)$$

we might call **under-equipped**. That is, since we can remove but not add text, we have not, under any sensible interpretation, solved the problem of text editing. An under-equipped system may well turn out not to be *reachable*, in the sense defined by Dix and others [60]. It is often possible to spot under-equipment by an appeal to symmetry: a window that scrolls up, but not down, for example. However, there cannot be a hard and fast formal judgement on this characteristic, since in some cases, as we have shown, the designer may wish the domain to be limited in this way. For example, for reasons of security users are not normally provided with a completely equipped set of operations on an operating or database system.

Lastly, it is equally possible for a system to be **over-equipped**. That is, there may be so much redundancy in the set of operations that it becomes a problem to remember which ones apply in which situation, and which ones to deploy as an optimal strategy (as in the example of the button-per-document editor above). It is possible to argue that the commands of the UNIX operating system or the Smalltalk class hierarchy fall into this category.

3.2.6   *Structuring*

Structuring is the second component of the design process, and comes into play after a set of abstractions which answers the problem domain has been differentiated. We look for generalisations and correspondences, and wield Occam's Razor. The criterion of usefulness remains relevant. Just as with differentiation, design as structuring is by no means mechanical. Certain correspondences, for example, reveal themselves in the unstructured set of operations in EDITOR. Yet the set yields alternative structures. It is possible to organise the specification to capture character manipulation (*via* the keyboard) versus block manipulation (*via* the mouse):

```
┌─ KEYBOARD_OPS ──────────────────────────────
│ INSERT
│ DELETE
│
└─────────────────────────────────────────────
```

```
┌─ MOUSE_OPS ─────────────────────────────────
│ CUT
│ PASTE
│
└─────────────────────────────────────────────
```

On the other hand it is equally possible to reorganise the specification

so that it expresses addition as against removal of text. This allows us
to redefine the insert and delete operations to use cut and paste:

```
┌─ NEW_INSERT ──────────────────────────────────
│  key? : CHAR
│  PASTE \ (sel?)
├─────────────────────────────────────────────
│  sel? = ⟨key?⟩
└─────────────────────────────────────────────
```

```
┌─ NEW_DELETE ──────────────────────────────────
│  CUT \ (pos2?)
├─────────────────────────────────────────────
│  pos2? = pos1?
└─────────────────────────────────────────────
```

The alternative organisation therefore is:

```
┌─ INSERT_OPS ──────────────────────────────────
│  NEW_INSERT
│  PASTE
└─────────────────────────────────────────────
```

```
┌─ DELETE_OPS ──────────────────────────────────
│  NEW_DELETE
│  CUT
└─────────────────────────────────────────────
```

This last structure is more compact, since we have *factored* the cut
and paste operations to cover also insertion and deletion of keyboard
characters. Structuring in this sense is entirely analogous to what
Stroustrup calls finding 'commonality' [180] in the design of classes
in object-oriented programming. As he notes, this is not a trivial process. In addition, structuring in Z exploits, in object-orientation terms,
a multiple rather than a single inheritance hierarchy, since a schema
can include (inherit) arbitrarily many others.

In general it is not clear that the most elegant structuring of the
abstract specification is the most appropriate for the implementation or
for use. Constraints on design become evident during implementation
and use which may force a radical restructuring (or even redesign).
This may occur because the structure becomes unsuited to the revised
types or operations, or alternatively because the criteria for structuring
change.

3.2.7   *The user interface*

By designating input and output channels, we gave
OBSERVABLE_SYSTEM a *user interface* (however rudimentary). Any
effective functionality has both 'users' and an 'interface' to those users.
The immediate users may simply be other functionality, as for instance
when applications call library subroutines, and the corresponding interface may be sparse and clean. Ultimately, however, human users,
and a tangible interface, will be involved. We use the term 'interface'
to a system in this wider sense.

The user interface provides access to the underlying operation(s).
But more importantly it generates a *model* within which the user interprets the effects of the operation. To put it another way, the denotation of the operation can only be inferred from its effect on external objects. N is therefore a model for the operation defined in
OBSERVABLE_SYSTEM. Notice, however, that as well as possibly
being constrained by the predicates within the abstract type, the model
also acts itself as a constraint on the abstract operation: in this case
negative and real roots are excluded. Excluding negative roots may
be a useful constraint, but excluding real roots is a limitation on the
usefulness of the operation (since we cannot therefore obtain the square
root of *any* natural number). The user's interpretation of this operation
is therefore strongly modified by its interface. There is no difference
between the effect of the type N on this operation, and the effect of,
for example, using a monochrome device to display colour raster operations: in both, the user's interpretation of the underlying operation
is altered, possibly significantly — on a monochrome screen, colour
distinctions may become equalities and output may be lost.

Such interface constraints on the operations, therefore, must also
become constraints on their design, since unless such effects are taken
into account, what the user perceives may be at odds with the designer's
abstract intentions. Thus, whereas the pure functionalist might regard
a user interface as a peripheral side-effect, there is a strong sense in
which it is fundamental to a *computer* system.

This section has examined design in Z as a *synthetic* process involving
differentiation and structuring. Z, as a model-based notation, invites
the designer to think firstly in terms of data structure, then in terms of
operations. Algebraic notations, on the other hand, invite functional
decomposition [146], emphasising operations over data structures. The

next section examines constraints on design that may arise after specification.

3.3   Constraints on design

The software engineering view of specification as an immutable document consequently models the production of an implementation as
refinement. Refinement is the process of generating implementations
(I) which satisfy specifications (S). That is:

$$I \Rightarrow S$$

The relationship between a specification and its implementations is,
however, not one to one:

$$refinement : S \leftrightarrow I$$

That is, a number of implementations may satisfy a single specification,
and it is conceivable that a number of specifications may be satisfied by
a single implementation. A complex system like an operating system
may satisfy a number of discrete specifications, for example.

Design choices, in the creative sense used above, must therefore enter
into any implementation. It has been argued by Dix and others [61,
84] that these design choices may be formalised into general design
principles:

$$refinement : S \times gueps \nrightarrow I$$

(i.e., by taking these principles into account the early stages of refinement become *deterministic*). To the extent that this is possible,
however, creative design is then simply hidden within the gueps.

This section argues that abstract design is not independent of design
issues arising during refinement. It identifies four classes of constraint
(soft, firm, hard, and environmental) which may reveal themselves during implementation and use, and may force a re-evaluation and reformulation of the abstract design.

3.3.1   *Soft constraints*

By *soft* constraints we mean constraints for which there is no good reason other than end-user preference or prejudice. There are two points

here: it is dangerous to escape these by erecting a barrier of formality, since the application may well turn out to be unused even if not unusable; and, while in some cases user objections may be trivial and easy to accommodate, in others they may attack fundamental structures of the formal specification or the implementation.

Trivial issues may be the style of highlighting: inverse video or underlining for text; shadowing or Macintosh-like 'handles' for graphical objects. The underlying notion of selection is largely independent of these presentation issues. Other issues, however, may strike deeper into the design. In Presenter, for example, selectability of a region was specified orthogonally to movability: it seemed a clean assumption that the end-user may wish in some cases to select a region (representing a button, say), and in other cases to move the region. However, Presenter's tree structure allows grouping of regions, indicated by selection of the common ancestor region. If that region is movable, then the whole group is moved. Application programmers wished to provide groups of regions which were directly movable by the user (i.e., without prior selection) — the simplest solution in the abstract seemed to be to modify the behaviour of the *movable* attribute so that (as happens with selection) the first movable region up the tree from the region which the user is attempting to move (with the second mouse button) is in fact the region that is moved. In this way, by judicious setting of the movable attribute, the application programmer could achieve the functionality wished. In practice the problem arose that users often found themselves unintentionally moving large groups of regions when trying to move an unmovable (descendant) component.

This problem forced a redesign of the semantics of the *selectable* attribute. In this current design, selectability operates as a guard not only for selection, but also for the movement and sizing operations. That is, when an attempt is made to move a leaf region, the first *selectable* region up the tree is found. If this is in addition movable (and only then), it is moved. Unexpected group movement can therefore be prevented by setting lower regions selectable but not movable, thus blocking the effect of a move operation, while *intentional* group movement can be permitted by explicit selection. In explanation this seems a subtle point, but it was an important factor in general usability. The original specification was not wrong — there were just factors of *scale* that it did not take into account. In this example, moving a *single* region unintentionally is simply remedied by moving the region back. However, this strategy is unacceptably time consuming and visually confusing when a large group of regions is moved. The solution was not just a 'hack', but a redesign: selectability was generalised to accessibility.

Other soft constraints may be less easy to accommodate. In Presenter, for example, the interactive paradigm is *object-based*, where the primary designation of function is selection of visible objects on the screen (buttons, for example). Some applications employ a *gesture-based paradigm* [206] in which the *path* of the mouse is significant. The Alternate Reality Kit [177], for example, allows users to 'throw' objects using the mouse. While Presenter allows the application to track the cursor if wished, it provides no constructs to do this conveniently. This is a policy decision rather than a design decision (since the space of possible interfaces must be reduced to a manageable size).

3.3.2   *Firm constraints*

The objects the user manipulates will have inherent characteristics. Such objects might be numbers, tree structures, tuples, files, or pieces of text. Their characteristics may be easy to model abstractly, as in the case of numbers, or rather difficult, as in the case of text. Dijkstra [53] quotes the example of dates, which refuse to fit tidily into square arrays. The temptation for the designer of a formal specification is to abstract away from recalcitrant objects like text. However, it may well turn out (during implementation) that the assumptions he makes in order to do this are invalid, or that the resultant specification is too general to be useful. The often intransigent characteristics of the basic objects impose *firm* constraints on design.

In order to obtain the clean specification of a text editor above, we made some severe abstractions from what we know heuristically are the features of computer-based text editing. In particular, we ignored issues of text formatting and text selection on the implicit assumption that formatting is a function that can be applied to text independently of the basic editing operations. However, there are three dangers: firstly, and most seriously, we may in fact not be able to abstract away from some levels because of a circularity in the operations. In the editor example, the edit operations depend on a text selection; this may in turn depend on format. This dependency is not evident in the current specification;

but what if user pressure (a soft constraint) had required a *line delete* operation? Lines are functions of the format, rather than inherent in the text sequence. Similarly, if we later supply a scroll operation on the format, there may be constraints on text editing unforeseen in the present specification — that only editing of visible text should be possible, for example. Here again, the abstract specification is constrained by its implementation.

Secondly, in ignoring formatting and selection, we are abstracting away from features which may be critical to the usability of the editor. In particular we leave open whether the text insertion point will be identified with the current text selection, and where text insertion will take place (before or after the caret). In an interactive system these considerations are not peripheral. In the implementation of Presenter, for example, the decision was taken (since it was not considered during specification) that the insertion point should be identified with the text selection. Only then was it obvious that if character insertion was implemented by a paste (as in NEW_INSERT above), and pasted characters remained selected (ergonomically sound), and there was at most one current selection (again ergonomically sound), then no pasted selection would survive the next insert — that is, as soon as a character was typed, it would become the text selection. Whereas the specification had assumed that selection and highlighting were trivial issues that would follow from the basic cut and paste operations, in practice a considerable amount of rethinking was involved.

Lastly, to abstract away from firm constraints on design, for example intransigent features of text such as left-right ordering, may encourage an unreal symmetry in the formal specification. In other words, usefulness and symmetry may conflict. Sufrin [181], for example, defines a *mirror* function, which maps a document to its textual mirror image. He composes this function before and then after a target function:

$$right, left : (DOC \times DOC) \rightarrow (DOC \times DOC)$$

$$right\ f = mirror \circ f \circ mirror$$
$$left\ f = f$$

where the target function (f) may be *move*, *delete*, or *insert*. By this strategy, he halves the number of definitions he has to make of these operations in their directional modes. For example,

> *left move*

and

> *right move*

fully define the directional modes of the single *move* function, which he gives an inherent leftward bias (since *left f = f*). However, it is by no means clear that under formatting and display constraints this symmetry is actually present in edited documents, nor that the range of derived operations (including left and right delete) is actually useful to the user. Usefulness may be being sacrificed to elegance of expression.

3.3.3   *Hard constraints*

The limitations or characteristics of the target hardware impose *hard* constraints on design. These are constraints, that is, that are imposed not by the objects themselves, but by the medium in which they will be manipulated. While it must be possible to abstract away from such constraints, it is dangerous not to take them into account during design.

Hard constraints will essentially be imposed by considerations of *efficiency* (in time or space), but other limitations (absence of colour or sound hardware, for example) will also be relevant. In real time systems, hard constraints like response time may be absolute limitations. In user interface design these will be less definitive, since users are more or less tolerant of such factors. Nevertheless, it is always possible to specify systems that turn out in practice to be uselessly slow or unpredictable in response. The use of double (or multiple) clicks as a distinguished event is now a fairly common overloading of mouse button functionality. While this is possible on a single-process machine like the Macintosh, it is problematic when application and interface are distributed over networks, due to the latency involved in the network traffic (how long do you wait for another click?). It is difficult to implement this in X [166], for example, since the X server has no double-click event. Considerable redesign might be involved to get round this.

Latency also makes 'mouse-ahead' problematic. A user requests a pop-up menu, for example, by pressing a mouse button, and then drags the mouse and releases the button on the menu item he wants. However, an expert user may know where the menu item is going to be, and is

capable of releasing the button before the screen manager has had time
to draw the menu. The danger is that the button release event will
be wrongly despatched to the application under the menu, rather than
to the menu process. A solution is to queue input, and in addition
provide a mechanism to freeze input processing (that is, so that input
is queued but not processed). Both X (*synchronous mode* [10]) and
NeWS (*blockinputqueue* [8]), for example, provide a mechanism to block
input in this way.

As Myers [130] notes, there is a converse problem, however, a *novice*
user may be confused by network latency into thinking that the system
simply has not responded (to a mouse button push, for example) and
repeat the action. Contrary to what he expects, his input is queued, and
he finds he has made multiple invocations of, say, some menu command.
A simplistic solution is to flush the buffer (resulting in a single-event
record rather than a queue) or to allow events some limited lifetime.
There is thus a conflict here between the needs of the novice and the
expert user. Whereas the expert user needs to be guaranteed that his
input is despatched to what he *predicts* is its target (a soon-to-pop-
up menu, for example), the novice user needs to be guaranteed that
events are despatched to what he *sees* is their target (for example, a
plain background against which he has no means of knowing that a
menu is about to pop up). These important hard constraints are easily
ignored in a formal specification in which atomic operations are treated
as instantaneous (if time is considered at all).

In Presenter's specification an image is defined simply on a (possibly
infinite) set of contiguous points in the real plane, over the closed unit
intervals:

$$POINTS \triangleq ([0,1] \times [0,1])$$
$$IMAGE : POINTS \twoheadrightarrow COLOURS$$

In graphical interfaces, however, screen limitations such as resolution
and size must be taken into account. It would not be possible, for
example, to display readably a full page of a large newspaper on a
Sun screen, because the number of pixels available per character would
hardly distinguish them, let alone be pleasant to read. If we wished to
develop a publishing application for newspapers, therefore, we would
be forced to adopt scrolling or holophraxis to subset or compact the
required space [15, 97]. This is a major addition to the design whose
need is not evident from the abstract image definition.

The original specification for Presenter also adopted a text model similar to the second structuring (INSERT_OPS and DELETE_OPS) above. This was cleaner and shorter. However, in the case of keyboard input, the *delete* operation is in fact an *insert* of a DEL character. In the implementation, therefore, deletion (but not cutting) had to be made a special case of the *paste* operation. Nor could this be restricted to single character inserts, since the possibility of character stream buffering means that delete characters may arrive in batches embedded in other text. In the face of this hard constraint the design had to be restructured.

3.3.4   *Environmental constraints*

An abstract specification encourages an isolated view of the task and its data. In real systems, on the other hand, tasks must share resources and cooperate with other tasks. Environmental priorities for maintaining the society of tasks may conflict with priorities as seen from the point of view of the abstract specification of a particular task.

We examine here three environmental constraints on design: factoring, independence and separation. The requirement for separation in user interface design is examined more fully in terms of dialogue abstraction and a new paradigm, surface interaction.

Factoring

Environmental constraints are likely to place a high priority on the *factoring* of resources among tasks. Programmer resources can be factored by providing mechanisms for reuse of program components (*data* abstractions). The formal paradigms we have discussed so far provide a basis for such an abstraction. A major strategy for handling hard constraints of time or space is also to factor *computational* resources by distributing certain tasks to specialised hardware or processes (*control* abstractions). Factoring with this motive has two benefits: computational load is shared; and separation of concerns encourages an examination of domains that may not have been immediately suggested by the application in isolation.

Independence

Environmental constraints may also require levels of *independence*. That is, it may be convenient to hide contingent levels (such as machine or

device configurations) from applications by requiring that they express
input and output in terms of some higher level constructs. These constructs can then be mapped to a variety of lower primitives. Ideally,
this binding should be performed as late as possible, for example so that
the user can modify the style and characteristics of his environment at
run time. Historically the most important level of independence has
been device independence [23]. This is usually accomplished by a level
of *virtual* [71] or *logical* devices [162]. Other levels have been suggested:
media independence [117], and *style* independence [110]. More recently,
dialogue independence has been explored, enabling expert or novice dialogues to be provided for the same functionality, either at the discretion
of the user [41], or automatically [19]. It is also possible [200] to identify
a level of *data* independence, whereby applications use a common data
representation.

Factoring and independence are orthogonal: it is possible to conceive
of a level of independence which has no practical use (files of just 365
characters, for example), as well as generally usable constructs which
are fully dependent on the machine level (colour imaging, for example).
Ideally, however, the constructs provided for factoring resources should
at the same time provide a level of independence. Thus a window
server like X [166] factors out display concerns, and at the same time
is mappable to a variety of display devices.

We might also identify two fundamental environmental paradigms
which provide for factoring and independence: the *linguistic* paradigm
and the *agent* paradigm. The linguistic paradigm derives from the
lexical, syntactic, and semantic levels of Foley's language model [69],
and has its fullest instantiation in the Seeheim model for User Interface
Management Systems (UIMS) [74, 75]. Its characteristic is a *layering*
of the environment along the linguistic levels. In the agent paradigm,
on the other hand, the only structuring principle is the agent itself,
which encapsulates data, computation, and input and output. Agents
are scheduled non-deterministically by user events (that is, there is no
dialogue abstraction). The 'device' models of Anson [11] and Bos [23]
are instantiations of the agent paradigm. Here the agent is composable,
such that at the top level the whole application is an agent. More recent
agent instantiations can be seen in object-oriented systems [180], and
in user interface toolkits [143, 156, 185, 49].

Separation

The *separation* of interface and application is a fundamental environmental constraint often applied. In general, proponents of the linguistic paradigm support strong separation, while proponents of the agent paradigm do not. The envisaged benefits of separation derive from factoring and independence:

- User interfaces and applications can evolve independently. It may be possible to analyse or prototype each in isolation from the other.

- The interface and the application may execute as separate processes, for example in a server/client relationship, and even over a distributed network.

- One interface can be made common to a range of applications, and thus interface consistency can be enforced, and code and development effort shared.

- A range of interfaces can be applied to the same application, so that user preference or designer experimentation can be catered for.

Disagreement over the very possibility of accomplishing separation (contrast the positions of [44] and [175]) often stems from a disagreement over terms. Separation may be performed logically, *via* a data abstraction such as program modules, libraries, or inheritable class definitions, or physically, *via* a control abstraction. For example, the internal and external control models of the 1982 UIMS workshop [198], and the concurrent control model of the 1986 UIMS workshop [116] vary in their physical separability.

Dialogue abstraction

Disagreement on separation also arises from differing interface application partitions. In particular, if dialogue is abstracted into the interface, as in the standard UIMS, then problems arise in specifying the dialogue syntax (the Syngraph UIMS was underused for this reason [142]), and also for the implementer in parsing user input accordingly [86]. It is also ironic that the more powerful the formal language for dialogue specification (in terms of the Chomsky hierarchy), the more prescriptive it is for the end user, in the sense that a more structured dialogue is often more moded. A prescriptive dialogue is particularly inappropriate in a direct manipulation interface. While a totally non-determined dialogue may not in some cases be a good thing (for beginners, for example [192]), direct manipulation encourages the user to be spontaneous in his actions.

On a glass teletype, it is difficult for the user to conduct a dialogue with more than one process at a time (although not impossible). On a bitmapped screen, on the other hand, dialogues may be spatially multiplexed. Typically a user may interact with different applications simultaneously *via* separate windows, but even within applications it is becoming common to provide non-deterministic dialogues *via* a range of discrete interactive components. The multi-threaded dialogues that result [187, 188] are difficult to model syntactically [91].

The dialogue is also not likely to be able to take account of all environmental conditions. For example, a window manager may have its own dialogue, which may interfere with application dialogues. Thus, application operations may become unavailable in the concrete interface because their representation has been occluded (a window has been popped by the user and hides the buttons), or because the mouse button is overloaded and has been usurped (for instance to move or size a window).

If the dialogue is in addition separated from application data, then the further problem arises of 'semantic feedback' [100]. This is particularly severe in direct manipulation interfaces, where the user expects a high degree of 'engagement' [102] between objects on the screen and the underlying semantic objects. This problem can be avoided by moving the application data into the interface [41], but at the expense of imposing a shared data representation on all applications [211]. Both Olsen [141] and Coutaz [46] have recently abandoned the separate dialogue component as an environmental constraint.

The only cases in which a dialogue abstraction might be useful involve processes which cannot be held responsible for their actions. Such processes might be a novice user who did not know, for example, that quitting from an editor did not automatically save his edited file; or a nuclear reactor that could not be expected to 'know' that obeying a command to simultaneously void its coolant and raise its damping rods would result in a melt-down. In both these cases the interface designer might wish to *impose* a structure on the dialogue for the good of the participants. That is, the traces of the basic functionality might be subjected to *external* temporal or logical constraints, resulting in what Thimbleby [192] calls a 'well-determined' dialogue. These, however, are constraints that could just as well be applied at the application level rather than the interface level, and are thus distinct from the problem of separation.

Surface interaction

A new environmental paradigm may be proposed, **surface interaction**. This seeks to move the emphasis away from a separable dialogue abstraction (where the UIMS model places it [75]), onto a separable presentation component. As Olsen notes ([142] p.135) presentation is 'sorely neglected'. Two fundamental recognitions may be made here. Firstly, the presentation domain provides broad scope for factoring interaction in user interfaces, both in terms of data abstractions and control abstractions. There is a natural separation in that at least the semantic level is independent of presentation (there may be many model-view mappings, for example). Secondly, the screen is a *shared resource*. In order to handle synchronisation constraints and provide optimal update, it is therefore necessary to have a *global* presentation component. This is in contradistinction to the agent paradigm, in which agents may encapsulate their own presentation, as in object-oriented interface systems like Smalltalk's MVC [30], or Szekely's 'presenters' [186]. In practice, screen synchronisation in object-oriented systems is handled by a global class, or by an underlying window manager, but this only supports the point. The agent paradigm therefore provides poor separation. The linguistic paradigm, on the other hand, is strongly separated, but has problems handling multi-threaded dialogues and semantic feedback. Surface interaction seeks to make a more pragmatic separation between surface (presentation) and deep (semantics).

A major premise of surface interaction is that the surface, in addition to providing operations to display and manipulate images (data abstraction), can be made to encapsulate a high proportion of graphical interaction (control abstraction) quite independently of application state transitions. We can think of the surface, that is, not just as a view mapping, but as itself having abstract functionality and control concerned with the manipulation and behaviour of surface objects like characters or images. This enables the notion of *equal access*, since both the user and the application can be thought of as clients of this surface functionality. It is therefore possible to develop a surface interaction model in the domain of geometric manipulation and graphical and textual editing, independently of any underlying functionality it might be called upon to represent or provoke. The surface need have no knowledge of application semantics, and thus can be common across a range of applications (although applications need to have knowledge of surface operations and events). At the same time it provides a powerful factoring of computational resources which can be modularised and distributed from applications in a server process. In addition, the surface interaction paradigm does not presuppose any structure to deep interaction: this may use a layered or an agent paradigm, for example.

The details of the particular surface model are critical to the success of the paradigm. Standard window managers already provide surface interaction: there are data types (windows and icons), operation on them (open, close, etc.), and there is a control abstraction by which window management operations can be interleaved with application operations. It may be, however, that the window management paradigm is in practice graphically and geometrically limited, and not sufficiently general to provide presentation constructs for a wide range of applications. This model instantiated in Presenter, and described formally in [200], is an attempt at such generality.

3.3.5 *Limitations of formal specification*

A formal specification allows the designer to be rigorous about proving the internal consistency of that design, and about proving implementations with respect to the design. Yet, as we have illustrated, there are a number of constraints which may, in the worst case, invalidate a 'proven' design. How do these problems arise?

Any formal system must depend on axioms that are assumed but are unproved. There is a temptation in formal specification to exploit this necessity by wrapping up any uncomfortable reality in a type name and 'not define it further'. The justification for this sort of packaging is that the specifier can thereby 'abstract away from' unnecessary details. Suppression of detail, however, may in fact hide recalcitrant real-world features. For example, EDITOR uses the type CHAR without further definition. In real terms, however, the user never edits a logical char-

acter like this. Instead he manipulates one of a set of possible images
varying in font, point size, and resolution. Each of these factors may
radically affect the denotation of the editing operations under the constraints of scrolling and formatting. Similarly the IMAGE definition in
Presenter hides the display limitations imposed by screen resolution.

There is also a danger that as specifiers we impute too much meaning
to our model in abstraction from its objects, either implicitly or explicitly by overloading the notation. For example, there is little (except
common sense and the textual explanations), to prevent interpreting
OBSERVABLE_SYSTEM as a text editor. s is the persistent underlying text, y? is keyboard input, x! is the screen, and the square function,
let us say, is a formatting constraint. If we lower our guard, there may
be many such homomorphic models for the specification, some of which
hold only analogously rather than rigorously. For example, to what extent is it wise to use the = relation between two CHARs, given the
observations of the type above? If we are not careful, there may also
be interpretations which are not only not expected, but nonsensical:
reverse-text editors, for example.

The choice of notation may also force the designer to ignore certain issues. In Z, for example, it is difficult to express timing constraints and
inter-object communication. In process algebras and dialogue grammars, on the other hand, it may be difficult to express functionality.

Ideally, a formal specification should be explicit at the level of the
primitive objects in its domain. In user interface systems, this means
taking full account of text fonts, formatting styles, and screen resolution, as well as timing constraints and the possibility of user errors
and interference from other applications. Even the simple square root
OBSERVABLE_SYSTEM is not fully explicit. For example, what happens in the case of input for which there is no integer square root? Such
an ideal specification has been called a *realisation* [109]. A realisation
is a formulation of a system which is concrete (that is, precise in its
details), but does not preclude further refinement for the sake of optimisation. For example, whereas Presenter's specification implies a global
update of the screen on each character insert, a clear optimisation is
incrementally to update the screen only in the areas of change. Other
than in improved performance, this is perceptually indistinguishable
from the realisation.

The degree of precision described above poses problems. Not least is the length and complexity of the specification: formatting of text under font and display area changes is not a trivial operation to define. There may also be important stages of interaction which take place *between* the initiation and completion of a defined operation. Presenter, for example, echoes a *move* or *size* of a region in one of two ways: a rubber box may track the cursor while the appropriate button is held down, and the region jumps to the new position or size upon button release. Alternatively, the region may follow the cursor movement smoothly. The atomic *move* or *size* operation of the specification, therefore, has in fact a continuous component. The current specification does not model either of these effects, largely because they entail a *time-based*, rather than state-based approach. That is, transitions of the system would be on time intervals rather than state intervals.

The distinction between realisation and implementation marks a limit of concreteness beyond which it is not necessary for specification to go. The programming language is an appropriate notation in which to express the transition from realisation to implementation. However, the realisation may be difficult to express because of its complexity or the limitations of the notation. The boundary between specification and programming is therefore not clear-cut.

3.4   Conclusions

Since no stage in the transformation from problem to product is thoroughly determined, design, in a creative sense, is involved at all levels. It is, moreover, dangerous to dissociate abstract design from design of the interface, because of the possibility of unexpected interpretations of the specification, the need to take fully into account asymmetries in the problem domain, and the danger that the abstract design may not coincide with the designer's intentions through constraints imposed by the interface. However, formal specification is a useful vehicle because it minimises unnecessary dependencies, and also allows transference of solutions from other problem domains. Software production should therefore be specification-centred rather than specification-driven. The aim of specification should be a *realisation* based on sound principles, but also taking account of soft, firm, hard, and environmental constraints. For this reason, a formal specification should ideally remain open to modification throughout the product development process.

CHAPTER FOUR

NON DETERMINISM AS A PARADIGM FOR UNDERSTANDING THE USER INTERFACE

ALAN DIX

4.1   Introduction

Although this chapter primarily presents conceptual and pragmatic
ideas about non determinism in user-interfaces there is another, higher
level, more important point to it. This chapter provides an example
of the subtle interweaving of formal and informal reasoning; the way
formal analysis can lead to new insights which influence the informal.

We start with an examination of problems arising from several formal
models of interactive systems. Chapter 5 gives a fairly detailed account
of one such model, however, here our treatment will be less formal, only
considering those features essential for the present discussion. These
features lead us to consider *non deterministic* models in order to express
properties of interest. The models are non deterministic in a purely
formal sense; the rest of this chapter considers the repercussions non
determinism has on our understanding of the user interface.

Non deterministic models contradict the general feeling that computer systems are deterministic, that they follow a fixed sequence of
instructions, so we might wonder whether there is any real meaning

to the use of the term non determinism, or whether it is a useful but essentially meaningless formal trick.

Here, we shall demonstrate four things about non determinism in user interfaces: it does exist; users deal with it; we can help them do this; and, finally, we can use it.

§4.4 and §4.5 deal with the first of these points. §4.4 shows that non determinism is in fact a common experience of users, and we focus on a notion of *behavioural* non determinism to square this with the normal deterministic model of computation. §4.5 catalogues various sources of non determinism in the user interface.

Further sections show how users, abetted by the designers of systems, can deal with non determinism. The final point of §4.6 reminds us how non determinism can be useful in the specification of systems, even if this non determinism is not intended to be a facet of the actual system, only a tool for development. §4.7 goes beyond this giving an example of how non determinism might be *deliberately introduced* into a user interface to improve performance. Without being prepared—by noting how supposedly deterministic systems behave as if they were non deterministic—the deliberate introduction of non determinism could seem preposterous! Instead we are able to assess it impartially and see how it can actually *reduce* apparent non determinism for the user.

To some extent the overall structure of the chapter (formal models; informal analysis; semi-formal application) is the opposite of the normal presentation where an informal problem leads to a formal statement and analysis. Our approach reflects the true historical development of the work: the formal models *did* arise originally from informal consideration of the systems they describe, but the issue of non determinism, and the recognition of it in various guises arose directly from the formal analysis. However, it did not remain in the formal sphere but enabled understanding beyond the aspects formally modelled.

4.2   Unifying formal models with non determinism

Several different interaction models have been developed at York to understand and express properties of various styles of interaction. These are abstract formal models: abstract in order to be generic over a range of similar systems and formal in order to be amenable to analysis. Here we are going to consider briefly three of these interaction models:

- PIEs [61]—a very general 'black-box' model intended to be applicable to almost all systems;

- *a temporal model* [56]—for considering real time properties of interactive systems;

- *view spaces* [57]—for modelling windowed systems.

In any particular system, we may want to apply properties expressed over several of these models and we could map them all onto the system independently, however, it is sensible to consider how these inter-relate at the abstract level, and if possible relate them all back to the general PIE model. This process will require a non deterministic version of the PIE model.

More details about these models and the principles that can be defined using them may be found in the papers cited above, and in my thesis [54].

4.2.1   *The PIE model*

The PIE model is a very simple model of single stream input/output interactive systems. The user enters a stream of commands from a set C. These commands can be at various levels, perhaps key-presses or mouse-clicks, or perhaps parsed command lines. The response of the system we call the effect, from a set E. Again this can be interpreted at various levels, perhaps the actual bitmap or character map seen by the user, or perhaps the underlying state of the system. When this latter is the case, there will typically be functions display: $E \to D$ and result: $E \to R$ giving the immediate display, and the final result of the system for a particular state. If these are present the model is called a **red-PIE**. The sequence of commands input (from the set $P = C^*$) is related to the effect observed by an interpretation function $I: P \to E$.

This model is used to express simple properties applicable to nearly all interactive systems. Although it is a simple model, it is surprising how complex the analysis can be. One of the first principles considered was related to predictability: "I have been using the system, I go away for a cup of tea, and upon returning have forgotten where exactly I am in the dialogue. Is there sufficient data available for me to proceed?" This question has been addressed at various levels of complexity and abstraction, but one of the simplest requirements is that the system be **predictable**:

$$\forall\, p, q, r \in P : I(p) = I(q) \Rightarrow I(pr) = I(qr)$$

This says that if two systems have the same current effect, then whatever further commands are entered, the systems will stay the same. If E is interpreted as the display this is usually too restrictive, whereas if it is the complete state, it says nothing at all. However, it does capture the flavour of more complex conditions. We will return to it later.

4.2.2   *Problems for temporal systems*

The above model does not tell us how long we have to wait for an effect, only what that effect will be when it comes and that it is deterministic. It does not allow us to describe real time phenomena, such as the buffering (or lack of buffering) of user input, or display strategies such as intermittent update (when some intermediate displays are skipped when typing fast) or partial update (when part of the screen is kept up to date, but the rest is allowed to lag behind the typing).

We can augment the model to allow us to describe real time phenomena by including in the possible inputs at any time the possibility of no input, represented by τ, a 'tick.' The resulting set of inputs is thus $C_\tau = C \cup \{\tau\}$. The sequence of inputs is the history $H = C_\tau^*$. The effect is as before, and the history and effect are related by an interpretation function $I_\tau : H \rightarrow E$. Formally this is identical to the PIE, but the connotations are different: P being sequences of actual user commands; H being a time series.

The user will be unaware of detailed timings; an abstraction of temporal behaviour is required. Clearly from any sequence of C_τ we can abstract a sequence from C by simply ignoring every τ. This is the user's view of the input (i.e., what was entered but not exactly when). It is not clear what effect should be associated with a particular input sequence but for the moment let's use the steady state effect. This is the effect that would result if all typing stopped, and we waited for the system to become quiescent or **steady**.

$$I_{steady}(h) = I_t(h\,\tau\tau\ldots)$$

Having removed timing from the temporal system the result is likely to be non deterministic. For instance, take a bufferless typewriter which requires a single time interval after each character to reset itself and ignores any characters being entered too fast. In this case $C = \mathrm{Ch}$, the set of characters, and $E = \mathrm{Ch}^*$ sequences of characters.

The interpretation function is defined as follows, ε being the empty sequence:

$$
\begin{aligned}
I_\tau(\varepsilon) &= \varepsilon \\
I_\tau(c) &= c \\
I_\tau(p\tau) &= I_\tau(p) \\
I_\tau(p\tau c) &= I_\tau(p)c \\
I_\tau(pc_1 c_2) &= I_\tau(pc_1)
\end{aligned}
$$

Thus, the input sequence abc with different timings may give rise to different effects:

$$
\begin{aligned}
I_\tau(\mathrm{a}\tau\mathrm{b}\tau\mathrm{c}) &= \mathrm{abc} \\
I_\tau(\mathrm{ab}\tau\mathrm{c}) &= \mathrm{ac} \\
I_\tau(\mathrm{abc}) &= \mathrm{a}
\end{aligned}
$$

We need a non deterministic version of the PIE model to model such behaviour.

4.2.3   *Problem for windowed systems*

A similar problem arises when considering the representation of windows. We can create a model similar to the PIE model to represent windowed systems. We associate with each window a label or handle from a set Λ. The possible states of the system are from a set S, and we can recover from this a combined result, **result**: $S \to R$, and for each window its display, **display**: $S \times \Lambda \to D$. Similarly each command is addressed to a particular window, and it is possible to derive a state updating operation **doit**: $S \times C \times \Lambda \to S$. In fact, the model needs to be a little more complex to deal with the way windows are created and destroyed, but this suffices for the moment.

The whole system may be regarded as a PIE with a command set $C \times \Lambda$. More often we would be interested in regarding each window as an interactive system in its own right.

If we 'freeze' all other windows we can give the functionality of a window λ in the state s as the result and display interpretations I_r and I_d:

$$I_r \quad = \quad \mathsf{result} \circ I_\lambda$$
$$I_d(p) \quad = \quad \mathsf{display}(I_\lambda(p), \lambda)$$

Where I_λ is the iterate of doit relative to λ:

$$I_\lambda(\varepsilon) \quad = \quad s$$
$$I_\lambda(pc) \quad = \quad \mathsf{doit}(I_\lambda(p), c, \lambda)$$

This definition is not very useful: it's not very interesting knowing the functionality of a window system when you only use one window. What we really want to know is the functionality of each window when other windows are being used also. To do this we would consider the possible effect of commands p to a window amidst all possible interleavings from other windows. Sometimes all commands are result and display independent in all contexts. The overall result, and the displays in the windows do not depend on the order of interleaving. In this case, we would obtain the same interpretation functions as above. In the general case, however, we would again obtain non deterministic functionality.

> *Meta-point: The various formal models have been developed out of our informal understanding of interactive systems. They are all deterministic but in each case we have found a purely deterministic model insufficient. We are now going to make the transition in the formal domain to consider non deterministic models.*

4.3   Non deterministic PIEs

We will now consider non deterministic generalisations of the PIE model. There are various ways of modelling non determinism, but one of the simplest is to substitute for some value a set of possible values. However, we have to be careful to choose the right representation of our model, and the right values to substitute. The simplest option is to assign to each input a set of possible effects. That is we modify the signature of the interpretation to $I_{ND}: P \to \mathbb{P} E$, where $\mathbb{P} E$ is the collection of sets of effects. Unfortunately this does not distinguish some systems that are clearly distinct. Consider I_{ND}, defined as follows:

$$\forall p \in P: I_{ND}(p) = \{0, 1\}$$

Does this describe a system that starts off with a value of 0 or 1 and retains this value no matter what the user enters? Does it represent a system that makes an independent choice after each command? Is it something in between? On the basis of the information given, we cannot decide. We therefore need to consider the trace of all effects generated by a command.

For any deterministic PIE we can always define a new interpretation $I^*: P \to E^*$ by:

$$I^*(\varepsilon) = \varepsilon$$
$$I^*(pc) = I^*(p) :: I(c)$$

where '::' is sequence concatenation.

That is, we define an interpretation giving the entire history of effects for each command history. This is the appropriate function to generalise for non determinism yielding an interpretation $I^*_{ND}: P \to \mathbb{P} E^*$. We could then distinguish the single random constant system with interpretation:

$$\forall p \in P: I^*_{ND}(p) = \{\text{zeroes}, \text{ones}\}$$
where
zeroes is a sequence of zeroes of length $\text{length}(p) + 1$.
ones is a sequence of ones of the same length.

From the multiple independent choice system:

$$\forall p \in P: I^*_{ND}(p) = \{0, 1\}^{n+1}$$
where
$n = \text{length}(p)$

We can see that necessary conditions for a valid interpretation I^*_{ND} are:

Effect history is right length for number of inputs:

$$\forall\, e^* \in I^*_{ND}(p): \text{length}(e^*) = \text{length}(p) + 1$$

History cannot change:

$$\forall\, q \leq p \in P, e_p \in I^*_{ND}(p)\; \exists\, e_q \in I^*_{ND}(q): e_q \leq e_p$$
where
$\leq$ is the initial subsequence relation: $q \leq p \doteq \exists\, r \in P: p = qr$

The first condition says that the effect trace must contain one member for each input command plus an initial effect, the second that if some sequence of effects has been the result of a sequence of commands then its first $m + 1$ entries must be a possible result of the initial m commands.

From now on we will call a triple $\langle P, I^*_{ND}, E \rangle$ satisfying these conditions a non deterministic PIE abbreviated ND-PIE.

We can say that a ND-PIE is deterministic if for all p there is at most one effect given by $I^*_{ND}(p)$. That is $\forall\, p \in P: \|I^*_{ND}(p)\| \leq 1$.

If any of the $I^*_{ND}(p)$ are empty then the resulting PIE has a language.

If we do not want our ND-PIEs to have input languages, then we have to put more restrictions on I^*_{ND}. It is insufficient in the general case to simply ask for I^*_{ND} to always be non-empty. Consider I^*_{ND} where:

$$\begin{aligned} I^*_{ND}(\text{ab}) &= \{000, 111\} \\ I^*_{ND}(\text{abc}) &= \{0000\} \end{aligned}$$

If we had typed **ab** and got the series of responses **111**, then there is no valid response if we typed a further **c**. That is the ND-PIE displays an non deterministic input language. The proper additional rule to prevent this is to ensure that for any input p there are possible extensions to this no matter what additional input we type:

$$\forall\, p \leq q \in P, e_p \in I^*_{ND}(p): \exists\, e_q \in I^*_{ND}(q): e_p \leq e_q$$
where
$\leq$ is again the initial subsequence relation.

Note the way this is a dual to the 'history cannot change' condition. Whether we want such a condition is debatable, it depends on the level of system description we are using and on whether there are any fundamental constraints to user input (like typing at non-existent windows, or trying to use a bank-teller when its cover is down). In fact each of the ND-PIEs we are going to derive will satisfy all these properties.

4.3.1   *Use for temporal systems*

We can now use the ND-PIE to represent the non deterministic functionality we required in §4.2.2, stated as:

$$I^*_{ND}(p) = \{I^*_{steady}(h) \mid \xi(h) = p\}$$

Where ξ is the function extracting the user commands from a sequence containing ticks:

$$
\begin{aligned}
\xi(\varepsilon) &= \varepsilon \\
\xi(h\tau) &= \xi(h) \\
\xi(hc) &= \xi(h)c & c \neq \tau
\end{aligned}
$$

With this definition the example of the typewriter which misses characters typed too quickly gives us:

$$
\begin{aligned}
I^*_{ND}(\mathrm{abc}) = \{&[\varepsilon, \mathrm{a}, \mathrm{a}, \mathrm{a}], [\varepsilon, \mathrm{a}, \mathrm{a}, \mathrm{ac}], \\
&[\varepsilon, \mathrm{a}, \mathrm{ab}, \mathrm{ab}], [\varepsilon, \mathrm{a}, \mathrm{ab}, \mathrm{abc}]\}
\end{aligned}
$$

Not only can we now define this functionality, but it gives us a new
way to look at the system. A perfectly buffered system with total
update (i.e., no intermediate displays skipped) is precisely a system
where I_{ND} is deterministic.

4.3.2   *Use for windowed systems*

We consider using a window (with handle λ) in isolation, ignoring possible interleaved commands to a second window (λ'). This yields a
projection from the handle space onto a ND-PIE:

$$
\begin{aligned}
I^*_{ND}(\varepsilon) &= \bigcup_{q \in P} \{[\mathsf{doit}^*(e, q, \lambda')]\} \\
I^*_{ND}(pc) &= \bigcup_{e^* \in I^*_{ND}(p), q \in P} \{e^* :: [\mathsf{doit}^*(\mathsf{doit}(e^*, c, \lambda), q, \lambda')]\}
\end{aligned}
$$

Here doit^* is the natural extension of doit to all members of P. This
may be used to give an alternative definition for result independence:
result independence between λ and λ' is precisely the condition that
$\mathsf{result} \circ I^*_{ND}$ is deterministic.

4.3.3   *Non deterministic properties of PIEs*

We have seen that properties over temporal models and handle spaces can be defined as determinacy properties of ND-PIEs. Are there any interesting ND-PIEs that can be abstracted from simple PIEs?

We considered the simple predictability property; a PIE is **monotone** if:

$$\forall p, q, r \in P : I(p) = I(q) \Rightarrow I(pr) = I(qr)$$

We examined this in the context of the 'gone away for a cup of tea' problem, where one has forgotten exactly what command sequence has been entered before the cup of tea. This suggests non determinism about the value of p. The ND-PIE generated by this is:

$$I_{ND}^*(s) \doteq \{I^*(ps)\}_{p \in P}$$

If this ND-PIE is deterministic then the PIE is rather uninteresting as its functionality is independent of the commands entered. It is a deaf system! The predictability condition can be stated using this ND-PIE as:

$$\forall s \in P, e_1^*, e_2^* \in I_{ND}^*(s) : \mathsf{first}(e_1^*) = \mathsf{first}(e_2^*) \Rightarrow e_1^* = e_2^*$$

This is a measure we could apply to any ND-PIE whether or not it is derived in this way. It is quite a strong requirement saying that although the system is non deterministic, one glance at the first effect resolves all future doubt. We could go on and give non deterministic equivalents to the more refined concepts of predictability.

One other ND-PIE suggested by the definition of I_{ND}^*, above, results if we substitute arbitrary PIEs for the collection I_p. For example, given two interpretations I and I' over the same domains P and E, we could define the non deterministic interpretation, $I_{ND}^*(p) \doteq \{I(p), I'(p)\}$. If this ND-PIE is deterministic, then I and I' are identical. Later we will see a real situation that could be described using this.

A specific case of this is where the interpretations are PIEs representing the 'same' system with different start data. If we consider the red-PIE, we will often have the case where there is a 'bundle' (tray!) of PIEs, each indexed by an element of the result, $\{I_r\}_{r \in R}$. Where each PIE starts with the appropriate result, and is related to the others:

$$\forall\, r \in R\colon \mathsf{result}(I_r(\varepsilon)) = r$$
$$\forall\, r, r' \in R\colon \exists\, p_r^{r'} \in P\colon \forall p \in P\colon I_{r'}(p) = I_r(p_r^{r'} p)$$

The ND-PIE generated from these interpretations,

$$I_{\mathrm{ND}}^*(s) \doteq \{I_r^*(s)\}_{r \in R}$$

represents non determinism about the starting value of the system. Subsequent sections will show how this arises informally.

4.3.4   *Summary—formal models and non determinism*

We have seen how a non deterministic model has been useful in unifying the description of various properties in diverse models.

The examples, above, share one common feature: in each case, the deterministic model is viewed *via* an abstraction which corresponds to losing some part of the available information. This leads to non deterministic behaviour. In each case the non deterministic model used to capture this behaviour was the ND-PIE, however, this is largely because the various models were derivatives and extensions of the basic PIE model. Different flavours of model could be dealt with similarly using different non deterministic models and perhaps using different methods of expressing the non determinism.

When viewed in the light of the previous discussion, properties such as predictability and non-interference of windows become efforts to control non determinism. Either they assert that in certain circumstances the effect is deterministic, or give procedures to resolve it.

> *Meta-point: Having made the formal transition from deterministic models to non deterministic ones, we are now going to shift back to the informal domain. What is the meaning here of the formal analysis?*

4.4   Non deterministic computer systems?

In the last section we found that formal models of non determinism are useful to describe certain abstract properties of interactive systems, however, we were left wondering whether this formal construction held any meaning for the user. We accept that the internal workings of some systems will be non deterministic, especially where concurrent processes are used, and even that some specialist applications like simulations and certain numerical methods will involve random number generation, but surely most real systems have a deterministic external interface.

4.4.1   *The tension for the user*

Do users perceive computers as deterministic? In fact the opposite is the case, most users expect a degree of randomness from the systems they use. Time and again they will shrug their shoulders in bewilderment, "Oh well it didn't work this time, I'll try the same thing again, it may work now." The apparently random behaviour of such systems conflicts with the alternative model of the computer as a deterministic machine relentlessly pursuing its logical course. Some users are able to cope with this. Expert users may treat this as a challenge, puzzling over the behaviour and experimenting until a logical reason is found. Pragmatists will accept the occasional strangeness circumventing it, and more awestruck users will regard it as part of the magic and mystery of modern technology. Others may have a more negative reaction. The self-confident may react, "this is silly" and lose all confidence in the computer, the self-deprecating may respond, "I'm silly" attributing their problems to their own lack of understanding, and possibly retiring from further use. Phrased in these graphic terms the problem seems extreme and demands investigation, but how can it be that thoroughly deterministic programs give rise to this apparent randomness.

4.4.2   *Levels of non determinism*

Very few systems are really random, even random number generators are usually based on deterministic algorithms, ERNIE (a random number generator used in a national lottery in the UK) being a possible exception. Programs that rely on external events could be classified as non deterministic, for instance the time when a printer signals that it has emptied its buffer, but even then the printer itself will probably behave deterministically. In fact what is usually termed non determinism reflects the things that the programmer either doesn't know or doesn't want to know. In other words, it is programmer-centred.

We could classify non determinism into several levels, depending on what they appear non deterministic to:

- *mechanistic world*—the atomic events measured by ERNIE and the actions of people would certainly be regarded as non deterministic, and are incapable of prediction even when considering the whole of the computer systems together. Even here, whether these events are *really* non deterministic can be argued, however—we are getting into the realms of metaphysics;

- *computer*—other events, like the printer signals are deterministic when we take the entire mechanism computer and printer together, but are not so from the point of view of the computer alone—unless it has a very sophisticated model of the printer, in which case it needn't bother with handshaking at all!

- *programmer*—program scheduling within a multiprogramming system is deterministic from the computer's point of view which is applying some scheduling algorithm (e.g., round robin, priority based etc.). From the programmer's point of view, however, this is non deterministic since in real time it may jump suddenly between adjacent program steps. Similarly file systems may change apparently non deterministically as other programs operate;

- *user*—even totally deterministic calculations such as: "is $579217^{11} - 1$ prime?" are non deterministic from the user's point of view [196], and are effectively the same as if the computer had tossed a coin to find the answer. Many systems do not use such obviously obscure formulae but manage to produce interfaces that are equally bizarre.

The theme that comes out of the above is that non determinism is relative, to both knowledge and reasoning abilities.

4.4.3   *Behavioural non determinism*

What should a user centred view of non determinism be? If we imagine two systems, they each have two possible prompts, each day they choose a different prompt for the day. One system bases its choice on whether the number of days since 1900 is prime or not, the other on the decay of a slightly radioactive substance. From the programmer's point of view (and the computer's), we would say that the former is deterministic and the latter not. From the user's point of view the two systems display equally non deterministic behaviour.

The user sits at the bottom of the hierarchy of knowledge, all the forms of non determinism are equally random, and should be treated equivalently. That is we are going to take a *behavioural* view of non determinism. This recognises that some system may be 'really' deterministic and others may be 'really' non deterministic according to some definition. If they behave the same, we will regard them as equally non deterministic. Not only does this mean that we regard some 'really' deterministic systems as deterministic, but also the other way round. For instance, if we had a music system with some random 'noise' that led to errors of one part per million in the frequency of notes, we would regard the system as being deterministic since the difference in behaviour would be undetectable.

We could demand tighter views of non determinism, but for the purposes of this chapter we will adopt the behavioural one. Again we could use a weaker word to represent behavioural non determinism, however, the use of the charged word concentrates the mind wonderfully.

> Meta-point: At this point we have made an important informal step, obtaining a new understanding of non determinism in this context.

4.5   Sources of non determinism

In the last section we decided that, taking a behavioural view of non determinism, it did make sense to describe interface behaviour in these terms. In doing so, we introduced some examples to argue the point. In this section we will catalogue informally some of the sources of non determinism in the user interface, giving more examples on the way. We will study these sources of non determinism under six headings:

- timing;

- sharing;

- data uncertainty;

- procedural uncertainty;

- memory limitations;

- conceptual capture.

The first two of these cover the informal equivalents of two formal problems that started this chapter in §4.2.2 and §4.2.3. The second two consider problems that appear even in the steady state functionality of single windowed systems, and cover lack of knowledge about *what* you are dealing with and *how* you should do it. These correspond to some of the ND-PIE's we considered in §4.3.3. The last two are to do with the more complex ways that human limitations can give rise to apparent non determinism. These two could be thought of as 'the user's fault,' but the system designer cannot wriggle out of it so easily; good system design should take into account the inevitable human limitations of its users.

This list is not complete, however, it does give a broad spectrum of different types of non determinism to which the reader can add.

4.5.1   *Non determinism due to timing*

A variety of problems, which users experience, can be viewed as manifestations of non determinism. When a user types quickly, intermittent and partial update strategies produce different output than if he had typed more slowly. If the user is unaware of this exact timing, then the system's behaviour is apparently non deterministic. This non determinism is usually deemed acceptable since the final display does not depend on the exact timing, and further, spells of fast typing may be regarded as single actions anyway. Intermittent update could be said to be less non deterministic than partial update, since at least all its intermediate displays would have arisen with slow typing. On the other hand, in partial update, a portion of the screen is always exactly as it would be if the machine were 'infinitely fast,' and this portion is therefore totally deterministic.

Similarly the problems associated with slow machines and buffering can be thought of as arising from non determinism. A machine that doesn't buffer and loses characters typed too quickly could be regarded as non deterministic on this score. This is exactly the non determinism captured by the formal model at the beginning of this chapter. However, a system with buffering can lead to a non deterministic feedback loop between user and computer, leading for instance to cursor tracking (where the user continually overshoots with the cursor).

Scheduling of multiple processes leads to non determinism. If for some reason a system makes explicit or implicit use of real time, then, when running on a time share computer, the run times of its components and hence possibly its functionality, will be non deterministic. More often than not this dependency on real time will be in the assumptions made about the relative speeds of certain components, or in the assumption that two statements following one another will be executed immediately, one after the other. The most innocuous case of this is when several concurrent processes print messages to the terminal in random order.

4.5.2   *Non determinism due to sharing*

Again the problem of sharing can be regarded as one of non determinism, reflecting exactly the formal treatment of handles. For instance, as I transact with one process which is my focus of interest, other processes may print error messages on the screen. Because I am preoccupied with the focal process, I may have forgotten that the others were running and thus be temporarily confused. In this case, I would not remain confused for long, as I would remember what other processes were running (or ask the system), and infer their behaviour. Thus, the non determinism could be resolved, but not soon enough to stop me acting (potentially disastrously) on a changing system.

This situation is in the middle of three levels of sharing. Each of these types of sharing can lead to non determinism.

Single actor—multiple persona. The user is simultaneously involved (perhaps *via* windows) with several dialogues, which may share data. When switching from one dialogue to another, the user may forget that actions in one dialogue may have repercussions in the other, thus causing apparent randomness. Literally the right hand may not know what the left is doing.

Single controller—several actors. The user sets off several concurrent processes that affect data common to each other and to the user's current view. This is the original case given above, and differs from the single actor case in that changes may actually occur as the user is actively involved in a dialogue, rather than during interruptions to the dialogue. Because of this, it is apparently more non deterministic since the system is changing as one tries to manipulate it.

Several independent actors. This is the case of the multi-user system where not only are several things happening at once, but they are not under your control. This is the most random of all, since the machine processes are at least in principle predictable, but from your point of view the other users are fundamentally non deterministic processes.

4.5.3   *Data uncertainty*

A user has a program on a system which was written a long time ago, the exact contents of it is now forgotten. He wants to make changes to this program and invokes his favourite editor by entering the command `edit prog`.

This is an example of **data uncertainty**, the user does not know the exact value of the data on which he is going to operate, and a major goal of the interactive session is to reduce the uncertainty, perhaps by scrolling through the file to examine it. This corresponds to the ND-PIE generated from the bundle of PIEs in §4.3.3.

Data uncertainty is of course common. The example given is typical of uses over many different types of task. However, it is not an unexpected problem: we do not expect to know all the data in a computer system by heart. The importance is in the user's ability to discover the information, in the *resolution* of the non determinism, a point we shall return to in the next section.

4.5.4   *Procedural uncertainty*

Consider the following two situations:

- a user is within a mail utility and has just read an item of mail which is only 10 lines long and is still completely visible on the screen. They want their reply to include a few selected lines from the message and achieve this by using the mail's e command in order to edit the text of the message. There are several editors on the system. "I wonder which it will use," they think;

- the user who is editing a program decides that the variable names a, b, c are not very evocative of their meaning and

decides to change them to day-total, week-total and year-
total respectively. They then realize they have forgotten the
method of achieving a global search/replace.

In the first situation, the exact nature of the data is known and it
is *procedural uncertainty* from which the user suffers. They will look
for clues using the knowledge they have of editors on the system. The
editor fills the entire screen so it can't be a line editor like **ed**, they
surmise. Neither can it be mouse based, like **spy**, for it doesn't have
menus all over the place. It could be either of the screen editors **ded** or
vi. Tentatively they type in a few characters to see if they're inserted
in the text. The editor beeps at them a few times, then deletes half the
text ... now they knows it's definitely **vi**.

This form of procedural uncertainty is captured by the ND-PIE which
chose between a set of interpretation functions. It is interesting that
the two situations which appear quite different informally, have such a
similar informal definition.

The second case is another example of procedural uncertainty of a
less extreme but more common form!

4.5.5   *Memory limitations*

As previously stated, one of the causes of non determinism is lack of
knowledge. This is exacerbated by the fact that people forget. Thus,
as the user attempts to amass information in order to resolve the non
determinism, their efforts are hampered by their limited memory. A
designer must consciously produce features which take account of this.
These could include general features, such as an online memo-pad and
diary, or more system-specific ones. Further the user is likely to interpo-
late the gaps and be unaware of which information is known and which
is inferred. This process is distinct from forgetting, we can think of it
as **degradation of information**. The designer may need to be aware
of where such degradation is likely and actually force this information
to the user's attention.

4.5.6   *Conceptual capture*

We are all familiar with the idea of capture, where, for example, one
walks home without noticing when one intended to go to the railway
station in the opposite direction. This occurs in computer systems
where commonly used sequences of keys can take over when one intends

to use another similar sequence. A similar process can also occur at the conceptual level. For example, in a display editor where long lines are displayed over several screen lines, the cursor up key might mean move up one screen line or one logical line. As most logical lines will fit on the one screen line the difference may not be noticed. Later when a long line is encountered the action of the system may appear random to a user who has inferred the wrong principle.

4.5.7   *Discussion*

Of the six headings which we have considered, the first four can be given formal expression, to some degree or other, using some of the models developed earlier in this chapter. The last two would require a more sophisticated model of human cognition, with its attendant problems of robustness. There is an obvious parallel between data uncertainty and degradation of information and between procedural uncertainty and conceptual capture. However, the second of each pair is far more dangerous. The major problem with both these situations when compared to procedural and data uncertainty is that the user may not be aware of the gaps in her knowledge. The situation where a user doesn't know something and *knows* she doesn't know it is still non deterministic, but the situation where the user thinks she knows what the system is going to do and then it does something completely different is downright random. We could say that failure in knowledge is far less critical than failure in meta-knowledge.

> *Meta-point: Some of the sources of non determinism we have discussed were the direct translation of properties derived from pure formal analysis. Some were not apparent in the formal analysis (perhaps unformalisable) but only appeared when we examined the corresponding informal concepts. Thus, the two strands together have led to an understanding of the situation that would have been impossible to achieve in isolation.*

4.6   Dealing with non determinism

We have seen that non determinism is a real problem in the user interface, and that it has many causes. How can we deal with the problems of non determinism. We will consider four options in this chapter, we can: avoid it; resolve it; control it; or use it. We now consider each of these options in turn.

4.6.1   *Avoid it*

The most obvious way of dealing with non determinism is to make sure it never arises. This can be done by designing a system with this in mind, or by adding functionality afterwards. We have already seen examples of this:

- *timing*—we have said that timing leads to non determinism. However, the information suggested in [56] to tell the user when the system is in steady state, and when commands will be ignored will reduce or remove this non determinism;

- *sharing*—using the definitions of independence between windows in [57] we could demand that systems have sharing properties that avoid non determinism. Alternatively, we can use one of the responses suggested there to make the sharing apparent, and hence reduce non determinism when interference occurs.

In both these solutions, we add information to the interface in order to avoid non determinism. This is of course a general technique restricted only by the display capacity. For instance, if procedural uncertainty is the fault of hidden modes, then we can make the modes visible *via* a status line.

We can attempt to avoid conceptual capture by making sure the models we use are either exact matches of the user's model or else where they match and where they don't is made obvious. This is of course very difficult advice to follow as it is difficult to predict what model the user will infer for the system. However, systems that propose a model (such as the desktop) but fail if the user follows it too far are obvious candidates for improvement. Another situation it would warn us to avoid is where two sub-subsystems have apparently similar semantic behaviour, but later diverge.

In most systems of any complexity it would be unreasonable to expect complete removal of non determinism, however, these techniques can reduce the non determinism or remove some aspect of it.

4.6.2   *Resolve it*

Assuming the user is in a situation of non determinism he can try to resolve that non determinism, attempting by observation or experiment to reach a deterministic situation.

Data uncertainty is an obvious candidate for this. The concept of strategies, introduced in [61], can be thought of as an attempt to resolve the non determinism. These are procedures that the user can use to investigate aspects of the current state, either just the objects of interest, resolving data uncertainty, or dialogue state resolving issues such as mode ambiguity.

The designer can help the user in the resolution of data ambiguity by reducing the conceptual and memory costs of strategies. This is aided by the fact that the user will only want to discover some part of the information. Typical techniques include:

- *improved navigation aids*—by easing the location of information the designer reduces the effort required of the user and makes it more likely that she will be able to remember sufficient information for the task at hand. Further, the job of refreshing memory can be significantly reduced. Mechanisms for this include, depending on the application: search commands in text editors, dependency trees in programming environments, cross referencing and indices;

- *place holders*—because of degradation the user will need continual refreshing of information. Uncommitted navigation aids can be augmented by the ability to lay marks at important positions to refer back to, comparable to bookmarks;

- *multiple windows*—in a similar vein, a system may allow several simultaneous views, thus making dispersed information simultaneously available. Due to the limited size of displays all the views will not be present at one moment, and thus we may regard windows as a form of sophisticated place holder;

- *folding mechanisms*—If the data is structured in a relevant manner, folding mechanisms can significantly aid navigation. Further, if the user has sufficient control over what is, and what is not, folded then unwanted information can be folded away and only the relevant information made visible. Effective folding can thus satisfy some of the requirements for the place holders. It should be noted, however, that in order to achieve these aims, either the user will require control of the structure of the folding, or the fixed structure must be very well chosen (arguably no fixed scheme would satisfy all needs).

Procedural uncertainty is more difficult to resolve. Help systems can be thought of as a way of resolving procedural uncertainty, however, they do, of course, have to make major assumptions about how much the user knows already. The one sort of procedural uncertainty that the help system definitely cannot resolve, is the method for invoking help. This underlines the need to use consistent and obvious rules (e.g, permanent icons, dedicated labelled key or the use of 'h' or '?').

4.6.3   *Control it*

Rather than try to remove non determinism completely, we can try to control it so that the non determinism experienced is acceptable in some way. This can obtain at the local or the global level. That is we can ask for complete determinism over a part of the system, or merely that some rules always apply for the system as a whole. We consider the local level first.

It is said that you ought to be able to use a system with your eyes shut. Extending this analogy somewhat, we could observe that blind people are able to navigate a familiar room quickly and confidently whereas they would use a totally different strategy for navigating a busy street. Similarly, when using a computer conferencing facility one might be able to touch type because the layout of the keys is fixed, and attention is fixed on the screen where unexpected changes will occur. Thus, in computer systems, as in real life, we need a solid base of determinacy in order to be able to concentrate on those areas where non determinacy will occur. We call this requirement **deterministic ground**. Record and file locking facilities are an example of how we might, for a period, enforce determinacy on a shared domain. Similarly protection mechanisms offer a more permanent way of ensuring some level of determinacy. However, if we look at the three levels of sharing, mentioned in §4.5.2, we see that only the multi-actor case is helped by having private files. So, if I have several windows, or have some background jobs running, they are all the same user, and hence the file system protection would fail to protect me from myself. As an example of this breakdown of security, consider the semantics of the line printer spooler. In some systems, the print command does not make a copy of the file to be printed in a system spool area, but merely makes a note of the request and the file to be printed. The user, however, after issuing the command may reach closure on that operation and then later go on to modify or even delete the file to be printed. Perhaps one could extend protection mechanisms to include files private to tasks and windows?

At the global level the effects of sharing are controlled by the accepted procedures that are used for updating them. Some of these are enshrined in the software, and some in organisational and social conventions. For instance, today my bank's teller machine might read £300, however, tomorrow it may read only £20. If I hadn't kept a close tally on my spending, I might not have expected the change and I would regard the change as essentially non deterministic, however, I would have enough faith in the banking system to believe that the change was due to some of my cheques clearing. If this belief were not widely held the non determinacy of bank balances would become unacceptable and the banking system would collapse. Similarly early in a day a travel agent may notice 5 seats free on a particular flight, later in the day, on trying to book one for a customer, the request might be refused. The conclusion drawn is that someone else has booked the seats in the meantime. Thus, we rely on the semantics of others transactions to make the apparent randomness of our view of data acceptable. If the changes we observe in the data are not consistent with our understood semantics we will lose confidence in the data.

I would argue, therefore, that in order to understand the problems of sharing from a user oriented view, we should concentrate on defining the semantically acceptable non determinism of a system. That is we are prepared to accept *limited non determinism*. We can apply this to other fields. For instance, if we look at buffering strategies. A perfectly buffered system may well be non deterministic because the screen does not reflect the current state of affairs, however, we might regard this as acceptable. In contrast a word processor which ignored all type-ahead would be regarded as exhibiting unacceptable non determinism. The predicate describing perfect buffering is a limit to the non determinism sufficient to make it acceptable. Similarly, we may not be too worried about the exact strategy a text editor uses when rearranging the display when the cursor hits the screen boundaries. It would be unacceptable if the cursor movement caused part of the document to be altered. (I have used a text editor which did exactly this!) Again the limitation that the cursor movement does not alter the document is sufficient (with others in this case) to make the non determinism acceptable.

4.6.4   *Use it*

We have just argued, that to a large extent controlled non determinism can be acceptable non determinism. Every user manual uses this fact, as it defines only the external behaviour of the system. So, for instance, different versions of a word processor could use different algorithms, be written in different programming languages and even run on different hardware in the same box! Similarly, formal specifications define only the interface behaviour leaving the internals undetermined. Thus, all specification is a use of non determinism. It is usually assumed that the systems described by formal specifications will be deterministic. It is just which particular consistent system chosen that is non deterministic. One could certainly have non deterministic systems which satisfy a given loosely defined specification, but this is not usually done. There is a paradox here, in order to make accurate statements about a system (and hence reduce non determinism regarding its behaviour) specifications are used which are non deterministic.

There is also a strange duality of non determinism within the interface. The computer system must, if it is to be useful, be non deterministic. A completely deterministic system would never tell the user anything that the user didn't know already. Not very useful! On the other hand, from the computer's point of view, the user is non deterministic, but if the user were not so, the system would always produce the same result. There is conflict between the two partners' search for determinism, and the programmer usually has the upper hand: forcing the user to answer in specified ways and in specified orders. From the programmer's point of view, this could be thought of as producing a more deterministic response from the user. From the user's point of view this is at best restrictive, and possibly may seem non deterministic because the programmer's arbitrary decisions may have little relevance at the interface. Thimbleby calls this excessive control by the programmer **over-determination** [192], and elsewhere I have proposed a technique for returning control of the dialogue sequence back to the user [55]. Not surprisingly this technique involves programs with non deterministic semantics and which regard the user as a non deterministic entity.

We could distinguish two aspects of interface non determinism based on the previous discussion. First are those that are part of the application, necessary to make the application useful. Second are those in the interface, resulting from arbitrary decisions and complexity, which are not wanted. On the other hand, we could use this to make the distinction between application and interface, discussed in the previous chapter, by saying that the application is what we want to be non deterministic and the interface is what we want to be deterministic.

4.6.5   *Summary—informal analysis*

We have seen how the user helped by the designer can avoid, resolve and control the non determinism of interactive systems. We have also seen that non determinism can be used in formal specification. Earlier we asked whether non determinism existed at the user interface or whether it was just a formal trick and decided that, yes, it is a real, meaningful phenomenon. We could parallel that now and ask: is the use of non determinism just a formal trick for interface specification or can it really be used to improve user interfaces? The next section will seek to answer that question.

> *Meta-point: Having discussed some techniques for dealing with non determinism largely at the informal level, we have seen that non determinism can be a useful concept. We make use of this by shifting back to the concrete formal domain, examining the introduction of non deterministic features to improve interactive response.*

4.7   Deliberate non determinism

So far, we have dealt with cases where non determinism has unintentionally arisen in the interface, and we have been mainly interested in removing it and its problems. In the last section, we saw that when developing systems, non determinism can actually be used to good effect.

In this section, we will consider a display update strategy that is deliberately non deterministic. We will call this strategy *non deterministic intermittent update*. It has considerable advantages over deterministic strategies from the point of view of efficiency, however, can such a deliberate policy of non determinism ever be acceptable?

In the first subsection we will consider a basic semi-formal framework in which we can consider update strategies. In the following sub-section, we will consider the expression in this framework of total and intermittent update strategies. Then, in §4.7.2 we extrapolate these strategies and define non deterministic intermittent update. Lastly, we consider whether or not it is an acceptable strategy from the user's point of view, and conclude that by deliberately adding non determinism to the interface we may actually *reduce* the perceived non determinism.

4.7.1   *Static and dynamic consistency*

Many interactive systems can be considered in the following manner: there is an object, (obj), which is being manipulated, and an associated screen display, disp. The way such a system is implemented is often as a state, $\langle \text{obj}, \text{map} \rangle$ consisting of the object and the additional information, map, required to calculate the current display. For example if the object were a text then map may be the offset of the display frame in the text. As the user issues a sequence of commands (which may be keypresses, menu selections or whole line commands, depending on the system), the state changes in a well defined and deterministic manner. Thus, as a sequence of commands are issued we get a sequence of objects o_i mapping states m_i and displays d_i.

$$
\begin{array}{ccccccccc}
d_0 & & d_1 & & d_2 & & d_3 & & d_n \\
\uparrow & & \uparrow & & \uparrow & & \uparrow & & \uparrow \\
o_0, m_0 & \xrightarrow{c_1} & o_1, m_1 & \xrightarrow{c_2} & o_2, m_2 & \xrightarrow{c_3} & o_3, m_3 & \cdots \xrightarrow{c_n} & o_n, m_n
\end{array}
$$

The earlier discussion on specification would lead us to question the *requirements* for this update sequence. Typically they fall into two categories:

> *static consistency*—at any stage we expect there to be a well defined relation between the object and the display. For instance, in the case of text with a cursor position and a simple character map display with its cursor, we would expect the characters to match if we overlayed the two aligning the cursors;

dynamic consistency—properties that hold between successive displays. Typical of this is the principle of display inertia that says displays should change as little as possible.

The designer will have some idea of which static and dynamic requirements are important for the particular system. However, these will rarely specify the map completely and thus additional *ad hoc* requirements will be added to define it uniquely. This is idealised, as often in practice these fundamental design decisions are made as the system is coded, with little reference to global impact. The additional requirements may themselves be either static or dynamic.

Bernard Sufrin's specification of a display editor [181] deliberately leaves the specific update strategy only partially defined, instead he supplies a static consistency requirement and a dynamic "inertia" requirement that if the new cursor fits on the old display frame then the frame doesn't change. Many editors follow this rule of thumb and add additional rules to fully specify the case when the cursor does not fit on the old screen, such as 'scroll just enough to fit in the cursor', 'scroll a third of a screen in the relevant direction' or 'centre the cursor in the new display'. All these rules have additional special cases at the top or bottom of the text, and in the case of the first two, when the movement of the cursor is gross.

4.7.2   *Intermittent update*

As already noted in §4.5.1 the time taken to compute the new map and update the display may lead to apparent non determinism for the user, such as cursor-tracking. Clearly we want to avoid this non determinism.

If, after all, other optimisations have been tried, the response is still unacceptable, a possible course is to use intermittent update as described in the previous section. This corresponds to suppressing some of the displays in the sequence:

$$
\begin{array}{ccccccccc}
d_0 & & & & & & d_3 & & d_n \\
\uparrow & & & & & & \uparrow & & \uparrow \\
o_0, m_0 & \xrightarrow{c_1} & o_1, m_1 & \xrightarrow{c_2} & o_2, m_2 & \xrightarrow{c_3} & o_3, m_3 & \cdots \xrightarrow{c_n} & o_n, m_n
\end{array}
$$

This is mildly non deterministic in that the sequence of displays depends on exactly how fast the user types. So, already we have a common example of deliberate use of non determinism.

Although this reduces traffic to and from the display device (critical on older, low bandwidth, channels), it still leaves the considerable expense of updating the map component. Is there any way we can reduce this overhead?

4.7.3   *Declarative interfaces*

When specifying the editor component of a simple hypertext system [59] a slightly different approach to the standard display inertia was taken. As usual, only basic static requirements were specified, and then to try a few additional requirements that could loosely be described as 'cursor inertia.' The first of these was strict cursor inertia, where the cursor position on the screen moved as little as possible. This is a dynamic requirement which had some very strange consequences, in particular, as the cursor began at the top of the document and hence at the top of the screen, it *always* tried to stay at the top of the screen! A second variation on this was to always position the cursor as near the middle of the screen as possible. In terms of its observed behaviour this requirement has its own advantages and disadvantages. However, it is important to emphasise that this is a purely static requirement. This means that the display map can always be calculated from the current text alone, it is a purely *declarative interface*.

In principle, one would expect a declarative interface to be very predictable. However, few interfaces adopt this style. Harold Thimbleby's novel calculator [195] does so, but users are often surprised at its features, perhaps because they are unused to the declarative style. The big advantage in performance terms of a declarative interface is that when one only updates the display intermittently, one need only update the `map` intermittently also.

$$
\begin{array}{ccccccc}
d_0 & & & & d_3 & & d_n \\
\uparrow & & & & \uparrow & & \uparrow \\
o_0, m_0 & \xrightarrow{c_1} & o_1, ? & \xrightarrow{c_2} & o_2, ? & \xrightarrow{c_3} & o_3, m_3 & \cdots & \xrightarrow{c_n} & o_n, m_n
\end{array}
$$

This technique ignores dynamic requirements entirely, so at first glance it appears to be relevant only to totally declarative interfaces. However, given the benefits in terms of performance, we must ask ourselves whether some similar technique could be developed for non-declarative interface?

4.7.4   *Non deterministic intermittent update*

It is usually the case (and is so in the text editor example) that static consistency is most semantically important. We can imagine then relaxing the demand for dynamic consistency. Normally, it applies between each state transition, but when we have intermittent update, we apply it only between displays that actually occur. That is, we effectively bunch a series of commands updating the object and then re-establish the display map based on static consistency, and modifying the dynamic requirements, to apply to these consistent epochs.

Put in formal terms: previously we would have demanded for each command, c_i, an object-map pair where each o_i is derived from the previous object *via* the command, where each $\langle o_i, m_i \rangle$ is consistent with respect to the static requirements, and where the successive pairs $\{\langle o_{i-1}, m_{i-1} \rangle, \langle o_i, m_i \rangle\}$ satisfy the dynamic requirements. Now we only ask for an object for each command, a set of epochs e_j and maps at these epochs only, such that at each epoch $\langle o_{e_j}, m_{e_j} \rangle$ is consistent and each successive epoch pair $\{\langle o_{e_j-1}, m_{e_j-1} \rangle, \langle o_{e_j}, m_{e_j} \rangle\}$ satisfies the dynamic requirements.

4.7.5   *Is it a good idea?*

What sort of effect would this have in practice? Imagine the text editor with display inertia. The cursor is on the second to last line of the screen, and we slowly enter **down, down, up** at the second **down** the screen would scroll to accommodate the new cursor position, then on the **up** it would stay (by display inertia) in this new position. If, however, we entered the commands quickly and they were bunched for processing, then after the three commands when the static and dynamic invariants are enforced, the new cursor position is within the original display frame and this is retained ... the result is non deterministic!! Comparing this to intermittent update, we see that in that case only the intermediate states of the screen differed, in this case the final state differs depending on the exact timing of input.

I would argue that the non determinism introduced is acceptable for two reasons. Firstly, because it is only non deterministic within the bounds of the static consistency, it is *limited non determinism*. Secondly, the exact operation of the dynamic requirements are usually unpredictable anyway, and thus the apparent non determinism will be no worse, and we may actually reduce it. This is especially true of the principle of display inertia. Its purpose is to ensure that the location of useful information changes as little as possible in order to aid visual navigation. If intermediate displays are not produced then the deterministic strategy leads to a changing display, whereas the non deterministic strategy leads to a fixed one; clearly the latter application of the principle is more in line with its intention, and for the user is probably *more* predictable than its application to imaginary intermediate displays.

> *Meta-point: In this final concrete example, we at a formal level appeared to introduce non determinism, however, when looked at with the wider viewpoint we have found that it actually reduces non determinism. The technique springs most readily to mind when looking at the problem in the formal sphere, yet if we had evaluated it only there, we would have been likely to reject it out of hand. Again the two perspectives have interacted in a way greater than either alone.*

4.8   Discussion

We have seen how formal non deterministic models are useful in describing interactive systems behaviour. We asked ourselves whether this had any real meaning. In §4.4.3 we saw that the appropriate user centred definition of non determinism was a behavioural one, and under this definition interfaces did display non deterministic properties. Further, we have seen many examples of how non determinism arises in practice. In §4.6 we found that users have many ways of dealing with non determinism, and that the designer can design systems to aid them in this. Finally, we have seen that it can be beneficial to deliberately introduce non determinism into the user interface, both to achieve other goals (in the example efficiency) but also to potentially reduce the non determinism of the interface.

What have we gained by this analysis?

First, by using the strong word 'non determinism' rather than weaker ones like 'unpredictable,' we see rather more the urgency of the problems considered.

Secondly, we have found that many different well recognised problems can be considered as manifestations of non determinism, this allows the possibility of cross-fertilisation between the domains.

Thirdly, by considering problems in this light, it enables us to see more clearly ways of expressing them. For instance, regarding problems of sharing as specifying acceptable levels of non determinism. Thus, we might describe a mail system, not in terms of multiple users and messages, but as a single user with a system displaying limited non determinism.

Finally, it has given us a more pragmatic view of non determinism and hence the ability to consider the idea of *deliberately* non deterministic interfaces.

> *Meta-point: It is precisely the way in which the formal recognition of non determinism leads us to recognise it as a common problem that enabled us to approach it in this pragmatic manner. It is also the formal parallels between the different phenomena that highlighted the parallels at the informal levels. That is we see formal methods not as a brute force technique for the aesthetically inarticulate, but as a source of imagery for a thinking mind.*

CHAPTER FIVE

A STATE MODEL OF DIRECT MANIPULATION IN INTERACTIVE SYSTEMS

MICHAEL HARRISON AND ALAN DIX

5.1   Introduction

A promising method for the design of interactive systems involves the initial development of an interaction model [60, 58]. This model of interactive behaviour represents abstractly the input and output characteristics of the proposed system in a form that is uncluttered by all the detail that would be required to produce an implementation. Such a model provides a basis for matching system characteristics of interactive behaviour with the user's perception of how the system works. Therefore interaction models have potential as a means of supporting the design of usable systems.

Being abstract, interaction models are appropriate generally across a range of application domains, and provide a basis for structuring the way the system interacts with the user. Our primary concern has been to use interaction models as a basis for the formulation and application of general principles of interactive behaviour [194] with scientifically based user validity. The intention is that interaction models should, when rendered into a form that is intelligible to designers, be used by them as they make decisions about features of interactive systems. Once appropriately defined, the interaction model may be refined into an efficient executable system. This refinement process takes two stages: first, a full specification is produced described in terms of an existing technique for the specification of computer systems (see Sufrin Chapter 6), then an implementation is produced. In this chapter we use a state-based interaction model to discuss properties related to direct manipulation. Elsewhere [59] we discuss the refinement issue with *module level* extensions so that we can move (preserving correctness) from the model, through a full specification, to an implementation that inherits the properties of the interaction model.

5.2   Direct manipulation

Direct manipulation [174, 102] is a desirable design goal for many types of interactive system, although what precisely constitutes such a style of interactive behaviour is often unclear. The chief features of such systems are that there is a close relationship between input and function (often one keystroke per command) and that the data manipulated by the user interface (and therefore the effects of all commands) are immediately, consistently and unambiguously visible.

It is argued that novices and experts alike benefit from the simplicity and directness of this style of interface. Simple models of system use may be communicated quickly by demonstration to novice users; intermittent users may recover a working knowledge rapidly each time they have a session. The simplicity, economy and directness of the user interface limits the amount of redundant information that may obstruct longer term expert use. All users have the benefit of a sense of direct contact with the data to produce a result, as opposed to generating indirect dialogues about the system, its data and function.

The character of a direct manipulation interface is in contrast with other styles of interface. The difference may be emphasised by means of a small example: an editor. A direct manipulation editor would support, for example, a single *rubout* key that uses the cursor to find the appropriate character for deletion; pressing the key will cause immediate deletion and its consequence will be clearly visible. This style may be contrasted with the alternative presentation to the user of a menu of options, including *rubout*. Subsequent additional dialogue would be essential to give the user the required confidence that the correct data is being deleted.

In practice it is not possible to maintain the simplicity of such a direct manipulation interface throughout. System function is often so complicated that a single key-to-function mapping is inappropriate. The data being manipulated are usually large making it impossible to display all changes at once. One mechanism for factoring this complexity is *mode* [193, 126]. Often mode is used in direct manipulation systems to cluster data with associated admissible operations and the display gives an unambiguous and consistent view of part of the data.[1] It is required within such a direct manipulation system that the cluster of data and operations that are available to the user should be entirely clear to the user. A useful model of direct manipulation systems should require graceful transition between modes, and deal properly with boundary issues that arise as a result of incomplete displays.

Our purpose is to give precision to notions that describe the relationship between state and display to aid design, implementation and evaluation.

5.3   Chapter plan

The plan of the chapter is as follows. §5.4 develops a formal model of interactive systems. §5.5 and §5.6 discuss the development of appropriate mechanisms for structuring input and output and their relation to direct manipulation style. §5.7 develops normal and exceptional models of interactive systems that prove helpful in clarifying where commands are difficult to use. We leave description of mode, and principles governing the transition between modes to a future paper.

5.4   A formal framework for direct manipulation

5.4.1   *Principles*

Even though recent developments [64] in the modelling of computer systems have led to a more precise understanding of design concepts,

---

[1]   Jacob [107] discusses these aspects of "modiness" in more detail, describing a particular notion of *interaction object* that captures screen devices such as buttons and icons.

these understandings have not yet been applied thoroughly to developing principles of design.

We may draw comparisons between what is being presented here, and the situation twenty years ago when semantic models of programming languages were used to clarify understanding of programming language concepts such as scope, extent, type and abstraction [190]. Modelling interactive systems lends precision to discussion of consistency in design with particular reference to certain well defined principles of interactive behaviour. It allows empirical testing of the value of these principles and their violations in particular cases. For example, currently we are investigating the complementary role of formal models of interaction and empirical evaluative techniques [83]. It is clear that principles such as those associated with direct manipulation do not have general applicability in all circumstances and for all application domains. Rather, we require mechanisms to allow the testing of certain choices and situations where the general application of principles fall down.

5.4.2   *The interaction model*

The direct manipulation paradigm is about the connection between what is input and what is seen. A tactile relationship is required between what is done and seen by the user, and the effect of the operation on the inner state of the system. We can define the inner workings in terms of a state-based model of computer systems defined by a set of states S, and a set of commands that transform states $C \subseteq S \rightarrow S$. Hence, commands are considered to be the inner functionality of a system without concern about how the functionality is invoked by the user or what visible effect is generated as a consequence. An initial state $s_0 \in S$ is also assumed. The model is widely applicable, for example:

- an *editor's* state may be defined as text, and cursor position. *insert(ch)*, *delete*, *up*, *left*, *down* and *right* transform the state. The initial state of the editor is the text provided as an argument to the edit operation, and a cursor pointing to the first character of the text;

- an *operating system's* state is heterogeneous, consisting of files, utilities, mail messages, and so on. *copy*, *run*, *login*, etc. all transform the state;

- a *simulation system* for the engine room of a ship. State consists of pipes, taps, tanks, boilers, turbines and so on. Commands switch on taps, start boilers etc.

On top of this minimal model of computer systems, layers may be added: (1) computer systems are often a hierarchy of nested subsystems; (2) the input and output systems are an outer shell to the model, thus:

(1) In reality, interactive systems involve a collection of contexts (subsets of commands that manipulate components of the state). A *context* consists of two components: part of the state required by the command (e.g., parameters cached for immediate use as would be the case when changing directory to a local directory); and a local set of commands available only within this context (editing commands are available only when the editor has been invoked and they relate specifically to the file being edited). Multiple contexts may be modelled by defining commands which can modify the command set as well as the state i.e., $C \subseteq S \to (S \times C)$. In addition it would be required that, associated with any command set, there is a state projection of the state that extracts the relevant data for the context.

(2) The model requires input and output within it, which we model by the sets: K of *physical inputs* (keystrokes, gestures, speech, touch etc.) and D of *displays*. Three mappings *parse*, *run* and *v* make the inner functionality of the model accessible to the outside world:

parse: $K^* \twoheadrightarrow C^*$

> *parse* maps a sequence of physical inputs into a sequence of state transforming commands.

run: $C^* \to C$

> The *run* mapping composes them into a single state transformation.

v: $S \to D$

> *v* (the view mapping) produces a visible display of the state.

So we have a *modeless* interactive system:

$$\langle s_0, S, C, K, parse, run, D, v \rangle.$$

It may be noted that in this chapter we do not model internal structure explicitly and that a number of further simplifying assumptions have been made:

- a single discrete sequential stream of input is assumed (without loss of generality since, for example, we can model mouse input as a sequence of discrete position coordinates interleaved with keyboard input);

- there is a single view mapping. Note that elsewhere [57] we have modelled windowed systems based on multiple view mappings. In this chapter we confine our attention to a single window on an interactive system;

- we also assume that all commands are simply state transforming. The interface at a level closer to the user deals with necessary parameters. For example, $insert : Char \rightarrow S \rightarrow S$ is modelled as a partially applied function $insert(ch) : S \rightarrow S$. The character parameter ch is dealt with by the *parse* mapping and will not be discussed in more detail.

Direct manipulation will be considered first in terms of the mapping from input to command (§5.5) and then in terms of the mapping from state to display (§5.6). Finally we will discuss the difficult issue of how universally direct manipulation properties must hold for a system to be a direct manipulation system. So far, the details of S and D are unimportant; the interaction model is general. Any interactive system will satisfy this model if it has a defined starting point, may be modelled by a fixed mapping between state and display, and supports "modeless" commands. In practice, of course, any particular interaction model will require more detailed specification of the nature of commands, states and displays.

The model is now sufficiently developed to use as a framework for discussing concepts in direct manipulation. We move from the model to properties of that model, in order to understand how the model should be used.

5.5 The relationship between input and command

In this section we consider the relationship between input and command in more detail; we shall consider the thickness of the intermediate structure. Modelling direct manipulation requires understanding of the relationship between key and command, state and display. A particularly salient requirement of direct manipulation input seems to be that single inputs map to complete commands. Hence, pressing the delete key deletes immediately; mouse movement moves the pointer; icon clicking invokes a function that corresponds in some sense to the meaning suggested by the icon. It is difficult to be precise about what direct manipulation is in terms of inputs and effects based on typical examples of direct manipulation systems. Contrast, for example, keystrokes representing *delete*, *insert* and cursor movement in a display editor; invoking *MacWrite* by clicking on a *MacWrite* file icon; pulling down a menu to change font. All these styles are described as direct manipulation but it is not clear that the properties that make them so are the same.

As can be seen in the examples of the previous paragraph stylistic (or syntactic) mechanisms, such as menus and command interfaces generate an additional layer of structure between the physical interface to the user (the lexical level) and the semantic innards of the interactive system [70]. The properties that we consider in this section relate the lexical to the semantic.

5.5.1 *Temporal ordering*

Our informal notion of direct manipulation requires some constraint on the connection between the physical and the functional that incorporates the extra layers required by menus and icons. A reasonable starting point for a definition would be to require that the ordering of physical inputs should reflect the ordering of command invocations. Our starting point is motivated by the requirement for *consistency* between physical action and command. An implication of this requirement is that there be no *intermediate* commands; for example, a command language based system typically provides a *second* level of commands to support *command editing*. Our ordering principle would require that inputs are interpreted immediately rather than delayed to the end of line for example.

A simple temporal relationship between input and invocation is as follows:

If $p, q \in K^*$ are input sequences such that p is a *prefix* of q written $p \leq q \doteq \exists r$ such that $p : r = q$ then *parse*(p) is a prefix of *parse*(q) (*parse*(p) $\leq$ *parse*(q)).[2]

This relationship, called *temporal* directness, gives a simple method of ensuring that nothing is happening behind the scenes to remove the tactile directness of the system. Examples such as the following do not satisfy the temporal directness relation:

- an *intelligent interface* where the interface is able to change the order of commands or insert and delete commands in order to achieve the same result more efficiently;

- a *command based* system which includes, at the syntactic level, a command editor.

Hence, temporal directness is useful, not only because it demands synchrony of input and effect but also because it prescribes that any intermediate syntactic layer does not reorder or modify the input stream.

5.5.2   *Contextual problems*

However, temporal ordering is not sufficient. This property does not adequately constrain the operation of the interface so that contextual ambiguities may not occur. Two illustrations will demonstrate a problem that arises because direct manipulation systems often use visual context to provide command parameters:

- an *inserting* editor inserts or deletes characters at a position in text dependent on the cursor position. So, a specific subsequence within a use of the editor might involve some cursor movement (using the mouse to move around the display for instance) that will vary depending on where the cursor was to start with. Hence, given any current result, since inserting editor commands are *local* (depending on status information as well as the result), there is no unique mapping between inputs and function[3]. This situation cannot be avoided since

---

[2] Here ":" denotes concatenation of tuples.

[3] By *result* we mean state that is the product of the system; *result* therefore ignores system status information such as cursor and display frame.

the notion of locality is an essential component of direct manipulation. The user can see what is being manipulated and uses tools to locate the data that are to be manipulated. Inserting editors are temporally directed according to our earlier definition but the mapping taking keys to function is context sensitive.

In the case of a *menu interface* we have a similar situation but this one conflicts with an intuitive understanding of direct manipulation. In this case the problem is that keys do not map uniquely to function.

- a *menu interface* replaces the direct invocation of commands by a combination of navigation commands and *do it* commands. Hence, executing a *copy* command will involve moving the cursor to the relevant position in the menu and then, *doing* the copy (this will include responding to requests to supply the required arguments). Despite the fact that the temporal relationship is preserved, this interface is not *direct* because *copy* is context dependent. We can say this more precisely: *parse* is not an injective mapping and, in particular, there is no way of discovering which function is involved from the input sequence. Many input sequences, depending on context, will map into the same command sequence.

These examples have illustrated a number of issues:

- it is useful to split the design of the function of the system and the commands available to the user between task function and interface function;

- it is necessary to formalise the binding between input sequences and commands invoked so that we can better understand context issues;

- it is also necessary to model the point at which input sequences are interpreted. A simple definition of *parse* and *run* may not be sufficient.

5.5.3   *Adding structure to the input model*

We can further develop our understanding of the relationship between physical input and command by introducing two extra interpretation functions:

interpret: $K^* \to C$

interpret transforms a sequence of physical inputs into a single command.

lex: $K^* \to K^*$

lex picks up the first well defined sequence that corresponds to a command invocation.

A more stringent directness requirement then could be expressed semi-formally as follows:

If $parse(p) = \langle c_1, c_2, ... \rangle$ then $interpret(lex(p)) = head(\langle c_1, c_2, ... \rangle) = c_1$. Hence, repeatedly applying interpret to the input sequence produces each command at the semantic level. It is at this level that the parameters supplied to a command may be dealt with so that its interpretation is a member of $S \to S$.

In summary we require both a direct temporal relationship between physical input sequences and state sequences and also a one-to-one correspondence of lexemes to functions thereby prohibiting the possibility of reordering deletion or insertion. Hence the order of invocation is directly related to the order of keystrokes; there is no intermediate level that reorders invocation in any way. In passing we have made a distinction between commands that appear at the functional level (after *interpret* and *lex*) and commands that appear at the interface level (after *lex* only). No attempt has been made to model these two levels because it is implicit in the notion of direct manipulation that there is no syntactic level. We have addressed this problem in our paper on window interference [57].

It may also be noted, in passing, that a *modeless* system must have the property that there is precisely one lexeme $l \in K^*$ such that $interpret(l) = c$ for each command $c \in C$.

5.6   Mapping state to display

An important notion within the direct manipulation style is the idea of articulatory directness [102]. A crucial component of any support for this notion is that the display gives a mirror representation of the manipulable state. As manipulations are performed on data, the effects of the manipulations are immediately visible in the display. As noted by Jacob [106], visible representation may, in practice, be a very abstract picture of the state. Take for example:

- a remote submersible — the *state* is the physical attitude, position, velocity and the environment of the submarine; the *display* consists of dials and other icons representing speed, direction and attitude, and a two dimensional view from a camera contained on board the craft;

- a simulated ship's steam engine [95] — the *state* is the simulation of the engine itself; the *display* schematic gives the status of flows and temperatures through the engine.

It may be appropriate to include the physical model being mirrored or monitored by the computer system. In the case of the submersible, state is outside the computer system. As operations affecting the display are invoked, the physical state of the submarine or ship's engine is modified.

In order to model the distinction between state and display in a direct manipulation system, we require two models (we may model them as algebras since both models will include objects, operations and axiomatic constraints): a state algebra (S, C), consisting of state and *commands* on the state; and a display algebra (D, O), that consists of display and *operators* that manipulate display. For example, in the case of the remote submersible a change of velocity is either a modification of the attitude, speed and direction of the submarine or a change of illumination in the dials and icons of the display plus a renewed picture from the camera. We view them as algebras because we will be interested in the possibility of defining axioms on the commands and operations that govern their behaviour. Initially we treat the visual representation as entirely separate from the state representation. In practice, of course, the models are related since they represent two different views of the same artefact, although each model will be limited by a different set of constraints. At this stage we are not interested in the details of the implementation of state, display or the operations upon them or how the two models arise. As the design progresses, structure will be added to these basic models; the designer's task is to avoid early design decisions that commit to particular interface styles or implementations. All the detail necessary at this point is that C is a set of state transformations $(S \rightarrow S)$ and O is the set of display transformations $(D \rightarrow D)$. It is assumed in both models that parameters (that is what the command requires in order to produce its result) have been dealt with at some other level, somewhere in the mapping between physical inputs and commands (see §5.5). The display may be considered to be a visual representation of some or all of the state (they are considered to be entirely independent) and might be, for example, an array of pixels (the details are not important).

The display is a view of some aspect of the state, so the view mapping $v: S \rightarrow D$ produces a visual representation of some or all of the state. The view mapping will also handle constant information to provide additional spatial information (we might call it template sugaring) to present to the user for example: a box outline of a data entry form, or menu, or information about mode. The two models may have a set of complementary commands in common, that is for $v : S \rightarrow D$, there exist two sets C' and O' of complementary functions. C' will include editing operations on text such as *insert*, *delete* and cursor movement, while O' consists of operations that change the state of pixels in the display, for example *cursor left* will move the illumination of the cursor one position to the left. These complementary sets may have the property that for any $c \in C'$ there corresponds an $o \in O'$, the **complement** of c, such that $\forall s \in S \; v(c(s)) = o(v(s))$, that is the commands are related by the view mapping, in a strong way (at least at this stage). It can be seen that an adequate description of mirroring is expressed in this coupling.

Two points emerge from the preceding discussion:

(1) the mapping from state to display, when complementary, affirms that the display is updated as the state is transformed by commands. Nothing is said about the user's understanding of the context in which commands are invoked. For example, does the user perceive an operation on display or a command on state? Commands may be invoked within the state metaphor or the display metaphor. Dix [54] describes a model in which a reverse mapping from display to state is used to map the effect of operation invocations into the state;

(2) typically, all the data of interest to the user cannot be represented adequately within a limited display. The design of an interactive system involves the development of techniques for

handling the whole, by showing an approximation of the data with enough detail for user purposes, and alternatively or additionally, by giving a partial view coupled with a strategy for revealing the whole.

It is the second of these points that we will pursue.

5.6.1   *Display resolution*

An important design problem is to develop an appropriate mechanism within an interactive system for presenting a partial picture of the state. We may think of the display as an approximation of the state in that it gives some detail of only part of the state. In this section, we discuss and refine what we mean by approximation in the context of the state and display models. Clearly, it is difficult to express the idea that a display is more approximate than a state, because displays and states are members of different domains (we are comparing state information with screen illuminations). One notion of resolution that may be adequate, but is too strong, is to say that, if one state s_1 is no less approximate than another s_2 (we abbreviate this by $s_1 \sqsubseteq s_2$) then of the images of the two states: $v(s_1)$ must be no less approximate than $v(s_2)$ as displays ($v(s_1) \sqsubseteq v(s_2)$). This definition of approximation is too strong if it demands that one state (or display) is *strictly* more approximate than the other state or display because it would require that any difference between the two states must be reflected in the two displays.

Part of the design process then, in such a framework, is to define an appropriate relation between states and between displays. The details of the relationship between states is not required in this account so we shall ignore it. In order to clarify the notion of approximation for displays, more information is required about the structure of the display. One example, a definition that will be used extensively throughout the rest of the chapter, is that the display is a mapping between co-ordinates and pixels $N \times N \to P$ and P is flat [168]. In other words elements of P are incomparable with any other element than $\perp$, the least defined or undefined element. One display will be no less approximate than another ($d_1 \sqsubseteq d_2$) if co-ordinate positions in d_1 are the same as d_2, or are undefined. One might imagine a least defined display as a display whose boundaries limit the display to nothing. A fully defined display, on the other hand, is a display that is able to encompass everything.

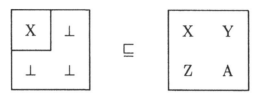

There are other more subtle approximation relations on displays that may be more appropriate in particular design cases. Systems often use icons to abbreviate information on the display. Icons are used to give brief visual references to information contained within the state that would otherwise use substantially more display space. Such an arrangement requires a notion of approximation in which an icon is considered to be more approximate than the full display form of the information that it represents. A co-ordinate based relationship would not provide an appropriate description of this notion of approximation.

For present purposes, part of the design modelling role, carried out as part of the specification of an interactive system, is to formalise an appropriate partial ordering both on state and display. One significant property, that will be required of such an ordering, is that if $s_1 \sqsubseteq s_2$ then $v(s_1) \sqsubseteq v(s_2)$; that is: v is **faithful** with respect to these partial orderings. This is a property that is not too strong if the orderings are not strict orderings.

Since how and when commands behave in an irregular manner is of major significance to the user, an important modelling issue will be how properties of commands or operations are affected at the boundary. It will help us to analyse this behaviour if we define the least approximation of state that produces the same display under v as the whole state would, that is $s' \sqsubseteq s$ and $v(s') = v(s)$ and if n is strictly less defined than s' then $v(n) \neq v(s')$. As long as v is a monotonic function mapping S to D there will be a unique s', which is the minimal state under v to produce d. We shall define a function $f_v : S \rightarrow S$ that produces the minimal state. The choice of ordering will depend on the particular application. Our purpose is to consider general principles, not particular device issues.

5.6.2   *Partiality*

An alternative and tighter formulation of the connection between state and display models may be constructed by means of a panoramic [58] or wide angle view of the whole state. We require that what can be seen of the state through the view v is an accurate reflection, but this requirement is not sufficient to ensure that a complete picture may be constructed by the user. We need to ensure adequate views at boundaries and that no holes may occur where the view will not show the state.

A notion of observability is required that ensures that the entire state may be made visible consistently and faithfully. A mapping $v^+ : S \to D$, that gives a complete picture of the underlying state is required; note we are not suggesting here that all interactive systems should be observable in this sense. The state of interest may be significantly smaller than the whole state. For example, in the case of the remote submersible mentioned earlier, a user is only interested in a partial picture of what is happening. He is only marginally interested in the internal workings of the submarine. However, on the other hand, an editor or spreadsheet system would require a more precise notion of predictability that incorporates a complete picture of the behaviour of the state.

In the following sections constructions will be described that ensure that the user can make up the whole display through a series of views. Hence v^+ should be constructible by means of passive commands that have no unwanted side effects.

Passivity

Passivity prescribes a set of commands that are harmless with respect to the part of state that contributes to the result of the system's execution. To produce a precise definition of passivity, more information is required about the state. The state may be structured by taking two mappings that extract some of the constituents of the state: $r: S \to R$ where R is the result and $f: S \to F$ where F is the set of frame information that defines, for example, what part of the state is displayed. A command, $c \in C$, is **passive** if for all $s \in S$, $r(c(s)) = r(s)$. In other words, the result part of the state remains unchanged.

Examples of passive commands may be found within a direct manipulation display editor such as: *cursor-left* and *page-forward*; and within an operating system, commands such as *list-files*. Notice that passivity is not completely harmless since, for instance, *delete*'s effect on state is not equivalent to *cursor-left* followed by *delete*.

Constructing v^+

The wide angle view v^+ will generate a display that mirrors the whole manipulable state (probably the result component) whether visible or invisible under v. v^+ should satisfy certain obvious properties, both of consistency and completeness.

Consistency properties

- $\forall s \in S : v^+(f_v(s)) = v(s)$;

- $\forall s_1, s_2 \in S : s_1 \sqsubseteq s_2 \Rightarrow v^+(s_1) \sqsubseteq v^+(s_2)$;

A more reasonable assumption than v being complementary would be that v^+ be complementary, that is $\forall s \in S$, if $o \in O'$ is the complement of $c \in C'$ then $v^+(c(s)) = o(v^+(s))$. This requires that the whole viewable state mirrors the effect of complementary commands, not simply that which is viewed by v.

Completeness properties

v^+ is constructed dynamically by introducing a principle of **observability**. v^+ is generated by a sequence of states $\{s_i\}$ (produced by passive commands) being the least upper bound of a set of images of s_i under v. The least upper bound of two displays $d_1 \sqcup d_2$ (with approximation ordering as already defined) may be illustrated by means of the following picture:

$$
\begin{array}{|c|c|}
\hline
\text{X} & \bot \\
\hline
\bot & \bot \\
\hline
\end{array}
\quad \sqcup \quad
\begin{array}{|c|c|}
\hline
\bot & \text{Y} \\
\hline
\bot & \bot \\
\hline
\end{array}
\quad = \quad
\begin{array}{|c|c|}
\hline
\text{X} & \text{Y} \\
\hline
\bot & \bot \\
\hline
\end{array}
$$

Hence, given a particular $s \in S$, we require a *strategy* $\{p_i\}$ (a set of command sequences $p_i = c_1^i; c_2^i; ...; c_k^i$ where ";" composes commands and each c_j^i is passive) to generate a set of states with the following completeness properties: that the entire state should be visible through the panoramic view, and the panoramic view should contain an unambiguous representation of the result. This may be made more precise:

- $r(\bigsqcup_{i=1}^{n} \{f_v(s_i)\}) = r(s)$

  The result components of the least upper bound of the sequence of minimal states is equal to the result component of the original state.

- $\bigsqcup_{i=1}^{n} \{v(s_i)\} = v^+(s)$. v^+ produces a display of the whole state s.

- $\forall s \in S : r(s)$ is contained within the display $v^+(s)$ in an unambiguous form.

A system that satisfies these properties is called *observable*. Observability is stronger than required for many interactive systems, in particular for examples such as the submersible and steamer. For a general partial ordering, since a least upper bound is included, observability also highlights the possibility of display ambiguity that may arise when different parts of the state are capable of generating displays that are indistinguishable. These indistinguishable displays will not contribute properly to the panoramic display (since $d \sqcup d = d$). Systems may be designed that avoid the problem by using an iconic scroll bar to indicate where the display is in the context of the larger state. In practice, the definition that we have used here, because it is based on co-ordinates, ensures that a display is placed correctly within its co-ordinate background. A display produced by v is framed within a space of co-ordinates that all map to undefined, $\bot$.

5.7   Localising properties of direct manipulation systems

We defined a connection between state and display that transcends the physical limitations of the display, in the sense that the effect of commands on the panoramic display is consistent with the state. In practice there are often clearly defined neighbourhoods in which specific properties hold.

We consider two ways of defining locality:

- properties that hold for certain limitations of the effect of operations;

- properties that hold across particular points of the state space.

5.7.1   *Visibility*

So far in this chapter, we have explored the distinction between keys and commands, and a state model and a display model without considering how these models may be used within a design methodology. In practice a designer's interest in the complementary effect of an operation is likely to be limited to subsets of states. For example when considering the behaviour of a command that uses a cursor to select parameter information from the state, one is interested in whether or not the required and resulting information is visible.

A more fruitful way of considering the complementary properties of state and display from a designer's point of view is to distinguish between an unlimited model of interactive behaviour, and a model that demonstrates the physical limitations of the display. For example, a designer might initially conceive of a text editor consisting of an arbitrarily long line with an associated cursor. At this level algebraic principles relating to state behaviour of the commands may be developed and applied, for example invertibility, commutativity etc. Physical constraints, imposed by dimensions of display or chapter structure, will produce a requirement for new operations such as *cursor up* and *cursor down*. Also new behaviour of the existing commands will be required to deal with exceptional effects at boundaries, possibly conflicting with the originally required algebraic properties (e.g., commutativity and the existence of inverses may not be true at display boundaries). Neighbourhoods of the state, such as where manipulated information is visible, will provide context for investigating the complementary relationship between commands and operations. The display algebra operations characterise the boundary effects of commands.

There is therefore now a different emphasis in the use of these models. We are concerned about particular states, and whether properties true in the state model continue to hold in the display model. Constraints on commands and states are now required that will enable neighbourhoods for the two algebras to be complementary.

One example of a property that constrains the neighbourhood in which complementary properties should hold is **visibility**. A command is visible for a particular state if the command modifies visible data only, and produces a result in which all effects of the command are visible.

A relation is first defined between states: for any pair of states $s_1, s_2 \in S$: $vis(s_1, s_2)$ is true if $v^+(s_2) - v^+(f_v(s_2)) \sqsubseteq v^+(s_1)$ and $v^+(s_1) - v^+(f_v(s_1)) \sqsubseteq v^+(s_2)$.

This relation is complicated because of possible effects that might arise as state, that was visible in the display, becomes invisible, and previously invisible state becomes visible. This property requires that:

- the visible part of s_2 ($v^+(f_v(s_2))$) may change, but the invisible part of s_2 (i.e., $v^+(s_2) - v^+(f_v(s_2))$ where "−" defines all the co-ordinates of $v^+(s_2)$ that do not correspond to the visible part of s_2) is more approximate than what was initially visible under v^+;

- a similar property relates the visible and invisible parts of s_1. In short $vis(s_1, s_2)$ asserts that the only differences between s_1 and s_2 are visible in the display under v. Visibility is a particular form of this relation. A command c is *visible* in a particular state $s \in S$ if $vis(s, c(s))$, hence we are relating the initial state to the state after the command has been executed.

It is then possible to specify that regular properties of commands hold in states when a command is visible, for example given any $c \in C$ there corresponds an inverse $\overline{c} \in C$ such that $\forall s \in S$ for which $vis(s, c(s))$: $\overline{c}(c(s)) = s$. We may then demand that all displays must be visible for every state; this is similar to the technical property of *predictability* in interactive systems [60].

Given these notions of neighbourhood we may now consider properties of operations.

5.7.2   *Local properties when commands are visible*

Given a computation sequence $s_0 s_1 s_2 \ldots$, the view function v permits the possibility of parallel reasoning about a corresponding display sequence $d_0 d_1 d_2 \ldots$. Here d_i is the image of s_i under v and represents a "window" onto the system. As we have discussed already, operations may affect the state without affecting the display information, or alternatively alter the display perspective without modifying the data that is basic to the system.

We now specify properties that should hold for commands within such localities specified by the visibility constraint. These properties hold when data transformed by the command remains inside the display, and produce consistent alternative behaviour otherwise.

One important feature of a direct manipulation system is that it gives immediate visible response to a user operation. Commands should be tractable; they should have algebraic properties, for example: the existence of inverses; commutativity; idempotence, as appropriate to the function of the operation. These algebraic properties may be confounded at the boundaries of the display. For example:

(1) *cursor left* and *cursor right* are inverses except at the screen boundary; e.g., at the boundaries different editors take different actions: some *beep* and do nothing; some change the position of the display frame;

(2) *cursor left* and *cursor right* are commutative, except at boundaries;

(3) *insert* has *delete* as right inverse except at the display boundary.

We may localise the property of a command by using the definition of visibility and saying that if *prop* is the algebraic property of a command $c \in C$ then if $vis(s, c(s))$ is true, $prop(c)$ is true. On the other hand we could also specify the effect when a particular command is not visible. For example:

- *existence of inverses*: If b is an inverse for c then we may require that, for all $s \in S$, if $vis(s, b(c(s)))$ and $vis(s, c(b(s)))$ then $c(b(s)) = b(c(s)) = s$;

- *idempotence*: for all $s \in S$, c is idempotent $\Rightarrow$ that if $vis(s, c(s))$ then $c(c(s)) = c(s)$. In this case we might also specify that for all $s \in S$, if *not* $vis(s, c(s))$ then c is modified so that $c(s) = s$.

5.7.3   *Exception models*

Properties such as *visibility* establish neighbourhoods of validity for complementary properties of algebras. However, as said in the introduction, it is likely that users distinguish between normal and exceptional properties of interactive systems with distinct mental models. Two models of an interactive system may be appropriate: the normal model which includes a number of algebras describing different normal properties of commands with more or less hindrance from the display or implementation; and the exception model that describes the effects of context and other factors generating discontinuities in the operation of user commands.

The *exception model* is concerned with the properties of commands as they are affected by display boundaries, cursor pointers and block boundaries (for example cut-and-paste boundaries). We will refer to these special points in the display or state as *pointers*. Given the example above, we may generalise the properties of commands that are expressed in the exception model. In many interactive systems, for example display editors, these pointer effects are dominant in the user's perception of interactive behaviour and are therefore crucial to the user's understanding of the system.

For our purposes, the exception model consists of an enumeration of cases that exhaust the possible effects on pointers. For example, taking a display editor [58] we notice that commands have exceptional effects (which may include complex interactions) in, among others, the following circumstances:

(1) *cursor pointers*: certain commands change the state by modifying the cursor only. Cursor movement although passive, will affect active commands. For example, $delete(uparrow(t)) \neq delete(t)$ for some $t \in T$;

(2) *display boundaries*: certain commands change the state by moving the display boundary, and have no other effect on state. Other result transforming commands have exceptional effects at the boundaries, and it is appropriate to describe these effects separately. For example the effect when a command touches or crosses a boundary might be to have no effect on the result (contrary to normal principles such as invertibility) and sound the alarm;

(3) *cut-and-paste boundaries*: special commands form and manipulate these boundaries. Commands will often have an ancillary effect to do the necessary work to accommodate these boundaries.

Types of exceptional case

The exception model should enumerate cases and prescribe generalised properties that occur at boundaries for example:

- *Commands whose only effect is to modify pointers.* It is necessary to express the interactions of these commands with other commands that use the state. We express these interactions as constraints: for any result transforming command $c : S \rightarrow S$ and a command $d : S \rightarrow S$ that modifies frame information only, $c(d(s)) \neq c(s)$.

- *Commands that have an exceptional effect as they cross boundary points.* Hence we express the behaviour of commands over a subset of the domain of the command. We require properties such as: if $c \in S \rightarrow S$ is a command that depends on the pointers generated by the *ptrs* function then for any $s' \in S$ such that $ptrs(s') \subseteq Bdry(s)$, c has the property that $c(s) = s$ and *bell* is sounded. Here $ptrs : S \rightarrow power(Ptr)$ generates cursors, *Ptr* is a set of pointers and $Bdry(s)$ is the set of boundary pointers for state s.

5.8   Conclusions

A simple state based model of interaction has clarified understanding of direct manipulation by aiding the structuring of relationships between inputs and commands, and display and state. Locality issues have been explored for these systems relevant to the principles of direct manipulation. We have introduced an interaction model appropriate for reasoning with some precision about properties of such systems valid from a user's perspective. This technique for the design and evaluation of interactive systems provides both a scientific framework that may be used as a basis for evaluation and an engineering basis for their effective design.

   We have already put the three tiered approach (interaction model, formal specification, implementation) into practice by implementing an interactive system based on an earlier interaction model [59] to explore notions of predictability. This system has been extended in various ways to support controlled experiments on browsing mechanisms [127]. The results of these experiments, since they have been the results of evaluations against principles, have been adequate to provide supporting evidence for decisions between design alternatives.

   We see that the state based model described in this chapter would provide an effective first stage in the design process, easing refinement to a full specification. Currently [83] we are investigating the use of interaction models, such as this one, as a basis for experimental evaluation of interactive systems against precise claims about system usability.

5.9   Acknowledgements

We thank Harold Thimbleby, Andrew Monk and Roger Took for ideas and comments on the chapter.

CHAPTER SIX

SPECIFICATION, ANALYSIS AND REFINEMENT OF INTERACTIVE PROCESSES

BERNARD SUFRIN AND JIFENG HE

6.1   Introduction

It has become widely accepted that it is a good idea to build an abstract mathematical description (formal specification) of an information system before building the system itself. One good reason for doing so is that it is possible to explore the validity of design choices by reasoning about the description, rather than building the system and only then discovering that we have compromised its usefulness by making a bad decision early in the design process.

We explore the validity of design choices by attempting to prove conjectures about their consequences. For example, suppose we are trying to design a text editor, and believe (perhaps because we took the advice of a psychologist) that a delete key should remove the last character typed at the editor. In other words, the effect of inserting a character, then pressing the delete key should be to leave us with the text that we started with. If the behaviour of the insert and delete keys were modelled by the text-to-text functions, *insert* and *delete*, then we would attempt to prove from the descriptions of these functions that:

$$\forall c : CHAR \bullet \forall t : TEXT \bullet delete(insert\ c\ t) = t$$

But what else should we try to prove about our editor? Clearly, there is a class of conjecture which is connected with the implementability of the description: but implementability is not the only desirable quality for an information system. In [194] and [61] the search for *user-engineering principles* is motivated. The idea is that these principles should be formalisable, and should record generally-desirable properties of information systems — for example, *completeness*: "the commands provided permit all possible documents to be delivered", *predictability*: "the effect of a command can be forecast by looking at the screen", *honesty*: "the effect that a keystroke just had can be determined by looking at the screen". When exploring the design of an information system, we should be able to check the principles it satisfies by reasoning from its abstract description.

In this chapter, we introduce and explore a mathematical model of interactive information systems. In the first section, we introduce a model of processes which permits both "state oriented" and "trace oriented" styles of specification as well as combinations of these two styles. In the second section, we introduce a special class of process, the *interactive process*, and classify some properties of the commands used to drive such processes. In the third section, we outline a series of laws which may be used to justify the refinement of interactive processes from their specifications. Next, we present a brief discussion of the relationship between our model and state-based system specifications expressed in the schema notation of Z. Finally, we specify a simple mouse-driven editor and analyse some of its properties, thereby exposing some rather bad design decisions.

6.2   Processes

A process evolves by participating in *events*, during which it undergoes a transition from one *state* to another. Since we shall be using our model of processes to reason about *specifications*, we must consider from the very beginning the possibility that the specification of an event might not completely determine the relationship between starting and ending states: in other words, we have to admit the possibility of *non deterministic* specifications. Non determinism may be present in a specification for a variety of reasons:

- to support the description of a system from one of a variety of perspectives;

- to avoid overconstraining implementations of the system being specified;

- to support abstraction from the complete history of a system. For example, when specifying a single user's session at a bank teller automat, we must leave undetermined the exact amount of money the teller has available at the start of the session.

6.2.1   *The simple model*

We shall denote the set of all possible states in which a process might be by S, and the set of all possible events by E. Given these sets, a process can be specified by giving its **alphabet** (the set of events in which it may participate), its **behaviours** (an alphabet indexed family of state-state relations), and its set of *initial* states. Outside its alphabet a process cannot participate in any events. We formalise this by defining a schematic structure which captures these essential characteristics and their relationships:

$$
\begin{array}{|l}
\hline
\_PROCESS_{[S,E]}\text{_____} \\
\quad \alpha: \qquad \mathbb{P}\,E \\
\quad \hat{\beta}: \qquad E \twoheadrightarrow (S \leftrightarrow S) \\
\quad \iota: \qquad \mathbb{P}\,S \\
\hline
\quad \alpha = \operatorname{dom} \hat{\beta} \\
\hline
\end{array}
$$

At the very beginning, the system starts in one of the states in ι, and whenever it is in state $s \in S$, it is ready to participate in any of the events in its alphabet for which a behaviour is specified. The relationship between the current state of a system and the events in which it is ready to participate may be captured by extending the schematic structure *PROCESS* as follows:

$$
\begin{array}{|l}
\hline
Ready: S \to \mathbb{P}\,E \\
\hline
Ready\ s = \{e: \alpha \mid s \in \operatorname{dom}(\hat{\beta}e)\} \\
\end{array}
$$

If it is in state s and participates in the event $e \in Ready\ s$, then it moves to one of the states specified by the behaviour for that event, namely $\{s' : S \mid (s, s') \in \hat{\beta}e\}$; but the state to which it moves cannot be influenced by its environment.

Examples:

1. The odometer on a car, which can participate in the events *OneMile* and *Reset*, and which counts up to 999 before "wrapping around" to 0 is defined by

   ┌─ *ODOMETER* ─────────────────────────────
   │ *PROCESS*
   ├────────────────
   │ $\hat{\beta}$ *OneMile* $= \{i \mapsto i + 1 \bullet i : 0..998\} \cup \{999 \mapsto 0\}$
   │ $\hat{\beta}$ *Reset* $i = 0$
   │ $\iota = 0..999$
   │ $\alpha = \{OneMile, Reset\}$
   └──

2. An odometer which wraps around at 999, but to an unpredictable value.

   ┌─ *BROKENODOMETER* ───────────────────────
   │ *PROCESS*
   ├────────────────
   │ $\hat{\beta}$ *OneMile* $= \{i \mapsto i + 1 \bullet i : 0..998\} \cup$
   │ $\{999 \mapsto i \bullet i : 0..999\}$
   │ $\hat{\beta}$ *Reset* $i = 0$
   │ $\iota = 0..999$
   │ $\alpha = \{OneMile, Reset\}$
   └──

□

We can extend the idea of behaviour from individual events to sequences of events, which we shall henceforth call *programs*. The state transition which the system undergoes when it participates in the program $\langle p_1, p_2, \ldots, p_n \rangle$ is given by the distributed relational composition of the behaviours of each of the events, except that if an event which is not in the alphabet of the process appears in a program, the corresponding state transition relation is empty:

$$\hat{\beta} p_1 \ ; \ \hat{\beta} p_2 \ ; \ \ldots \hat{\beta} p_n$$

where

$$e \in \alpha \Rightarrow \hat{\beta} \ e = \hat{\beta} \ e$$
$$e \notin \alpha \Rightarrow \hat{\beta} \ e = \{\}$$

More formally

$$\beta : \mathrm{seq}\ E \rightarrow (S \leftrightarrow S)$$

$$\overline{\beta \ p \ = \ ; / (p \ ; \ \hat{\beta})}$$

We can (partially) specify processes by defining the behaviour of *programs*, rather than of individual events.

Examples:

1. Adding a "one-ply" *Undo* event to a process P amounts to saying that the behaviour of any two-event program whose last event is *Undo*, is the identity on states.

   $$PUndo \ \hat{=} \ P \ | \ Undo \in \alpha \wedge \forall \, e : \alpha \bullet \beta\langle e, Undo \rangle = id$$

2. Adding a checkpoint and restart facility to a process P.

   ┌─*PCheckpoint*────────────────────────────
   │ P
   │ ───
   │ $\{Check, Restart\} \subseteq \alpha$
   │ $\forall \, p : \mathrm{seq}(\alpha - \{Check, Restart\}) \bullet$
   │ $\beta(\langle Check \rangle \ ^\frown p \ ^\frown \langle Restart \rangle) = id$
   └──

   In fact, we will argue later that in an interactive system, both these specifications may constrain an implementation more than is necessary to achieve user satisfaction.

□

6.2.2   *Traces*

A process *trace* is a sequence of events in which the process can successfully participate, starting from one of its initial states. The set of traces of a process is the set of all possible sequences of events in which that process can participate

$$
\begin{array}{|l}
\hline
Trace : \mathbb{P}(\text{seq } E) \\
\hline
p \in Trace \Leftrightarrow \beta\, p (\!(\iota)\!) \neq \{\,\} \\
\hline
\end{array}
$$

It is a fundamental, and easily proven, consequence of the definition of *Trace*, that it is *prefix closed*: in other words if t is a *Trace*, then every initial subsequence of t is also a *Trace*.

The relations $\hookleftarrow$ ("prefixes"), $\hookrightarrow$ ("suffixed by"), and $\overset{\cdots}{\hookrightarrow}$ ("contains"), will be useful for describing constraints on traces, as will the function **Prefixes** which maps a sequence to all its prefixes.

$$
\begin{array}{|ll}
\hline
\hookleftarrow : & \text{seq } E \leftrightarrow \text{seq } E \\
\hookrightarrow : & \text{seq } E \leftrightarrow \text{seq } E \\
\overset{\cdots}{\hookrightarrow} : & \text{seq } E \leftrightarrow \text{seq } E \\
Prefixes : & \text{seq } E \rightarrow \mathbb{P}\,\text{seq } E \\
\hline
s \hookleftarrow t & \Leftrightarrow \quad \exists\, r : \text{seq } E \bullet s \frown r = t \\
t \hookrightarrow s & \Leftrightarrow \quad \exists\, r : \text{seq } E \bullet r \frown s = t \\
t \overset{\cdots}{\hookrightarrow} s & \Leftrightarrow \quad \exists\, r, r' : \text{seq } E \bullet r \frown s \frown r' = t \\
Prefixes\ t & = \quad \{ s : \text{seq } E \mid s \hookleftarrow t \} \\
\hline
\end{array}
$$

6.2.3   *The need for an improved model*

Suppose we want to insist that the first *ODOMETER* event is always a *Reset*. One would be to redefine the state and behaviours of *Reset* and *OneMile* in such a way that the odometer cannot engage in *OneMile* before engaging in a *Reset*. Such a formulation would be a little clumsy, however, since it would require us to build more mechanism into the state, the presence of which might distract readers from the essence of the specification.

We could leave the current specification as it is, but make an explicit constraint on its *traces*, namely that each nonempty trace is prefixed by $\langle reset \rangle$:

$$
\forall\, t : Trace \mid t \neq \langle\,\rangle \bullet \langle reset \rangle \hookleftarrow t
$$

Given the present definition this constraint is unsatisfiable. The traces are *completely determined* by β, and the extra constraint contradicts them.

If we are going to adopt a *hybrid* approach to process specification, then we need a definition of processes which allows us to constrain the traces of a process *independently* of our constraints on its state transitions.

6.2.4   *The improved model*

In the following model, a process is specified by: its alphabet; a description of the state transition relations corresponding to its events; its initial states; and its traces. The essential difference between this model and the simple model is that behaviour which is permitted by the state-transition part of a specification, may be excluded by placing restrictions on traces:

PROCESS

$\alpha :$　　　$\mathbb{P}\, E$
$\hat{\beta} :$　　　$E \nrightarrow (S \leftrightarrow S)$
$Trace :$　$\mathbb{P}\,(\mathrm{seq}\, E)$
$\iota :$　　　$\mathbb{P}\, S$

$\alpha = \mathrm{dom}\, \hat{\beta}$

$\forall\, s, t : \mathrm{seq}\, E \bullet s \,\widehat{}\, t \in Trace \Rightarrow s \in Trace$

As a process evolves, it "keeps track of its own history", and when in state $s \in S$, with history $h \in Trace$, it is ready to engage in an event e only if the behaviour of e is defined at s, and if $h \,\widehat{}\, \langle e \rangle$ is also a *Trace*.

$Ready : S \times \mathrm{seq}\, E \rightarrow \mathbb{P}\, E$

$Ready(s, h) = \{e : E \mid \exists\, s' : S \bullet (s, s') \in \hat{\beta} e\, \wedge$
　　　　　　　$\{h, h \,\widehat{}\, \langle e \rangle\} \subseteq Trace\}$

If the process is in state s, and has had history $h \in Trace$, and participates in event $e \in Ready(s, h)$, then it moves to one of the states $\{s' : S \mid (s, s') \in \hat{\beta} e\}$ and now has history $h \,\widehat{}\, \langle e \rangle$. Its **effective behaviour** $\bar{\beta}$ can be defined by

$$\bar{\beta} : E \rightarrow (S \times \text{seq } E \leftrightarrow S \times \text{seq } E)$$

$$\bar{\beta}\, e = \{(s, h), (s', h') : S \times Trace \mid (s, s') \in \hat{\beta}e \wedge h' = h \,\widehat{}\, \langle e \rangle\}$$

and the state transition βp of a program $p \in \text{seq } E$ is defined by

$$\beta : \text{seq } E \rightarrow (S \leftrightarrow S)$$

$$\beta\, p \;=\; \{s, s' : S \mid \exists\, h, h' : Trace \bullet ((s, h), (s', h')) \;\in\; \raise.5ex\hbox{$\scriptstyle\circ$} /(p \,\raise.5ex\hbox{$\scriptstyle\circ$}\, \bar{\beta})\}$$

The story of a process is completed by explaining where it all begins, namely at some initial state:

$$\forall p : \text{seq } E \bullet p \in Trace \Leftrightarrow \beta p(\!(\iota)\!) \neq \{\,\}$$

We can now specify a process with a combination of predicates over its state transition relations, and predicates over its traces.

Every specification in which a constraint on *Trace* appears is equivalent to one in which no such additional constraint is present, but whose state space and transition relations may be more complex. The additional complexity of the state space is what is required to "police" the *Trace* constraint.

Examples:

1. All nonempty traces begin with a $\langle Reset \rangle$.

$$\forall t : Trace \mid t \neq \langle\rangle \bullet \langle Reset \rangle \;\hookleftarrow\; t$$

2. A *crash* must never directly follow a *bang*.

$$\not\exists t : Trace \bullet t \;\hookrightarrow\; \langle bang, crash \rangle$$

3. Every *crash* must be preceded at some stage by a *bang*

$$\forall t : Trace \bullet t \;\hookrightarrow\; \langle crash \rangle \Rightarrow$$
$$\exists p : Prefixes\, t \bullet p \;\hookrightarrow\; \langle bang \rangle$$

$\square$

6.2.5   *Failures*

It is sometimes convenient to specify properties of processes by forbidding certain kinds of failure. If R is a set of events, a trace t is said to **Fail** at R if after the trace t the process *might* be in a state where none of the events in R are acceptable to it:

$$
\begin{array}{|l}
\_Fails\_ : \mathrm{seq}\ E \leftrightarrow \mathbb{P}\ E \\
\hline
t\ Fails\ R \Leftrightarrow \\
\qquad t \in Trace\ \wedge \\
\qquad R \subseteq \alpha\ \wedge \\
\qquad \exists\,s : S \bullet s \in \beta t (\!(t)\!) \wedge \forall r : R \bullet r \notin Ready(s, t)
\end{array}
$$

Examples:

1. Between a *bang* and the next *crash*, the process must always be prepared to accept at least one of the events in *Progress*.

$$
\begin{aligned}
&\forall\,s, t : Trace \bullet \\
&\quad s \hookrightarrow \langle bang \rangle \wedge (s \smallfrown t)\ Fails\ Progress \Rightarrow \\
&\qquad t \overset{\cdots}{\hookrightarrow} \langle crash \rangle
\end{aligned}
$$

2. Between a *start* and the next *stop*, the process must always be prepared to accept an *interrupt*.

$$
\begin{aligned}
&\forall\,s, t : Trace \bullet \\
&\quad s \hookrightarrow \langle start \rangle \wedge (s \smallfrown t)\ Fails\ \{interrupt\} \Rightarrow \\
&\qquad t \overset{\cdots}{\hookrightarrow} \langle stop \rangle
\end{aligned}
$$

□

If t fails at R and $R' \subseteq R$, then t also fails at R'. Thus every trace t fails at $\{\,\}$, and the traces of a process are related to its failures by:

$$
\forall\,PROCESS \bullet Trace = \{t \bullet (t, R) : Fails \mid R = \{\,\}\}
$$

6.2.6   *Sequential processes*

A **sequential process** is a process which can terminate; it has the special event $\sqrt{}$ (pronounced "tick") in its alphabet, and communicates the fact that it has terminated to its environment by being prepared to engage in $\sqrt{}$ as the last thing it does.

Termination doesn't change the state of a sequential process, and the process can do nothing at all after it has terminated:

```
┌─ SEQPROCESS ──────────────────────────────────────
│ PROCESS
│ ────────────────────────────
│ √ ∈ α
│
│ β̂√ ⊆ id[S]
│
│ ∀ t : Trace • t ↪ ⟨√⟩ ⇒ ∄ t' : Trace • t ≠ t' ∧ t ↩ t'
```

Example: A lolly-vending machine which starts full and terminates when it runs out of lollies:

$E ::= coin \mid lolly \mid \sqrt{}$
$S ::= coinpresent\langle\!\langle 1..20 \rangle\!\rangle \mid coinabsent\langle\!\langle 0..20 \rangle\!\rangle$

```
┌─ VM ──────────────────────────────────────────────
│ SEQPROCESS
│ ────────────────────────────
│ α            = { coin, lolly, √}
│ β ⟨coin⟩     = { coinabsent n ↦ coinpresent n • n : 1..20}
│ β ⟨lolly⟩    = { coinpresent n ↦ coinabsent (n − 1)
│                    • n : 1..20}
│ β ⟨√⟩        = { coinabsent 0 ↦ coinabsent 0}
│ ι            = { coinabsent 20}
```

The specification of this process is more complicated than it need be because we have made explicit in its state a mechanism by which it determines whether a coin has been supplied. In the next section, we introduce a method of specification which will allow us to be less explicit.

6.2.7   *Constructive specification of traces*

As we have shown, it may be convenient to specify the traces of a process independently of the effect each event has on process state. This can be done in a number of ways, the most effective of which is to define a set of operators which construct sets of traces. In [93] a very rich set of such operators is presented, but here we shall be content with just a few.

First, we define a **history** as a prefix closed set of sequences of events, and note that the set of traces of a process is indeed a process history:

$HISTORY \triangleq \{H : \mathbb{P}(\text{seq } E) \mid \forall\, a, b : \text{seq } E \bullet a \,\frown\, b \in H \Rightarrow a \in H\}$

The process which does nothing at all but terminate has a history which we shall call *skip*

$$skip \triangleq \{\langle\rangle, \langle\surd\rangle\}$$

If A is a set of events not containing $\surd$, and H is the history of process P, then $A \rightarrow H$ is the history of a process whose first event is from the set A, and which subsequently behaves like P.

$\_ \rightarrow \_ : \mathbb{P}(E - \{\surd\}) \times HISTORY \rightarrow HISTORY$

$A \rightarrow H = \{\langle\rangle\} \cup \{\langle a\rangle \,\frown\, h \bullet a : A;\ h : H\}$

Examples:

1. The history of a process which accepts *login* and then will accept only *logout* before terminating is:

   $$\{login\} \rightarrow \{logout\} \rightarrow skip$$

2. The history of a sequential process $A^{\otimes n}$ which accepts exactly n events from the set A, and then terminates is defined by:

   $$A^{\otimes n} \triangleq Prefixes \{s \,\frown\, \langle\surd\rangle \bullet s : \text{seq } A \mid \#\, s = n\}$$

3. The history of a sequential process $A^{\otimes}$ which accepts any number of events from the set A and then terminates is defined by:

   $$A^{\otimes} \triangleq \bigcup \{A^{\otimes n} \bullet n : \mathsf{N}\}$$

4. An odometer constrained to start with a *Reset*, and then continue with any number of *OneMile* or *Reset* events

$$ODOMETER \mid Traces = \{Reset\} \rightarrow \{OneMile, Reset\}^{\otimes}$$

□

If H_1 is the history of P_1 and H_2 is the history of P_2, then the history of a process which behaves like P_1 or like P_2 is denoted $H_1[]H_2$.

$$\underline{\quad}[]\underline{\quad} : HISTORY \times HISTORY \rightarrow HISTORY$$

$$H_1 \; [] \; H_2 = H_1 \cup H_2$$

If T is a term in which x appears free, a more evocative notation for the union of the family of histories $\{T \bullet x : X\}$ is defined by:

$$[]x : X \bullet T \triangleq \bigcup \{T \bullet x : X\}$$

If H_1 is the history of a sequential process P_1, and H_2 is the history of P_2, then the history of the process which behaves like P_1 until P_1 terminates, and then behaves like P_2 is written[1] $H_1 \, \fatsemi \, H_2$:

$$\underline{\quad}\fatsemi\underline{\quad} : HISTORY \times HISTORY \twoheadrightarrow HISTORY$$

$$H_1 \, \fatsemi \, H_2 =$$
$$\{s_1 \frown s_2 \quad \bullet \; s_1 : H_1; \; s_2 : H_2 \mid s_1 \frown \langle \surd \rangle \in H_1 \} \cup$$
$$\{s_1 \qquad \bullet \; s_1 : H_1 \qquad \mid s_1 \not\frown \langle \surd \rangle \qquad \}$$

Examples:

1. The history *Dump* in which a tape is chosen and mounted, any number of files are written, and the *same* tape is dismounted:

$$Dump \triangleq \bigcup \{Mount \; t \rightarrow Write^{\otimes} \, \fatsemi \, Dismount \; t \rightarrow skip \bullet t : Tape\}$$

---

[1] The symbol $\fatsemi$ is also used to denote relational composition; the two uses can easily be distinguished by context.

2. An alternative notation for the same history

$Dump \triangleq [] \ t : Tape \bullet Mount \ t \rightarrow Write^{\otimes} \ ; Dismount \ t \rightarrow skip$

☐

If H is the history of a sequential process P, then the history of a sequential process which behaves like P exactly n times before terminating is denoted $H * n$. The process which behaves like P zero or more times before terminating is denoted $H*$:

$$
\begin{array}{l}
\_ * \_: \quad HISTORY \times \mathsf{N} \twoheadrightarrow HISTORY \\
\_ * : \quad\quad HISTORY \twoheadrightarrow HISTORY \\
\hline
H * 0 \quad\quad\quad = skip \\
H * (n+1) \ = H \ ; H * n \\
H* = \bigcup \{H * n \bullet n : \mathsf{N}\}
\end{array}
$$

Examples:

1. The history *Session*, which accepts a *login*, any number of *Commands* and then terminates after a *logout* can be defined by:

   $Session \triangleq \{login\} \rightarrow Commands* \ ; \{logout\} \rightarrow skip$

2. The history *Workstation*, which accepts any number of *Sessions* or *Dumps* before terminating:

   $Workstation \triangleq (Session \ [] \ Dump)*$

3. The history *Command*, which accepts any number of *key strokes* or menu selections, followed by an *enter*:

   $Command \triangleq (keystroke \ [] \ menu)* \ ; enter \rightarrow skip$

4. A different definition of *Command*, in which commands specified by menu selections do not require a separate *enter*:

   $Command \triangleq (keystroke* \ ; enter \rightarrow skip \ [] \ menu)$

5. A *keystroke* involves pressing a key and then releasing the same key:

$$keystroke \,\hat{=}\, [] \; k : Key \bullet press \; k \,\rightarrow\, release \; k \,\rightarrow\, skip$$

6. A simple bank-teller

$$S \,\hat{=}\, \{onhand : \mathsf{N}; \; req : \mathsf{N}\}$$
$$E ::= card \mid digit \langle\!\langle 0..9 \rangle\!\rangle \mid ok \mid no \mid money \mid \surd$$

At the beginning of the session the teller may be in any state at all. The teller accepts the client's card, then allows the client to enter a request for money, digit-by-digit. The client may then confirm the amount and (if the teller has sufficient funds) get the money, or may cancel the transaction:

$$\iota = S$$

$$Trace = \{card\} \rightarrow$$
$$([] \; n : \mathsf{N} \bullet digit \; n \rightarrow skip)* \rightarrow$$
$$(ok \rightarrow money \cdot\rightarrow skip[]no \rightarrow skip)$$

$$
\begin{array}{llll}
\beta\langle card\rangle & (onhand, req) & = & (onhand, 0) \\
\beta\langle digit \; d\rangle & (onhand, req) & = & (onhand, req \times 10 + d) \\
\beta\langle no\rangle & (onhand, req) & = & (onhand, 0) \\
\beta\langle ok\rangle & = & \{(o, r) \mapsto (o - r, 0) \bullet o, r : \mathsf{N} \mid r \leq o\}
\end{array}
$$

The system must refuse *ok* if the teller has insufficient funds; the only action open to the client at this point is to cancel the transaction (with a *no*).

7. Another lolly machine with the same behaviour as our original. It doesn't really matter what the state space is (providing it has at least one element), since the constraint on the traces of the machine ensures the appropriate behaviour.

$$E \quad ::= coin \mid lolly \mid \surd$$

$$\begin{array}{|l}
\hline
\_VM\ \underline{\hspace{8cm}} \\
\quad SEQPROCESS \\
\quad \underline{\hspace{3cm}} \\
\quad \beta\langle coin \rangle = \beta\langle lolly \rangle = S \times S \\
\quad \beta\langle \sqrt{} \rangle = Id_{[S]} \\
\quad Trace = (\{coin\} \rightarrow \{lolly\} \rightarrow skip) * 20 \\
\quad \iota = S \\
\hline
\end{array}$$

□

6.3   Interactive processes

An **interactive process** is a process driven by a user. The events
in which it is prepared to participate include some which are known
as *commands*. Although our model of processes does not allow us to
formalise any idea of cause, we assume that the user causes commands
by presenting them to the process, and that the process causes the
remaining events to occur. We also assume that the user is always ready
to participate in any non-command which the system offers, whereas
the system must only participate in *commands* which it is ready for.

As each command is accepted, the process moves autonomously from
its current state through a succession of one or more states until it is
ready to show the user some visible indication of its state, which it does
"just after" engaging in one of the events △, (pronounced "**show**"). In
addition to this, the process is sometimes prepared to yield the user a
result of some kind, which it does "just after" engaging in one of the
events ▽ (pronounced "**yield**").

Thus, in order to turn a process specification into an interactive
process specification we need to describe:

- the events which the user can initiate (the *commands*);

- the △ events;

- the view which is seen after a △;

- the ▽ events;

- the result which a ▽ yields when it happens.

We shall denote the set all possible **indications** by V and the set of all possible results by R. When we look at the view provided by a system, it may be that certain aspects of it are irrelevant or inessential. Consider, for example, a system which shows the current date and time as part of *every* view. Likewise, there will be certain aspects of the results provided by a system which are essential, and others which are irrelevant. When inspecting a view or using a result, a user, or an implementer may have in mind notions of *equivalence up to irrelevant detail*. Rather than complicate the present work by representing such equivalences explicitly, we shall assume that such equivalences have been taken into account in the choice of V and R:

```
┌─INTERACTIVE──────────────────────────────────
│   command :  P E
│   △ :        P E
│   ▽ :        P E
│   view :     S ↔ V
│   result :   S ↔ R
│   PROCESS
├───────────────────────────────────────────────
│   ∀t : Trace;  e : △ | t ⌢ ⟨e⟩ ∈ Trace •
│                     β(t ⌢ ⟨e⟩)⟨|ι|⟩ ⊆ dom view
│
│   ∀t : Trace;  e : ▽ | t ⌢ ⟨e⟩ ∈ Trace •
│                     β(t ⌢ ⟨e⟩)⟨|ι|⟩ ⊆ dom result
└───────────────────────────────────────────────
```

Examples:

1. The bank teller always shows the amount of the client's request; the result event is *money*, and the result thereby yielded is the amount requested:

$$
\begin{array}{lcl}
V & \widehat{=} & \mathbb{N} \\
R & \widehat{=} & \mathbb{N} \\
command & \widehat{=} & \{card, ok, no\}\cup \\
         &   & \{digit\ n \bullet n : 0..9\} \\
\triangle & = & command \\
\nabla & = & \{money\} \\
view(onhand, req) & = & req \\
result(onhand, req) & = & req
\end{array}
$$

2. The teller gives an indication if the amount requested goes beyond what is on hand: all that needs to be changed is the definition of V and *view*:

$$V \; ::= \; enough \langle\!\langle N \rangle\!\rangle \mid notenough \langle\!\langle N \rangle\!\rangle$$
$$view(onhand, req) = enough \; req \Leftrightarrow req \leq onhand$$
$$view(onhand, req) = notenough \; req \Leftrightarrow req > onhand$$

3. A terminal handler, which supports simple editing operations such as delete and cancel, and which yields the line it has been constructing whenever *enter* is pressed. It refuses *delete* at the beginning of a line:

$$
\begin{array}{lll}
S & \triangleq & seq \; CH \\
R & \triangleq & seq \; CH \\
V & \triangleq & seq \; CH \\
E & ::= & ins \langle\!\langle CH \rangle\!\rangle \mid delete \mid cancel \mid enter
\end{array}
$$

__TH__ _____

  INTERACTIVE

$$
\begin{array}{ll}
command & = E \\
\beta \langle ins \; ch \rangle \; l & = l \,^\frown \langle ch \rangle \\
\beta \langle delete \rangle \; (l \,^\frown \langle ch \rangle) & = l \\
\beta \langle cancel \rangle \; l & = \langle \rangle \\
\beta \langle enter \rangle \; l & = l \\
\triangle & = E \\
view \; l & = l \\
\triangledown & = \{enter\} \\
result \; l & = l
\end{array}
$$
---

4. This handler will not accept *delete* when the line is empty. We now want our handler to accept *delete* when the line is empty but to *bleep* immediately afterwards (and only then):

$$\beta \langle delete, bleep \rangle = \{ \langle \rangle \mapsto \langle \rangle \}$$
$$\forall t : Trace \bullet t \; \hookrightarrow \; \langle bleep \rangle \Rightarrow t \; \hookrightarrow \; \langle delete, bleep \rangle$$

5. A simple line editor, which allows some cursor movement within the line being edited. The only constraint on the view is that it show no more than 50 characters, and that they be around the current cursor position. (The designer has forgotten to include a command which moves the cursor right):

$$
\begin{aligned}
S &\;\hat{=}\; \{leftofcursor, rightofcursor : \text{seq } CH\} \\
R &\;\hat{=}\; \text{seq } CH \\
V &\;\hat{=}\; \{leftview, rightview : \text{seq } CH \mid \\
  &\qquad \#leftview + \#rightview \le 50\} \\
E &\;::=\; ins\langle\!\langle CH \rangle\!\rangle \mid delete \mid left \mid enter
\end{aligned}
$$

$\_SLE\_$
$\quad$ *INTERACTIVE*

$$
\begin{aligned}
command &= E \\
\beta\langle ins\ ch\rangle(l, r) &= (l \,\widehat{}\, \langle ch\rangle, r) \\
\beta\langle delete\rangle(l \,\widehat{}\, \langle ch\rangle, r) &= (l, r) \\
\beta\langle left\rangle(l \,\widehat{}\, \langle ch\rangle, r) &= (l, \langle ch\rangle \,\widehat{}\, r) \\
\beta\langle enter\rangle(l, r) &= (l, r) \\
\triangle &= E \\
(l, r)\,view(lv, rv) &\Leftrightarrow l \hookrightarrow lv \wedge rv \hookleftarrow r \wedge \\
  &\qquad \#lv + \#rv \le 50 \\
\triangledown &= \{enter\} \\
result(l, r) &= l \,\widehat{}\, r
\end{aligned}
$$

6. The following specification, intended to provide an undo operation for the original terminal-handler, is *infeasible*:

$$
\forall\, cmd : E \bullet \beta\langle cmd, undo\rangle\ l\ =\ l
$$

In this case, the given state space is too small to remember the state of the handler before each command. We will not pursue this matter any further.

□

6.3.1   *Experimenting with views and results*

When users work with an interactive system, they are unable to discern the details of its internal construction, nor to influence any internal non deterministic choices it may make. A detailed description of the internal states and transitions of a system may be important to us when designing and building it, and may even be important in explaining or predicting its behaviour to an end user. The only means of evoking behaviour at a user's disposal are commands, and the only consequences of the commands which can be inspected are results and views, so the form our predictions take will always be a description of the relationship between command sequences issued by a user, and the results and views to which they (may) give rise.

A sequence of commands p is said to **cause** a result r if it is the largest sequence of commands embedded in a trace which ends in a ∇ and yields r; in this case we write $p \xrightarrow{R} r$. If p is the largest sequence of commands embedded in a trace which ends in a $\triangle$, and leads to the view v we say that p causes v, and write $p \xrightarrow{V} v$. To capture these ideas formally we extend the schematic structure *INTERACTIVE* as follows:

$$
\begin{array}{|l}
\_ \xrightarrow{V} \_ : \operatorname{seq} E \leftrightarrow V \\
\_ \xrightarrow{R} \_ : \operatorname{seq} E \leftrightarrow R \\
\hline
p \xrightarrow{V} v \Leftrightarrow \\
\quad \exists\, t : Trace \bullet last\ t \in \triangle \wedge t \upharpoonright command = p\ \wedge \\
\qquad\qquad\qquad\qquad\qquad\qquad v \in view\,(\!|\beta t\,(\!|\iota|\!)\,|\!) \\
\\
p \xrightarrow{R} r \Leftrightarrow \\
\quad \exists\, t : Trace \bullet last\ t \in \nabla \wedge t \upharpoonright command = p\ \wedge \\
\qquad\qquad\qquad\qquad\qquad r \in result\,(\!|\beta t\,(\!|\iota|\!)\,|\!)
\end{array}
$$

The result of a system is **command-determined** if a sequence of commands which yields a result always yields the same result: in other words, if $\xrightarrow{R}$ is a function. This property seems to be very desirable; but consider, for a moment, a text editor with a command which inserts the current date in the document being constructed. The presence of this command means that the result isn't command determined, but if it is the only such command, the system "nearly" has this desirable property. So rather than labelling the whole system deterministic or not, we shall label subsets of its commands:

$$Deterministic^R : \mathbb{P} \, \mathbb{P} \, E$$
$$Deterministic^V : \mathbb{P} \, \mathbb{P} \, E$$

$$ES \in Deterministic^R \Leftrightarrow (\text{seq } ES \lhd (\_ \xrightarrow{R} \_)) \in \text{seq } E \twoheadrightarrow R$$

$$ES \in Deterministic^V \Leftrightarrow (\text{seq } ES \lhd (\_ \xrightarrow{V} \_)) \in \text{seq } E \twoheadrightarrow V$$

Any subset of a deterministic set of commands is itself deterministic, but it is possible for the union of two deterministic sets of commands not to be deterministic. (e.g., one command may generate the potential for another to act capriciously).

Examples:

1. The teller and terminal handler commands are $Deterministic^V$ and $Deterministic^R$.

2. The editor commands are $Deterministic^R$ but the only non empty subset of them which is $Deterministic^V$ is $\{enter\}$.

□

A set of commands is *complete* if they can be used to generate all results. If the completeness is a consequence of the possibility that they might generate every result (depending on initial state and internal nondeterministic choices of the system) then this *weak* completeness is in general not very useful:

$$WeakComplete : \mathbb{P} \, \mathbb{P} \, E$$

$$ES \in WeakComplete \Leftrightarrow$$
$$\text{ran}(\text{seq } ES \lhd (\_ \xrightarrow{R} \_)) = R$$

A stronger, and generally more desirable, form of completeness arises when every result can be generated by at least one command sequence, and every command sequence which generates that result is guaranteed *always* to generate it:

$$Complete : \mathbb{P}\,\mathbb{P}\,E$$

$$ES \in Complete \Leftrightarrow (\text{seq }ES \vartriangleleft (\_ \xrightarrow{R} \_))^{-1} \ ;$$
$$(\text{seq }ES \vartriangleleft (\_ \xrightarrow{R} \_)) \ = \ Id_{[R]}$$

Any *Complete* set of commands is also *WeakComplete*. Furthermore, any weakly-complete set of commands which is *Deterministic*^{R} is complete.

A subset of a complete set of commands is not necessarily complete. If the union of two complete sets of commands is deterministic, then it *will* be complete.

Examples:

1. The bank tellers' E are weakly complete but not complete, because a teller may have insufficient funds available at the start of a session to meet the user's request.

2. Any subset of the editor's commands which includes $ins(|CH|)\cup \{enter\}$ is complete. The sequence of characters s will be yielded by the sequence of commands $(ins \circ s) \,\widehat{\,}\, \langle enter \rangle$.

☐

The commands which are present in every complete set of commands are called the *Essential* commands; for none can be omitted from an implementation without rendering it incomplete:

$$Essential : \mathbb{P}\,E$$

$$Essential = \bigcap Complete$$

A command sequence is **fruitless** if it cannot be extended to cause a result; the inclusion of fruitless sequences in a system is highly undesirable:

$$Fruitless : \mathbb{P}\,(\text{seq }E)$$

$$p \in Fruitless \Leftrightarrow \forall s : \text{seq } command \bullet p \,\widehat{\,}\, s \notin \text{dom}(\_ \xrightarrow{R} \_)$$

6.3.2   *Equivalence of command sequences*

In order to discuss a number of important aspects of system behaviour we need to define various equivalences between command sequences. Two command sequences are *result equivalent* ($\overset{R}{\approx}$) if they cause the same set of results; they are *view equivalent* ($\overset{V}{\approx}$), if they cause the same set of views:

$$
\begin{array}{|l}
\_ \overset{R}{\approx} \_ : \text{seq } E \leftrightarrow \text{seq } E \\
\_ \overset{V}{\approx} \_ : \text{seq } E \leftrightarrow \text{seq } E \\
\hline
p_1 \overset{R}{\approx} p_2 \Leftrightarrow (\_ \overset{R}{\dashrightarrow} \_)(\{p_1\}) = (\_ \overset{R}{\dashrightarrow} \_)(\{p_2\}) \\
p_1 \overset{V}{\approx} p_2 \Leftrightarrow (\_ \overset{V}{\dashrightarrow} \_)(\{p_1\}) = (\_ \overset{V}{\dashrightarrow} \_)(\{p_2\})
\end{array}
$$

Extending a pair of equivalent command sequences by a single command may make them inequivalent, but two equivalent command sequences which can be extended indefinitely without becoming inequivalent are called **indistinguishable** ($\equiv$):

$$
\begin{array}{|l}
\_ \overset{R}{\equiv} \_ : \text{seq } E \leftrightarrow \text{seq } E \\
\_ \overset{V}{\equiv} \_ : \text{seq } E \leftrightarrow \text{seq } E \\
\hline
p_1 \overset{R}{\equiv} p_2 \Leftrightarrow \forall s : \text{seq } command \bullet p_1 \,\widehat{\,}\, s \overset{R}{\approx} p_2 \,\widehat{\,}\, s \\
p_1 \overset{V}{\equiv} p_2 \Leftrightarrow \forall s : \text{seq } command \bullet p_1 \,\widehat{\,}\, s \overset{V}{\approx} p_2 \,\widehat{\,}\, s
\end{array}
$$

Sequences of deterministic commands which are result (view) equivalent are also result (view) indistinguishable.

Examples:

1. Consider the editor. Given a character sequence s, and a character ch the command sequence $(ins \circ s) \,\widehat{\,}\, \langle ins\ ch, delete \rangle$ is result indistinguishable from $(ins \circ s)$. In fact, if $p_1 \overset{R}{\equiv} p_2$, then $(p_1 \,\widehat{\,}\, \langle ins\ ch, delete \rangle) \overset{R}{\equiv} p_2$.

2. Consider the terminal handler. The same sequences of commands are both view and result indistinguishable.

3. Consider the bank tellers. Almost all that can be said of them is that the amount of money required can be prefixed with any number of zeros without changing the effect:

$$\forall s : seq\ E \bullet \langle card, digit\ 0 \rangle \frown s \overset{R}{\equiv} \langle card \rangle \frown s$$
$$\forall s : seq\ E \bullet \langle card, digit\ 0 \rangle \frown s \overset{V}{\equiv} \langle card \rangle \frown s$$

□

6.3.3   *Side-effects*

A command sequence p_1 is said to *have* **side-effects** *on* (or, for short, **affect**) a command sequence p_2 if there are situations in which p_1 does not immediately alter the result, but may change the effect of a subsequent p_2 on the result:

$$\_affects\_ : seq\ E \leftrightarrow seq\ E$$

$$
\begin{array}{l}
p_1\ affects\ p_2 \Leftrightarrow \\
\quad \exists\, p, q : seq\ E \bullet \\
\qquad p \frown p_1 \overset{R}{\approx} p \\
\qquad p \frown p_1 \frown q \frown p_2 \overset{R}{\not\approx} p \frown q \frown p_2
\end{array}
$$

A command sequence which has no side effects at all is called a **browse**:

$$browse : \mathbb{P}(seq\ E)$$

$$p \in browse \Leftrightarrow \not\exists\, q : seq\ E \bullet p\ affects\ q$$

6.3.4   *Restartability*

One of the strategies employed by a user who has become confused by the behaviour of a system is to try and start again from scratch. A command sequence is *restartable* if it is possible to extend it so that it becomes result-indistinguishable from the empty sequence of commands:

$$Restartable : \mathbb{P}(seq\ E)$$

$$p \in Restartable \Leftrightarrow \exists\, s : seq\ command \bullet p \frown s \overset{R}{\equiv} \langle\rangle$$

An interactive system is restartable if all command sequences it offers are restartable and is nonrestartable if none are. It seems highly desirable for a system to fall into one of these two categories, and for its users to know which. If elimination of a (small) set of commands would render a system restartable, then it is probably a good idea to advise new users which they are.

Example:

> The editor is neither restartable nor nonrestartable! Once a $\langle\mathit{left}\rangle$ has been accepted by the system, it is impossible to remove characters to the right of the cursor.

□

6.3.5   *Relating views to results*

It is generally accepted that the view offered by a system should help the user to determine the nature of the result which is under construction. The slogan "what you see is what you get" is hard to achieve literally, but a number of other forms of visual consistency are worth examining.

A system is **visually consistent** if its view indistinguishable command sequences are result equivalent: the corresponding slogan is "what you can find out determines what you have got now":

$$VC \triangleq INTERACTIVE \mid (\_ \overset{V}{\equiv} \_) \subseteq (\_ \overset{R}{\approx} \_)$$

A system is **strongly visually consistent** if its view indistinguishable command sequences are result indistinguishable: "what you can find out determines everything you are going to be able to get". We believe that, in general, this is what people mean by "what you see is what you get":

$$SVC \triangleq INTERACTIVE \mid (\_ \overset{V}{\equiv} \_) \subseteq (\_ \overset{R}{\equiv} \_)$$

A system is **transparent** if view equivalent command sequences are result indistinguishable: "what you can see now determines everything you are going to be able to get":

$$TRANSPARENT \triangleq INTERACTIVE \mid (\_ \overset{V}{\approx} \_) \subseteq (\_ \overset{R}{\equiv} \_)$$

A system is **goal-determines-view** if result equivalent command

sequences are view indistinguishable: "what you have got now determines what you are going to be able to find out":

$$GDV \mathrel{\widehat{=}} INTERACTIVE \mid (\_ \overset{R}{\approx} \_) \subseteq (\_ \overset{V}{\equiv} \_)$$

A command sequence is **directly predictable** if it has the same
effect on the result in situations which look the same; it is **predictable**
if it has the same effect on the result in situations which are visually
indistinguishable:

$$
\begin{array}{l}
DirPredictable : \quad \mathbb{P}(\text{seq } E) \\
Predictable : \quad\quad \mathbb{P}(\text{seq } E) \\
\hline
p \in DirPredictable \quad \Leftrightarrow \forall\, p_1, p_2 : \text{seq } E \bullet p_1 \overset{V}{\approx} p_2 \Rightarrow \\
\quad\quad\quad\quad\quad\quad\quad\quad\quad p_1 \mathbin{^\frown} p \overset{R}{\equiv} p_2 \mathbin{^\frown} p \\
p \in Predictable \quad\quad \Leftrightarrow \forall\, p_1, p_2 : \text{seq } E \bullet p_1 \overset{V}{\equiv} p_2 \Rightarrow \\
\quad\quad\quad\quad\quad\quad\quad\quad\quad p_1 \mathbin{^\frown} p \overset{R}{\equiv} p_2 \mathbin{^\frown} p
\end{array}
$$

Although it is a good idea for a designer to ensure that as many individual commands as possible are *directly* predictable, this is not always
easy to achieve. Consider, for example, the result of a "systematic-
substitution" command in an editor, where the best that can be guaranteed is that it be predictable.[2]

A command sequence is **honest** if when it has affected the result, it
gives some immediate indication that it has done so. It is **trustworthy**
if it allows the user to find out that it has affected the result:

[2] It was for this reason that in [181] we chose to eliminate systematic-substitution
from our editor specification, in favour of individual *find* and *replace* commands: *find*
moves the cursor to an instance of a pattern, and replace performs a substitution at
the cursor only if the cursor is positioned at an instance of the *find* pattern. Both
find and *replace* are therefore directly predictable.

$$Honest: \quad \mathbb{P}(\operatorname{seq} E)$$
$$Trustworthy: \quad \mathbb{P}(\operatorname{seq} E)$$

$$p \in Honest \Leftrightarrow \forall p_0 : \operatorname{seq} E \bullet (p_0 \frown p) \overset{R}{\not\equiv} p_0 \Rightarrow (p_0 \frown p) \overset{V}{\not\approx} p_0$$

$$p \in Trustworthy \Leftrightarrow \forall p_0 : \operatorname{seq} E \bullet (p_0 \frown p) \overset{R}{\not\equiv} p_0 \Rightarrow$$
$$(p_0 \frown p) \overset{V}{\not\equiv} p_0$$

As direct consequences of the definitions we have:

$$p \in Honest \qquad \wedge (p_0 \frown p) \overset{V}{\approx} p_0 \Rightarrow (p_0 \frown p) \overset{R}{\equiv} p_0$$
$$p \in Trustworthy \ \wedge (p_0 \frown p) \overset{V}{\equiv} p_0 \Rightarrow (p_0 \frown p) \overset{R}{\equiv} p_0$$

Clearly, all honest sequences are trustworthy, and trustworthiness seems to be an *essential* quality of all individual commands; it is nevertheless a very good idea to try to make all individual commands honest as well.

6.3.6 *Undoing*

Earlier in the chapter, we gave a tentative definition of undoing which required that after following a command with an undo, the system be in the same *state* as it was in before the command. This requirement was unrealistically strong, since the user is in the end only interested in the result, and cannot discriminate amongst states which yield the same result.

A command sequence p_2 is said to **weakly undo** a command sequence p_1 if running p_2 immediately after running p_1 leaves the system in a result equivalent state; if the system is left in a result indistinguishable state, then p_2 said to **strongly undo** p_1. We write p_2 *undoes*$_\approx$ p_1 and p_2 *undoes*$_\equiv$ p_1 respectively. The difference is that weakly undoing a sequence of commands does not guarantee the undoing of any side effects which the sequence had, whereas strongly undoing a sequence undoes its side effects as well:

$$\_undoes_{\approx}\_ : \operatorname{seq} E \leftrightarrow \operatorname{seq} E$$
$$\_undoes_{\equiv}\_ : \operatorname{seq} E \leftrightarrow \operatorname{seq} E$$

$$p_2 \ undoes_{\approx} \ p_1 \Leftrightarrow \forall p : \operatorname{seq} E \bullet p \frown p_1 \frown p_2 \overset{R}{\approx} p$$
$$p_2 \ undoes_{\equiv} \ p_1 \Leftrightarrow \forall p : \operatorname{seq} E \bullet p \frown p_1 \frown p_2 \overset{R}{\equiv} p$$

It is easy to show that when $p_1 \frown p_2$ has no side effects on any command, then p_2 *undoes*$_\equiv$ p_1.

A *general undo* is a single command which undoes the effect of all other single commands:

$$
\begin{array}{|l}
GeneralUndo : \mathbb{P}\,E \\
GeneralWeakUndo : \mathbb{P}\,E \\
\hline
c \in GeneralUndo \Leftrightarrow \forall c_0 : E - \{c\} \bullet \langle c \rangle\, undoes_{\equiv} \langle c_0 \rangle \\
c \in GeneralWeakUndo \Leftrightarrow \forall c_0 : E - \{c\} \bullet \langle c \rangle\, undoes_{\approx} \langle c_0 \rangle
\end{array}
$$

In the absence of a system-wide generalised undo, it is a good idea for most commands to have specific commands which undo them. Whilst strong undoing is preferable, weak undoing will often be satisfactory — especially in situations where the side effects of commands are easy to understand and remember.

6.4   Interactive process refinement

In this section we present, without proof, some laws which may have validity when a process specification is being refined to(wards) an implementation. We leave their justification to a future paper.

6.4.1   *A refinement ordering*

If a relation S is used to specify the behaviour of a program, then its domain $(\mathrm{dom}\,S)$ characterises those states from which the program will terminate if started; if the relation is a function, then the corresponding program is deterministic. A relation R is said to *refine* the relation S if it terminates when started in any state from which S would terminate, and whenever it terminates, does so in a state permitted by S. When this is the case we write $S \sqsubseteq R$:

$$
\begin{array}{|l}
=\![X, Y]\!= \\
\hline
\_\sqsubseteq\_ : (X \leftrightarrow Y) \leftrightarrow (X \leftrightarrow Y) \\
\hline
S \sqsubseteq R \Leftrightarrow \mathrm{dom}\,S \subseteq \mathrm{dom}\,R \wedge (\mathrm{dom}\,S \lhd R) \subseteq S
\end{array}
$$

This definition corresponds to a notion of refinement which allows an implementation to "do anything" when invoked in situations where the precondition of its specification is not satisfied, provided it always satisfies the postcondition of the specification when started in situations which *do* satisfy the precondition.

It is easily shown that $\sqsubseteq$ is a partial order. This is important, because it ensures that refinement may be carried out in steps.

We noted earlier (§6.3.1) that the only way in which users may detect differences between interactive processes is by performing experiments. The relations $P. \xrightarrow{V} \triangleright$, $P. \xrightarrow{R} \triangleright$, and $P.\mathit{Fails}$ are abstractions which correspond to the totality of the information which it is possible to gain by performing such experiments on process P. We say that a process P *view-refines* a process S if it yields a view for any sequence of commands for which S would, and the view is one of those which S might have yielded in response to the same sequence of commands. When this is the case we write $S \stackrel{V}{\sqsubseteq} P$. The process P *result-refines* the process S if it yields a result in response to every sequence of commands for which S would, and if that result is one of those which S might have yielded in response to the same sequence:

$$
\begin{array}{|l}
\_\stackrel{V}{\sqsubseteq}\_: \mathit{INTERACTIVE} \leftrightarrow \mathit{INTERACTIVE} \\
\_\stackrel{R}{\sqsubseteq}\_: \mathit{INTERACTIVE} \leftrightarrow \mathit{INTERACTIVE} \\
\hline
S \stackrel{V}{\sqsubseteq} P \Leftrightarrow (S. \xrightarrow{V} \triangleright) \sqsubseteq (P. \xrightarrow{V} \triangleright) \\
S \stackrel{R}{\sqsubseteq} P \Leftrightarrow (S. \xrightarrow{R} \triangleright) \sqsubseteq (P. \xrightarrow{R} \triangleright)
\end{array}
$$

A process P *failure-refines* a process S if its failures are included in those of S, we write $S \stackrel{F}{\sqsubseteq} P$ when this is so:

$$
\begin{array}{|l}
\_\stackrel{F}{\sqsubseteq}\_: \mathit{PROCESS} \leftrightarrow \mathit{PROCESS} \\
\hline
S \stackrel{F}{\sqsubseteq} P \Leftrightarrow S.\mathit{Fails} \supseteq P.\mathit{Fails}
\end{array}
$$

When P failure-refines S it is "better" in the sense that when it can do something undesirable, S can also do it, and when it can refuse to do something, then so can S.

Proposition 1. $\stackrel{V}{\sqsubseteq}, \stackrel{R}{\sqsubseteq}$ and $\stackrel{F}{\sqsubseteq}$ are partial orders.

We are now in a position to define a single refinement ordering for interactive processes. We say that an interactive process P refines an interactive process S when it view-refines, result-refines, and failure-refines S. As is customary, we will call S the specification, and P the implementation, even though P may not yet be in the form of a program:

$$
\begin{array}{|l}
\hline
\_refines\_ : INTERACTIVE \leftrightarrow INTERACTIVE \\
\hline
P\ refines\ S \Leftrightarrow S \stackrel{V}{\sqsubseteq} P \wedge S \stackrel{R}{\sqsubseteq} P \wedge S \stackrel{F}{\sqsubseteq} P
\end{array}
$$

Proposition 2.   The relation *refines* is a partial order.

6.4.2   *Properties preserved by refinement*

Refinement respects many of the properties defined earlier. In the following propositions, we will consider two interactive processes, a specification S, and an implementation P.

Refinement preserves view and result determinism; it also preserves completeness. An implementation may have more fruitless commands than its specification.

Proposition 3.   If P refines S then:

1. $S.Deterministic^{V} \subseteq P.Deterministic^{V}$

2. $S.Deterministic^{R} \subseteq P.Deterministic^{R}$

3. $S.Complete \subseteq P.Complete$

4. $S.Fruitless \supseteq P.Fruitless$

When results are specified completely and deterministically, that is when $S. \stackrel{R}{\longrightarrow}$ is a (total) function, then result equivalence and result indistinguishability mean the same in the implementation as they do in the specification; the undoing properties of commands are also identical.

Proposition 4. If P refines S and $(S. \xrightarrow{R}) \in (\text{seq}.E \to R)$ then:

1. $(S. \overset{R}{\approx}) = (P. \overset{R}{\approx})$

2. $(S. \overset{R}{\equiv}) = (P. \overset{R}{\equiv})$

3. $S.undoes_{\equiv} = P.undoes_{\approx}$

4. $S.undoes_{\approx} = P.undoes_{\approx}$

5. $S.GeneralUndo = P.GeneralUndo$

6. $S.GeneralWeakUndo = P.GeneralWeakUndo$

When views are specified deterministically, then view equivalence and view indistinguishability mean the same in the implementation as they do in the specification.

Proposition 5. If P refines S and $P. \xrightarrow{V} \in (\text{seq } E \twoheadrightarrow R)$ then:

1. $(S. \overset{V}{\approx}) = (P. \overset{V}{\approx})$

2. $(S. \overset{V}{\equiv}) = (P. \overset{V}{\equiv})$

When both views and results are specified totally and deterministically, then the various forms of visual consistency are preserved by refinement.

Proposition 6. If P refines S and $\{S. \xrightarrow{R}, S. \xrightarrow{V}\} \subseteq (\text{seq } E \to R)$ then:

1. $S \in VC \Rightarrow P \in VC$

2. $S \in SVC \Rightarrow P \in SVC$

3. $S \in TRANSPARENT \Rightarrow P \in TRANSPARENT$

4. $S \in GDV \Rightarrow P \in GDV$

5. $S.DirPredictable = P.DirPredictable$

6. $S.Honest = P.Honest$

7. $S.Trustworthy = P.Trustworthy$

6.4.3   Verification

The present definition of refinement is a bit too "large" for us to be able to verify easily that one process refines another. In this section, we present some sufficient conditions for a process P to refine a process specification S.

Refinement without change of representation

First, we will examine the situation where specification and implementation have the same state space: ST. When this is so, it is sufficient for the view and result relations of the refinement to refine those of the specification.

Proposition 7. P refines S if they have the same state-transition relation β, and the same initial state set ι, and satisfy:

1. $S.view \sqsubseteq P.view$

2. $S.result \sqsubseteq P.result$

When specification and refinement have the same state space and the same view and result relations, it is sufficient for the state transition relation of the refinement to be more deterministic than that of the specification, provided that it does not deadlock in places forbidden by the specification.

Proposition 8. P refines S if they have the same *view* and *result* relations, and satisfy:

1. $P.\iota \subseteq S.\iota$

2. $P.ready(P.\iota) = S.ready(S.\iota)$

3. $\forall e : \alpha \bullet P.\beta\ e \subseteq S.\beta\ e$

4. $\forall e : \alpha \bullet \mathrm{dom}(P.\beta\ e) = \mathrm{dom}(S.\beta\ e)$

5. $\forall e : \alpha;\ s : ST \bullet P.ready (\!| P.\beta\ e (\!|s|\!) |\!) = S.ready (\!| S.\beta\ e (\!|s|\!) |\!)$

Refinement by change of data representation
We would like to be able to refine processes by choosing machine-oriented representations for the abstract information structures used in our specifications. This form of refinement is usually known as *data refinement* and is explained in detail in [109] and [128].

The basic idea is to establish a correspondence between the two state spaces, then to check that the behaviour of the implementation adequately simulates the behaviour required by the specification under this correspondence. In the classical formulation of data refinement, the correspondence is given as a relation, called the *abstraction relation* between the state space of the implementation and that of the specification.

Definition: Downward Simulation
Let S and P be interactive processes with state spaces respectively SST and PST[3].

A pair of relations:

$$abs : PST \leftrightarrow SST$$
$$rep : SST \leftrightarrow PST$$

is called an *downward simulation* from P to S when the following conditions are satisfied:

1. Each initial state of the concrete process represents a starting state of the abstract process. Each starting state of the abstract process has a concrete initial representation:

$$abs (\!| P.\iota |\!) \subseteq S.\iota$$
$$P.\iota \supseteq rep (\!| S.\iota |\!)$$

_____

[3] It is customary to call a state $ps \in PST$ a *concrete state* and a state $ss \in SST$ an *abstract state*; we will extend this terminology and call P the *concrete* process, and S the *abstract* process.

2. The effect of a concrete event on a concrete state is consistent with the effect of the corresponding abstract event on corresponding abstract states:

$$\forall e : E \bullet$$
$$P.\beta\ e\ \mathbin{;}\ abs \supseteq abs\ \mathbin{;}\ S.\beta\ e$$
$$rep\ \mathbin{;}\ P.\beta\ e \subseteq S.\beta\ e\ \mathbin{;}\ rep$$

3. Concrete views and results are consistent with their abstract specifications:

$$rep\ \mathbin{;}\ P.view\ \subseteq\ S.view$$
$$rep\ \mathbin{;}\ P.result\ \subseteq\ S.result$$

4. When the abstract process is ready to engage in a particular event, the concrete process should also be ready to engage in it:

$$\forall ps : PST;\ ss : SST \bullet$$
$$ps\ abs\ ss\ \Rightarrow (\forall e : E \bullet ss \in \text{dom}\ S.\beta\ e \Rightarrow$$
$$ps \in \text{dom}\ P.\beta\ e)$$

Most explanations of data refinement require the relation *rep* to be the inverse of the relation *abs*, and *abs* itself to be a function; in these circumstances the definition above can be correspondingly simplified.

6.4.4   *A strategy for refinement*

The two main results of this section provide us with a strategy for refinement of interactive processes.

Proposition 9.   Soundness of downward simulations
  If there is an downward simulation from P to S then P refines S.

Proposition 10.   Stepwise refinement
  If (rep_1, abs_1) and (rep_2, abs_2) are downward simulations, then their composition $(rep_1 \mathbin{;} rep_2, abs_2 \mathbin{;} abs_1)$ is also an downward simulation.

6.5   Specifying processes in Z: an example

In this section we illustrate the relationship between our model of interactive processes and systems specified in the schema notation of Z[182, 179, 178]. We do so by defining a line editor in this notation, then translating it into the corresponding interactive process.

Our specification is in three sections: in the first, we explain how the *TEXT* which will be the result of editing may be manipulated; in the second, we explain the display and the mouse; in the third, we explain how the display and mouse relate to the text.

6.5.1   *Text manipulation*

The editor will support manipulation of a *text*, which is divided into three sections. The middle section is called the *selection* and can be manipulated in various ways. The editor also keeps track of the last chunk of text which was deleted, which is called the *cut*.

The state of a system is usually described by a schema in which "observable" information structures are declared and their invariant relationships are defined. There is no implicit commitment that *all* the information structures, so declared, will have an explicit representation in an implementation, indeed at the topmost level of a specification the use of redundancy is encouraged, and we exploit this below:

$$
\begin{array}{|l}
\_\textit{TEXT}_____ \\
\quad \textit{left}: \qquad \text{seq } CH \\
\quad \textit{selection}: \quad \text{seq } CH \\
\quad \textit{right}: \qquad \text{seq } CH \\
\quad \textit{text} \qquad \quad \text{seq } CH \\
\quad \textit{cut}: \qquad \quad \text{seq } CH \\
\hline
\quad \textit{text} = \textit{left} \,^\frown \textit{selection} \,^\frown \textit{right}
\end{array}
$$

Events are described by schemas in which the relationship between the state "just before" and the state "just after" the event is described. The name of each attribute of the state appears twice in such schemas: in its undecorated form, it denotes the value of the attribute just before the event; decorated with a dash (') it denotes the value of the attribute just after the event. Although each event in the editor affects the *TEXT*, it is guaranteed to do so in a way which maintains the declared constraints. So, every event in the editor can be described by suitable additions to the following schema:

```
┌─ΔTEXT───────────────────────────────────────────
│  left, left' :                 seq CH
│  selection, selection' :       seq CH
│  right, right' :               seq CH
│  text, text' :                 seq CH
│  cut, cut' :                   seq CH
├──────────────────────────────────────────────────
│  text = left ⁀ selection ⁀ right
│  text' = left' ⁀ selection' ⁀ right'
└──────────────────────────────────────────────────
```

In the schema notation, the above definition is expressed much more concisely as:

$$\Delta TEXT \cong TEXT \wedge TEXT'$$

Inserting
When the character *ch?* is inserted in the document it is inserted at the end of what was the selection and replaces it, thereby extending the text:

```
┌─ins─────────────────────────────────────
│  ch? : CH
│  ΔTEXT
├──────────────────────────────────────────
│  selection'  = ⟨ch?⟩
│  left'       = left ⁀ selection
│  right'      = right
│  cut'        = cut
└──────────────────────────────────────────
```

Note that we need not specify the value of *text*, explicitly, since the constraint *text'* = *left'* ⁀ *selection'* ⁀ *right'* is already present. This flexibility permits redundant predicates to be omitted from event specifications, helping to focus attention on essentials.

Pointing
Pointing at the text extinguishes the selection without altering the text:

```
┌─ point ──────────────────────────────────────────────
│ pos? : N
│ ΔTEXT
├──────────────────────────────
│   text'       =   text
│
│   left'       =   (1..pos?) ◁ text
│
│   selection'  =   ⟨⟩
│
│   cut'        =   cut
└──────────────────────────────────────────────────────
```

Dragging

Dragging the pointer to the right or left extends the selection in the appropriate direction without altering the text:

```
┌─ dragright ──────────────────────────────────────────
│ dist? : N
│ ΔTEXT
├──────────────────────────────
│   text'        =   text
│
│   left'        =   left
│
│   #selection'  =   dist?
│
│   cut'         =   cut
└──────────────────────────────────────────────────────
```

```
┌─ dragleft ───────────────────────────────────────────
│ dist? : N
│ ΔTEXT
├──────────────────────────────
│   text'        =   text
│
│   right'       =   right
│
│   #selection'  =   dist?
│
│   cut'         =   cut
└──────────────────────────────────────────────────────
```

Deleting

Pressing the *delete* key removes the selection from the text, and transfers it to the *cut*:

```
┌─ delete ─────────────────────────────────────────────────
│ ΔTEXT
│ ────────────────────────────
│   left'       =   left
│
│   right'      =   right
│
│   cut'        =   selection
│
│   selection'  =   ⟨⟩
└──────────────────────────────────────────────────────────
```

Pasting

The *paste* key exchanges the *cut* for the selection:

```
┌─ paste ──────────────────────────────────────────────────
│ ΔTEXT
│ ────────────────────────────
│   left'       =   left
│
│   right'      =   right
│
│   cut'        =   selection
│
│   selection'  =   cut
└──────────────────────────────────────────────────────────
```

Initial state

The editor initially has an empty *text* and an empty *cut*:

```
┌─ init ───────────────────────────────────────────────────
│ TEXT
│ ────────────────────────────
│   text = cut = ⟨⟩
└──────────────────────────────────────────────────────────
```

6.5.2   *Translating to a process*

The specification, presented above, is equivalent to a $PROCESS$ whose state space is the set of **bindings**[4] denoted by $TEXT$, and whose events have behaviours characterised by the schemas which include $\Delta TEXT$. The initial state of this process is the (unique) $TEXT$ binding denoted by *init*.

The parameterless events *paste*, and *delete* denote relations $\widehat{paste}$, and $\widehat{delete}$ which could be specified directly by:

---

[4] The bindings denoted by a schema correspond, roughly, to the set of models which satisfy the signature and predicate of the schema. For a more detailed explanation see [178]

$$\_\widehat{paste}\_ : TEXT \leftrightarrow TEXT$$
$$\_\widehat{delete}\_ : TEXT \leftrightarrow TEXT$$

$d \ \widehat{paste} \ d' \Leftrightarrow$
$\qquad d'.left = d.left \wedge d'.right = d.right \wedge$
$\qquad d'.selection = d.cut \wedge d'.cut = d.selection$

$d \ \widehat{delete} \ d' \Leftrightarrow$
$\qquad d'.left = d.left \wedge d'.right = d.right \wedge$
$\qquad d'.selection = \langle \rangle \wedge d'.cut = d.selection$

They may be defined more concisely as follows:

$$\widehat{paste} \ = \ \{ \ \theta TEXT \mapsto \theta TEXT' \quad \bullet \ paste \}$$
$$\widehat{delete} \ = \ \{ \ \theta TEXT \mapsto \theta TEXT' \quad \bullet \ delete \}$$

The events with input parameters (those whose names end in a "?") correspond to *families* of $TEXT \leftrightarrow TEXT$ relations indexed by the input parameter(s). For example, *ins* corresponds to a CH-indexed family of relations:

$$\widehat{ins} : CH \to (TEXT \leftrightarrow TEXT)$$

$$\widehat{ins} \ = \ \lambda \, ch? : CH \bullet \{ \ \theta TEXT \mapsto \theta TEXT' \bullet ins \}$$

Now that we have indicated how to translate events into the corresponding relations, all that remains is for us to describe the alphabet of the process, and give the correspondence between its elements and these relations. First, we define the set of events:

$E ::= \textbf{paste} \mid \textbf{delete} \mid \textbf{ins}\langle\!\langle CH \rangle\!\rangle \mid \textbf{point}\langle\!\langle N \rangle\!\rangle \mid \textbf{dragleft}\langle\!\langle N \rangle\!\rangle \mid \ldots$

whose elements have names spelled identically (but in a different font in order to avoid confusion) to the schematically-specified events.

Finally, we present the correspondence between the relations derived from our schematic descriptions of events, and the behaviour of the corresponding process:

$$\alpha = E$$
$$\beta\langle\mathbf{paste}\rangle = \widehat{paste}$$
$$\beta\langle\mathbf{delete}\rangle = \widehat{delete}$$
$$\forall\ ch? : CH\ \bullet$$
$$\beta\langle\mathbf{ins}\ ch?\rangle = \widehat{ins}\ ch?$$
$$\forall\ pos? : \mathsf{N}\ \bullet$$
$$\beta\langle\mathbf{point}\ pos?\rangle = \widehat{point}\ pos?$$
$$\forall\ dist? : \mathsf{N}\ \bullet$$
$$\beta\langle\mathbf{dragleft}\ dist?\rangle = \widehat{dragleft}\ dist?$$
$$\ldots$$

This sort of correspondence is so obvious that we will take it for granted in what follows. Since we usually discuss one process at a time, we will express constraints on its traces by means of predicates in which *Trace* appears as a free variable: the implicit understanding is that it denotes the set of traces of the process under discussion.

For example, we can insist that dragging only be permitted immediately after a *point* by specifying that:

$$Trace = (\ \ []\ \ ch : CH\ \bullet\ insert\ ch \to skip$$
$$[]\ \ drag$$
$$[]\ \ \{delete, paste\} \to skip$$
$$)\ \ *$$

where

$$drag = []p : \mathsf{N};\ n : \mathsf{N}\ \bullet$$
$$point\ p \to (dragleft\ n \to skip\ []\ dragright\ n \to skip)*$$

6.5.3   *Display and mouse*

In order to turn the editor process into an interactive process we need to add a display component. Our display shows an image, which is a line of 80 characters, some of which are highlighted; it also has a cursor, and a mouse-position indicator.

```
┌─ DISPLAY ─────────────────────────────────────────
│  image :      seq CH
│  highlight :  F(1..80)
│  cursor :     0..80
│  mouse :      0..80
│ ─────────────────
│  #image = 80
└───────────────────────────────────────────────────
```

The user may point at any position on the image, or drag the mouse from one position on the image to another:

```
┌─ displaypoint ────────────────────────────────────
│  ΔDISPLAY
│  pos! : 0..80
│ ─────────────────
│  pos! = mouse'
└───────────────────────────────────────────────────
```

If the new position of the mouse is to the left of its old position, this constitutes a *DragLeft* event, otherwise it's a *DragRight*:

```
┌─ displaydragleft ─────────────────────────────────
│  ΔDISPLAY
│  dist! : 0..80
│ ─────────────────
│  dist! = mouse − mouse'
└───────────────────────────────────────────────────
```

```
┌─ displaydragright ────────────────────────────────
│  ΔDISPLAY
│  dist! : 0..80
│ ─────────────────
│  dist! = mouse' − mouse
└───────────────────────────────────────────────────
```

6.5.4   *Putting the components together*

The complete state of the editor consists of the display and the text, together with an indication of the origin of the display. The display may show any part of the *text* being edited, provided that the *cursor* indicates the position of the right hand end of the *selection*, and the highlighted characters on the display are those of the selection:

$\_$ *STATE* $\_$
> *DISPLAY*
> *TEXT*
> *origin* : $\mathbb{N}$

> $image = \{i \mapsto SPACE \bullet i : 1..80 \ \}$
> $\oplus ((origin \ .. \ origin + 80) \overset{seq}{\lhd} text)$
>
> $origin + cursor = \#(left \frown selection)$
>
> $highlight = (origin + \#left) \ .. \ (origin + \#selection)$

The *view* shown by the system is the complete *DISPLAY* and the *result* is the text:

> $view : STATE \rightarrow DISPLAY$
> $result : STATE \rightarrow seq \ CH$
>
> ---
>
> $view = \lambda \, STATE \bullet \theta \, DISPLAY$
> $result = \lambda \, STATE \bullet text$

The *origin* (and hence the display) is not necessarily fully determined by the *text*. An implementer must choose a method of determining the origin so that the following constraints are always satisfied:

> $origin + cursor = \#(left \frown selection)$
> $cursor \in 0..80$

It is possible to achieve this trivially (always setting $cursor = 0$), but such a method of displaying the text might be disturbing to a user — no left context is ever visible, and the whole display would have to change whenever a character is inserted or removed. A better strategy would be to change the origin only when not to do so would cause the constraints to be violated.

The effects of the events of the complete system are specified below in a way which preserves the non determinism in the display:

$$
\begin{aligned}
Insert &\;\;\hat{=}\;\; ins \\
Delete &\;\;\hat{=}\;\; delete \\
Paste &\;\;\hat{=}\;\; paste \\
Point &\;\;\hat{=}\;\; [point \wedge displaypoint\;| \\
&\qquad pos? = pos! + origin]\backslash(pos?, pos!) \\
DragLeft &\;\;\hat{=}\;\; [dragleft \wedge displaydragleft\;| \\
&\qquad dist? = dist!]\backslash(dist?, dist!) \\
DragRight &\;\;\hat{=}\;\; [dragright \wedge displaydragright\;| \\
&\qquad dist? = dist!]\backslash(dist?, dist!) \\
Quit &\;\;\hat{=}\;\; \Delta STATE\;|\;\theta STATE' = \theta STATE
\end{aligned}
$$

We have hidden the channels by which the display component communicates mouse position and movement to the text component, so the event repertoire of the interactive process can be defined by:

$$
\begin{aligned}
E ::=\;&\mathbf{Insert}\langle\!\langle CH \rangle\!\rangle \\
&|\;\;\mathbf{Delete} \\
&|\;\;\mathbf{Paste} \\
&|\;\;\mathbf{Point} \\
&|\;\;\mathbf{Dragleft} \\
&|\;\;\mathbf{Dragright} \\
&|\;\;\mathbf{Quit}
\end{aligned}
$$

All events are commands:

$$
commands = E
$$

The initial state is uniquely determined:

$$
Init \;\;\hat{=}\;\; STATE \wedge init
$$

The system yields a view after every command, but a result only after *Quit*:

$$
\begin{aligned}
\triangle &= command \\
\triangledown &= \{Quit\}
\end{aligned}
$$

6.5.5   *Analysis of the editor*

Next, we analyse some of the properties of the editor. In the course of our analysis we will discover that despite its simplicity our design is not ideal.

Completeness and Restartability

Since the effect of every command on the *text* is deterministic, and since there are no "internally generated" events, it is easy to show that the result available at any point is determined by the sequence of commands.

Property 1 *The set E of editor commands is Deterministic^R*

Since any text $t \in seq\ CH$ can be inserted into an empty document with the sequence of commands **Insert** t_1, **Insert** t_2, ...

Property 2 *The set of commands* ran **Insert** $\cup\ \{Quit\}$ *is WeakComplete*

Since no other commands may be used to insert characters, the same set is *Essential*.

Since the editor commands are *Deterministic^R*,

Property 3 *The set of commands* ran **Insert** $\cup\ \{Quit\}$ *is Complete.*

Whatever state the editor is in it is possible to restart it by "selecting" (*i.e.* pointing then dragging) and deleting until the text is empty, so

Property 4 *All command sequences are Restartable.*

Undoing

Because **Paste** just exchanges the *cut* and the *selection*

Property 5 $\langle$**Paste**$\rangle\ undoes_{\equiv}\langle$**Paste**$\rangle$

Because **Delete** changes the *cut*, its effects are only weakly undone by **Paste**.

Property 6 $\langle$**Paste**$\rangle\ undoes_{\approx}\ \langle$**Delete**$\rangle$

On the other hand,

Property 7 $\langle$**Delete**$\rangle\ undoes_{\equiv}\ \langle$**Paste**$\rangle$

There is no command which strongly undoes a simple insertion, but

Property 8 ⟨**Delete**⟩ *undoes*$_{\approx}$ ⟨**Insert** *ch*⟩

It probably ought to be possible to strongly undo a "small" command such as **Insert**, so we should consider having **Delete** simply remove the last character of *left* ⌢ *selection* without affecting either the *cut* or the rest of the *selection*. We would need to add a **Cut** command to obliterate the *selection*, saving its previous value as the *cut*.

It may not be possible to undo the effect of a **Point**, directly because the display origin may change, thereby removing the original cursor position from view. In fact, if the choice of *origin* for the display is inappropriately made by the implementation, then it might become impossible to view all the text!

Visual Consistency

Since the result is directly derived from the text, and the commands are *Deterministic*^{R} we are tempted to claim that all command sequences are trustworthy. But the specification does not guarantee that we can "explore" the complete text[5], so it is possible to change it at a place which becomes inaccessible.

Property 9 *Not all command sequences are trustworthy.*

Similar reasoning leads us to the conclusion that

Property 10 *The editor is not SVC (strongly visually consistent)*

The fact the same material can be replicated at different places in the text (a property which most text editors share) means that

Property 11 *Only* **Point** *and* **Drag** *are directly predictable.*

Happily the requirement that the right hand end of the selection always be visible ensures that

Property 12 *Each individual command is honest.*

---

[5] We can only point to a position which is already visible, and there is no way in general to *force* the display module to show material which is to the right of the selection.

6.5.6   *Summary*

The problems uncovered during our analysis flow from the fact that it may not be possible to navigate the entire text. This could be remedied by imposing stronger requirements on the display, but it would be better remedied by providing a more complete set of "navigation" commands. These would have to be independent of the display, and we leave their specification as an exercise.

6.6   Further work

In this chapter, we have introduced a model of interactive systems which supports their specification, and a number of ways of classifying sets of commands in such systems. We have also presented refinement rules to support the development of correct implementations from more abstract specifications. But the work as it stands is incomplete: the following areas seem particularly worthy of investigation:

- the prospect of conducting formal proofs of some of the visual consistency properties of an interactive system of other than trivial complexity is rather daunting. It would be better to recognise that one of the classical ways of constructing an interactive process is to factor it into an application module, an input manager and a display manager. Having specified the application module, and decided upon a visual consistency requirement, the designer can *calculate* the weakest specification for the display manager;

- the present classifications of sets of commands were not chosen arbitrarily, but there may be other useful ones worth formalising. For example, a set of commands which may be used to examine the current result without changing it;

- it seems likely that a given application area (document editing, mechanical and electrical CAD, etc.) will yield application specific classifications. The notion of semantic coherence of the result being generated is important, but has not been explored here. Programs such as structure editors often allow intermediate results to be generated which are not completely semantically coherent. How would the explicit presence of a notion of semantic coherence affect our classification?

6.7   Acknowledgements

The present work is an attempt to improve on an earlier note [183], in which a deterministic state-based characterisation of interactive systems was presented; that note was directly inspired by [61, 84, 6]. Thanks to Geraint Jones, Ian Page, and Jim Woodcock for their advice and encouragement, and to Gregory Abowd for many useful discussions.

Glossary

Sets, relations, and functions

N	the set of natural numbers
$m..n$	$\{i : \mathsf{N} \mid m \le i \le n\}$
$\mathsf{P}\,X$	all subsets of X
$\mathsf{F}\,X$	all finite subsets of X
$\#X$	number of elements in a (finite) set X
$X \times Y$	cross-product of X and Y
	$(x, y) \in (X \times Y) \Leftrightarrow x \in X \wedge y \in Y$
$X \subseteq Y$	X is a subset of Y
$X \leftrightarrow Y$	binary relations between X and Y
	$X \leftrightarrow Y \;\hat{=}\; \mathsf{P}(X \times Y)$
$x \mapsto y$	a pair of elements
	$x \mapsto y \;\hat{=}\; (x, y)$
xRy	the relation $\_R\_$ holds between x and y
	$xRy \Leftrightarrow (x, y) \in \_R\_$
$\_R\_$	relation R "quoted" (*i.e.* used as a set)
R^{-1}	inverse of relation R
	$yR^{-1}x \Leftrightarrow xRy.$
$R \,\mathbin{;}\, S$	forward composition of relations R and S
	$\forall R : X \leftrightarrow Y;\ S : Y \leftrightarrow Z \bullet$
	$\quad x(R \,\mathbin{;}\, S)z \Leftrightarrow \exists y : Y \bullet xRy \wedge ySz$
$R(\!(S)\!)$	image of set S through relation R
	$R(\!(S)\!) \;\hat{=}\; \{y : Y \mid (\exists x : S \bullet xRy)\}$
$Id_{[X]}$	identity relation on X
	$id_{[X]} \;\hat{=}\; \{x \mapsto x \bullet x : X\}$
$dom\ R$	domain of relation R
	$dom\ R \;\hat{=}\; \{x : X \mid \exists y : Y \bullet xRy\}$
$ran\ R$	range of relation R
	$ran\ R \;\hat{=}\; \{y : Y \mid \exists x : X \bullet xRy\}$
$X \nrightarrow Y$	partial functions from X to Y ($\subseteq X \leftrightarrow Y$)
	$X \nrightarrow Y \;\hat{=}\; \{R : X \leftrightarrow Y \mid R^{-1} \,\mathbin{;}\, R \subseteq Id_{[Y]}\}$
$X \rightarrow Y$	total functions from X to Y
	$X \rightarrow Y \;\hat{=}\; \{f : X \nrightarrow Y \mid dom\ f = X\}$
$R \oplus S$	override relation R with relation S
	$x(R \oplus S)y \Leftrightarrow xSy \vee (xRy \wedge \neg xSy)$
$S \vartriangleleft R$	restrict domain of relation R by set S
	$x(S \vartriangleleft R)y \Leftrightarrow xRy \wedge x \in S$
$R \vartriangleright S$	restrict range of relation R by set S
	$x(R \vartriangleleft S)y \Leftrightarrow xRy \wedge y \in S$

Sequences

seq X finite sequences of elements of X
$$\text{seq } X \triangleq \{f : \mathbf{N} \nrightarrow X \mid \exists\, n : \mathbf{N} \bullet \text{dom} f = 1..n\}$$
$\langle\rangle$ empty sequence
$s \frown t$ concatenation of sequences s and t
$\#s$ length of sequence s

$;/s$ distributed composition of a sequence of relations
$$;/\langle\rangle = Id$$
$$;/\langle R\rangle = R$$
$$;/(s \frown t) = (;/s)\,;\,(;/t)$$

$s \upharpoonright S$ restriction of the range of sequence s to set S
$$\langle\rangle \upharpoonright S = \langle\rangle$$
$$(s \frown t) \upharpoonright S = (s \upharpoonright S) \frown (t \upharpoonright S)$$
$$\langle x\rangle \upharpoonright S = \begin{cases} \langle\rangle, & \text{if } x \notin S \\ \langle x\rangle, & \text{if } x \in S \end{cases}$$

$S \stackrel{seq}{\lhd} s$ restriction of the domain of sequence s to
the numbers in S
$$S \stackrel{seq}{\lhd} s = resequence(S \lhd s)$$
where
$resequence : (\mathbf{N} \nrightarrow X) \rightarrow (\text{seq } X)$
$sort : \mathbf{P}\,\mathbf{N} \rightarrow (\text{seq } \mathbf{N})$
$increasing : \mathbf{P}(\text{seq } \mathbf{N})$
$resequence \; R = sort(\text{dom}R)\,;\,R$
$ran(sort \; S) = S$
$increasing(sort \; S)$
$s \in increasing \Leftrightarrow \forall\, i,j : (dom \; s) \bullet i < j \Rightarrow s_i < s_j$

Set comprehension

$\{declaration \mid predicate\}$ comprehension, for example
$$\{x : \mathbf{N};\; y : \mathbf{N} \mid x > y\}$$
$\{term \bullet declaration \mid predicate\}$ term comprehension, for example
$$\{(x^2 - y^2) \bullet x : \mathbf{N};\; y : \mathbf{N} \mid x > y\}$$

CHAPTER SEVEN

FROM ABSTRACT MODELS TO FUNCTIONAL PROTOTYPES

COLIN RUNCIMAN

7.1   Introduction

The technique of *rapid prototyping* is often proposed as a way to check
the validity of constructive specifications before developing a refined
implementation. For many applications, prototyping by direct evaluation of a specification is adequate; it does not matter that execution
costs greatly exceed those required of the final program. But for *interactive* systems, a prototype with extremely slow response is at best
tedious to evaluate and at worst useless. Some degree of refinement
may, therefore, be essential for an interactive prototype, but the refinement process needs to be as quick and cheap as possible.

One method of accurately refining specifications into programs is to
use the rules of a *transformation system* [123]. There may be many
ways in which such rules could be applied and it is rarely possible to
express an appropriate strategy for their use as a machine algorithm.
So, transformational refinement is a discipline for the human programmer, not an optimisation routine in a fully automatic system. It is a
powerful technique, but can demand a lot of effort— too much effort,

one might think, for rapid prototype refinement. However, this chapter considers *partially evaluating* (prefabricating, if you like) transformational strategies that are applicable to a whole *class* of specifications. The members of this class are all instances of a particular abstract model of interactive systems—the *PiE* [61]. By this means, a good deal of the work required for transformational refinement can be done once and for all, and then exploited in a variety of different prototypes.

§7.2 explains the kind of functional programming used, including the basics of transformation. §7.3 explains the *PiE* model. §7.4 casts the *PiE* model in a functional mould, and uses it to specify some simple examples. §7.5 deals with transformational techniques for *PiE*-based prototyping. §7.6 summarises and concludes.

7.2   Functional programming

There are various reasons for choosing a purely functional programming system as the setting for this work. Transformational techniques are simplest and most thoroughly investigated in functional languages. This is hardly surprising, since functional languages are typically small and regular, with formal semantic definitions that are manageable (e.g., see Meira's definition [124] of KRC), yet they have considerable expressive power. Developments such as *non-strict* functional languages with *lazy evaluation* further add to the attractions of functional programming. On the one hand, expressive power is increased — of particular importance for the present chapter, computation can be defined over potentially infinite sequences, such as the sequence of characters entered at a keyboard. On the other hand, the proof theory is simplified — programs become *fully substitutive* [203]. In comparison, conventional imperative languages and programs are complex and irregular; reasoning about them formally is correspondingly harder. Readers needing further persuasion in favour of functional programming are directed to papers by Hughes [101] and Turner [202].

Notation
This chapter uses the functional programming notation of *Glide* [165], similar constructions can be expressed in most lazy functional programming languages. Program symbols and their meanings are summarised below.

`->`	is by definition
`[]`	empty list
`h:t`	non-empty list with head `h`, and tail `t`
`::`	concatenation operator between lists
`p.q`	a pair (not a list) of values `p` and `q`
`o`	functional composition — `(f o g) x = f (g x)`
`(⊕)`	operator ⊕ as a function — `(⊕) x y = x⊕y`
`(x⊕)`	partial application to left operand — `(x⊕) y = x⊕y`
`(⊕y)`	partial application to right operand — `(⊕y) x = x⊕y`

The following symbols will also be used. They are not part of the Glide language but are used to express properties of programs:

$\Rightarrow$	evaluates to
$\perp$	undefined value

7.2.1   *Recursively defined functions over lists*

Functional programming languages are well equipped to express computations over sequences. Often, sequences can be represented as finite lists. List-processing functions can be defined recursively, taking an empty list argument as the simple case, and a non-empty list as the recursive case decomposed into its head (first item) and its tail (list of remaining items). The following examples define functions that will be used later on:

```
sum [] -> 0
sum (h:t) -> h + sum t

reverse [] -> []
reverse (h:t) -> reverse t :: [h]
```

The meaning of the primitive `::` operator for list concatenation can also be expressed by recursive definition, as follows:

```
[] :: s -> s
(h:t) :: s -> h : (t :: s)
```

Some functions are defined only for non-empty lists. Their definitions typically take a singleton list as the simple case and a multi-item list as the recursive case. Once again, the examples will be useful later. The function **foot** yields the final item and **body** yields the list of all items but the final one:

```
foot [f] -> f
foot (a:b:x) -> foot (b:x)

body [f] -> []
body (a:b:x) -> a : body (b:x)
```

7.2.2   *Higher order functions*

Functions are *the* components from which functional programs are built.
They can be combined in a rich variety of ways by the application of
higher order functions whose arguments and/or result are themselves
functions. As Hughes [101] expresses it, these higher order functions
are the "glue" used to assemble functional components. Definitions of
list-processing functions can often use standard patterns of recursion
encoded into higher order functions. For example, map applies its functional argument, f, to each item in a list and yields the list of results;
fold generalises a binary operation b to one that operates over lists:

```
map f [] -> []
map f (h:t) -> f h : map f t

fold b z [] -> z
fold b z (h:t) -> b h (fold b z t)
```

An alternative definition for sum uses the technique of *partial application* to specialise fold by fixing the first two arguments. The result is
a function of a single argument corresponding to the third argument of
fold:

```
sum -> fold (+) 0
```

7.2.3   *Infinite lists and lazy evaluation*

In functional programming systems with *lazy evaluation*, sequences may
also be represented as *infinite* lists. For example, the infinite sequence
of natural numbers can be defined by recursion:

```
nat -> 0 : map (+1) nat
```

Some recursive definitions of functions computing over finite lists also
define a useful function over infinite lists, the [] case being simply

redundant. Functions built using map, for example, are like this. But many functions yielding well-defined results for finite lists may not be defined over infinite lists. The function sum is one such:

> sum nat $\Rightarrow \perp$

A standard mathematical technique in such circumstances is to regard the infinite computation as the limit of a series of finite computations. A result in this series provides an *approximation* to the infinitely expensive result that cannot be obtained. One way to use this technique in a functional program is to define a function prefixes that computes the sequence of finite prefixes of an infinite list:

> prefixes (h:t) -> [] : map (h:) (prefixes t)

> prefixes nat $\Rightarrow$ [[], [0], [0, 1], [0, 1, 2], ...]

If f is a function taking a finite list argument, then

> map f (prefixes s)

yields a sequence of increasingly good approximations to the value of f s which may not itself be computable:

> map sum (prefixes nat) $\Rightarrow$
> [0, 0, 1, 3, 6, 10, 15, ...]

In a more general form this scheme provides something like fold that can be applied to infinite lists:

> folds f z s -> map (fold f z) (prefixes s)

7.2.4   *Strictness*

A function f is said to be *strict* if the result is undefined when f is applied to an undefined argument:

> f $\perp \Rightarrow \perp$

More generally, f is strict in its nth argument if the result is undefined for every application of f in which the nth argument is undefined—no matter what the other argument values are:

f ... ⊥ ... ⇒⊥

Effective definitions about infinite lists rely on a ":" operator for list construction that is *non-strict* in its second argument. For example, computing:

head (0 : *infinite list of numbers*) ⇒ 0

must not (and does not) require the *infinite list* to be evaluated. Otherwise, this evaluation would be unending, and an endless computation producing no value is a form of ⊥.

Argument patterns

When it comes to functions explicitly defined by clauses, there is an important link between argument patterns and strictness. The presence of a pattern, other than a simple variable in some argument position, forces strictness. This is because the matching process implicit in the application of a function defined by cases cannot successfully evaluate a ⊥ argument to determine its constructive form: so the choice of clause (and hence the result) must be undefined. This principle can be illustrated with the familiar example of the conditional:

```
if True  x y -> x
if False x y -> y
```

Here **True** and **False** are definite values — the boolean constants — whereas **x** and **y** are just variables. So, the function **if** is strict in its first argument, but non-strict in the other two. This non-strictness corresponds to the intuitive observation that a conditional can yield a well-defined result, even though one of its alternatives, taken alone, would give only an undefined result.

7.2.5   *Reasoning about programs*

Reasoning about functional programs requires a combination of substitution by definition and some form of induction. In this chapter, lists are the dominant subjects of computation. For finite lists *structural induction* [31] can be used: to prove some property holds for all finite lists **x** prove first that it holds for the basic case **x=[]** and then, assuming as an inductive hypothesis that it holds for some list **t**, prove that it also holds for **h:t** for all **h**.

The procedure is almost as simple for infinite lists, but the principle behind it is more sophisticated, resting on a lattice-theoretic view of data structures [169]. To prove a property holds for all infinite lists **y**, prove first that it holds when **y** $=\perp$, the *undefined* value. The inductive step is as for finite lists: assume the result holds for some list **t** and show that it must therefore hold for (**h:t**). It follows that a property may be proved true for *all* lists, finite and infinite, by establishing both [] and $\perp$ base cases together with the common inductive case.

Further explanation and examples of inductive proof about lists can be found in one of Turner's papers [203].

Subsequent sections appeal to various *equivalence laws* relating functional expressions over lists, and these laws are summarised in an appendix. Their proofs rest on the kind of inductive techniques just described.

7.2.6   *Transformation of programs*

The same properties that make it easy to reason about programs also ease *program transformation*. The basis of most transformation methods in functional programming is the *fold/unfold* system of Burstall and Darlington [32].

This involves the manipulation of selected *instances* of defining clauses, corresponding to particular argument patterns. In each such instance, one first evaluates the definitive expression symbolically, as far as possible, by applying the defining clauses for functions that it uses. The resulting expression may then be re-arranged, by making use of equivalence laws, so that it can be contracted to a new form that takes better advantage of available definitions.

If the program involved may be used interactively, it is important to ensure that after transformation not only is the total output produced for a given total input unchanged, but also the correct interleaving of input and output is preserved. This means that the strictness of transformed functions must be respected. Replacing a variable by a pattern to form a clause instance is only valid if the originally defined function is strict in that variable [164].

Example: transforming `folds`

As an example, consider how `folds` may be made more efficient. Recall the definition of `folds` given earlier:

```
folds f z s -> map (fold f z) (prefixes s)            (1)
```

We shall transform this definition without making any assumptions about the functional argument f. The starting point is an instance of (1) in which the list argument s is non-empty. That this is a valid instance (indeed, the only one that need be considered at all) can be shown by symbolic evaluation as follows:

```
  folds f z ([] or ⊥ )
= map (fold f z) (prefixes ([] or ⊥ ))
= map (fold f z) ⊥
= ⊥
```

So let's formulate an instance of (1) for non-empty s and evaluate it as far as possible:

```
  folds f z (h:t)
= map (fold f z) (prefixes (h:t))
= map (fold f z) ([] : map (h:) (prefixes t))
= fold f z [] : map (fold f z) (map (h:) (prefixes t))
= z : map (fold f z) (map (h:) (prefixes t))
```

Law *M1* (see Appendix) allows us to replace such a double application of map by a single application to a composite function:

```
= z : map (fold f z o (h:)) (prefixes t)              (2)
```

The tail of (2) is *similar* to the *RHS* of (1). The difference is the presence of o (h:). Adopting the *promotion* strategy of Bird [20] we seek a functional expression *expr* satisfying the following equation:

```
fold f z o (h:) = expr o fold f z
```

The following lemma provides a solution:

Lemma (**folds** *promotion*)
```
        fold f z o (h:) = f h o fold f z
```
Proof
```
  (fold f z o (h:)) x
= fold f z (h:x)
= f h (fold f z x)
= (f h o fold f z) x
```
□

Picking up (2) once again, and resuming the main transformational development of `folds`, the lemma can be used to obtain a directly recursive definition, as desired:

```
z : map (fold f z o (h:)) (prefixes t)
= z : map (f h o fold f z) (prefixes t)
= z : map (f h) (map (fold f z) prefixes t)
```

which by (1)

```
= z : map (f h) (folds f z t)
```

and we obtain a transformed definition of `folds` as follows:

$$\texttt{folds f z (h:t) -> z : map (f h) (folds f z t)} \qquad (3)$$

Comparing (3) with (1), the auxiliaries `fold` and `prefixes` are no longer needed.

7.3   The *PiE* model

The *PiE* interaction model [61] was originally proposed as a simple, abstract way of looking at interactive systems. It formalises the perspective that an interactive system is a deterministic closed world: machine behaviour is entirely determined by preceding user actions. In the model, *command* sequences (also called *programs*) are entered by a user, causing corresponding *effects*. Calling the set of all possible programs P, and the set of effects E, the determination of effects is expressed in the definition of an *interpretation* function i from P to E yielding for any command sequence its net effect.

Despite its simplicity, the *PiE* model provides a sufficient framework for the definition of various classes of system. For example, a system may be termed *predictable* if it has a *PiE* model in which the interpretation function i obeys the following law:

$$\forall\, p_1, p_2.i(p1) = i(p2) \Rightarrow \forall p.i(p_1\, p) = i(p_2\, p)$$

That is, command sequences are completely characterised by their net effect. Therefore, the effect of subsequent commands depends only on the effect achieved so far, and not on the particular commands used to achieve it. Or, a system may be termed *reachable* if:

$$\forall\, p_1, p_2.\, \exists\, p.i(p_1\, p) = i(p_2)$$

which guarantees, among other things, that no desired effect can be irretrievably lost.

7.3.1   *Displays and results*
The *PiE* model can be enriched by distinguishing between that part of an effect which determines a *display* continually presented to the user and that which would determine a *result* if use of the system were to cease at a particular point. The set of possible displays is called D and the set of possible results R. Two mappings projecting effects onto displays and results are defined:

$$d : E \rightarrow D$$

$$r : E \rightarrow R$$

This produces the so-called *RED PiE* model depicted in the following diagram:

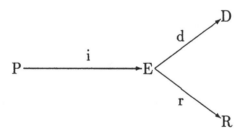

Since one frequently wants to refer to the display (or result) obtained after a sequence of commands, it is convenient to give names to the compositions of i with each projection:

$$di \rightarrow d \circ i$$

$$ri \rightarrow r \circ i$$

This enrichment of the model greatly enlarges the class of design properties that can be expressed. For example, the distinction can now be made between *active* command sequences that change the result and *passive* sequences that do not:

$$passive(p) \equiv \forall\, p'.ri(p'\,p) = ri(p')$$

Using this definition of *passive*, a system with *result-connected display* could be characterised as follows:

$$\forall\, p_1, p_2.ri(p_1) = ri(p_2) \Rightarrow \exists\, p'.passive(p') \wedge di(p_1\,p') = di(p_2)$$

This says that the current display must be one of a set determined entirely by the current result (regardless, for example, of the particular sequence of commands used to obtain it). Any other element in this set must be displayable without disturbing the result. This is achieved by giving an appropriate passive sequence of commands.

7.3.2   Uses of the model

The *PiE* model is intended primarily to serve as a framework within which to express general requirements of principle for interactive systems in a precise way, and to examine the formal relationships between such requirements. It has also been used to provide structure in formal specifications of particular interactive systems [59, 56].

7.4   PiE as a higher order function

Let's now review the *PiE* model in programming terms. For a given interpretation function i computing the overall effect of a finite sequence of commands, we want pie i (say) to map a sequence of commands to a sequence of effects. This is strongly reminiscent of the **prefixes** idea, and our first effort at a definition of the **pie** higher order function is as follows:

$$\text{pie i p -> map i (prefixes p)} \tag{4}$$

$$\text{prefixes (h:t) -> [] : map (h:) (prefixes t)} \tag{5}$$

The following paragraphs discuss possible objections to this definition, leading to a reformulation of it.

Avoiding restricted prefixes

We want to leave open the question of whether command sequences are finite or infinite, since an interactive system may be used for sessions of limited duration (*e.g.*, word-processing), or it may operate perpetually (*e.g.*, monitoring a transport network). In the latter case, the specification of an indefinitely long interaction is given by a sequence of approximations specifying the effect of longer and longer initial sections of that interaction. This is just the kind of use to which prefixes was put earlier. But given an argument of finite length n, the prefixes function defined by (5) yields a list whose first n items are indeed the prefixes of lengths 0 to $n - 1$ but whose structure after the nth item is undefined. To remedy this position, it is enough to extend the definition of prefixes by a second clause stating that [] is its own sole prefix.

$$\text{prefixes (h:t)} \rightarrow [] : \text{map (h:) (prefixes t)} \qquad (5)$$
$$\text{prefixes []} \rightarrow [[]] \qquad (6)$$

Now, given an argument of length n, prefixes yields appropriately the $n + 1$ initial subsequences of lengths 0 to n.

However, this still leaves a further problem to do with prefixes. Given a *complete* sequence of commands, it correctly yields all the initial subsequences each of which can be suitably interpreted in the pie context. In an interactive system, computation cannot be postponed until a complete sequence of commands is available — it must proceed as far as possible given the commands entered so far, producing results whose display is interleaved in time with the entry of further commands. Even assuming lazy evaluation, the prefixes function defined by (5) & (6) falls down in this respect because it is needlessly strict. One practical consequence of this in the pie context is that the initial effect (e.g., an introductory message and prompt) could not be computed until the first command, if any, has been entered.

To avoid such problems, one should use patterns for case analysis of sequence arguments only where a function is *necessarily* strict in the corresponding argument. Often, an auxiliary function can be introduced to shift the point of case analysis appropriately. For prefixes, the definition can be amended as follows:

$$\text{prefixes x -> [] : prefixes' x} \tag{7}$$

$$\text{prefixes' [] -> []} \tag{8}$$
$$\text{prefixes' (h:t) -> map (h:) (prefixes t)} \tag{9}$$

Interpreting history

A second objection to the originally proposed definition of `pie` concerns i, and is based primarily on grounds of inconvenience. The interpretation function i must be defined to accept as argument a finite sequence of commands presented in the standard list form:

first-command : subsequent-commands

The interpretation function must compute the net effect of this sequence. To determine this effect, it is often more natural to start with the command just applied and work backwards as necessary to determine relevant context. That is, commands are more conveniently regarded as history, arranged in reverse order of their application:

latest-command : previous-commands

This objection has a simple remedy, build in explicit reversal to the interpretation part of `pie`:

$$\text{pie i p -> map (i o reverse) (prefixes p)} \tag{10}$$

Abstract vs. *efficient*

The third objection defines a central issue of this chapter. Isn't the proposed definition of `pie` hopelessly inefficient? How can such an abstract formulation provide a suitable basis for prototyping? A detailed reply to this objection, showing how transformation methods can be used to improve performance, will be given in §7.5.

7.4.1   *PiE enrichments and composed partial applications*

Adding the distinction between display and result requires no change to the `pie` definition. It is enough to supply the result of a partial application of `pie` as a functional argument to a further higher-order function. Other arguments of the new function correspond to the display and result projections:

$$\text{red pie d r -> pair (map d) (r o foot) o pie} \qquad (11)$$

Every identifier in this definition denotes a function. This is a most important factor determining the flexibility and power of component combinations [13]. The auxiliary `pair` is just pairing lifted to the functional level:

```
pair f g x -> f x . g x
```

Input/output representations

Up to this point, the *representations* of commands, displays and results have not been considered. At the working level of `pie` and `red`, we should prefer to choose whatever representation is most convenient for the formulation of the interpreting and projection functions. For prototyping purposes, however, these representations must be translated by parsing from, and formatting to, the representations required at the user interface. Once again, this can be expressed without disturbing the existing definitions, by introducing a further higher order function whose arguments will include a program parser (**pp**), a display formatter (**df**) and a result formatter (**rf**):

```
hci redpie pp df rf ->
( let (displays . result) -> redpie (pp user)
  in map df displays . rf result )
```

The value **user**, here supplied as argument to the parser, is separately defined (for keyboard interfaces) as the sequence of characters keyed by the user during program execution. The production of displays will be correctly interleaved with the entering of commands, assuming that **pp** is so defined that, under lazy evaluation, each abstract command can be computed as soon as the full text of its concrete counterpart is available in **user** (but no sooner). The choice of pairing to combine the display sequence and final result for presentation to the user is an arbitrary one. (It is important that pairing is evaluated lazily, however, since otherwise nothing would be presented to the user until the final result was available.)

Teletype interaction

The hci function leaves unspecified some characteristics of the interface at the device level. For purposes of illustration it is convenient to define a particular instance of its use corresponding to a simple line-by-line teletype interface. Lines of **user** are taken as commands, and each display or result is presented as a line:

```
tty redpie -> hci redpie lines asline asline

lines [] -> []
lines (c:cs) -> if (c = '\n') ([] : lines cs)
                    ((c:l):ls where (l:ls) -> lines cs )

asline x -> x . '\n'
```

It is assumed that the output driver of the functional programming system lazily produces a character sequence representation of values omitting all structural punctuation.

7.4.2   *Specific PiE examples*

There are at least two approaches to the choice of illustrative examples. The first is to plug in some simple values as arguments for the higher-order functions of the model, and see what system results. The second is to select a simple interactive application, and show how it can be expressed using the model.

Ghosts

This first example owes something to both approaches. The arguments of **red** and **pie** are two particularly simple functions, namely the identity **id** and a function **none** whose result for all arguments is empty:

```
id x -> x

none x -> []

ghosts -> red (pie id) id none                            (12)
```

Since **id** is supplied to **pie** as the interpretation, the effect of entering a sequence of commands will be just the history of such entries—the same sequence in reverse. Since **id** is also supplied as the display projection, this history is what is displayed after each command is entered. Since **none** is the result projection, there is no final result yielded.

If single letters are used as commands, the program can be used for a two-player word game, called *Ghosts*. Call the two players A and B. Each in turn adds a letter to the front of an initially empty string until the next player (A say) *either* points out that B has formed a word *or* challenges B to name a word that ends in the current string of letters. The aim is *not* to complete a word, and yet to answer (or deter!) any challenge for a word-ending. The game is called Ghosts because each player's mind is haunted by half-formed words (most of which vanish as the string of letters changes). In the following game, the first player tries to set a trap but carelessly inflicts self-defeat:

```
tty ghosts
s
s
t
ts
s
sts
o
osts
h
hosts
```

Wordcount

To motivate trainee typists, a program is required to respond to each line typed with the number of words on that line. At the end of a typing session, the program should report the total number of words. This program can be modelled as a *PiE* by regarding each line of text as a command and letting the effect be a history of word counts for all lines so far. Display and result projections are then provided by **head** and **sum** respectively:

```
wordsin line -> 1 + blanksin line

blanksin [] -> 0
blanksin (c:cs) -> (if (c=' ') 1 0) + blanksin cs

wordcount -> red (pie (map wordsin)) head sum      (13)
```

```
tty wordcount
0
a sun without a sphere
5
a sea without a shore
5
(eof)
10
```

At first sight, the computational workings of this program might seem to put it in the "hopelessly inefficient" category, because the interpretation of *each* line is defined by mapping **wordsin** over *all lines* entered so far! However, under lazy evaluation, the computation *actually performed* as each line is entered is driven by the display function **head**, which demands a count only for this most recent line. (This does not mean that lazy evaluation renders transformational improvement unnecessary, but it does illustrate that, even before transformation, at-a-glance estimates of computational costs may be unduly pessimistic.)

7.5   Transformational refinement

Despite the remarks on the last example about the savings of lazy evaluation, only the simplest *PiE* models expressed by direct application of the higher order functions defined in the above ways are likely to perform acceptably as prototypes. So let's turn now to a detailed examination of how this problem might be overcome by transformational methods.

An important general principle to note is that the improvement obtained by transformation is commensurate with the degree of commitment [167] made to a particular model and its parameters. The more information there is available at transformation time, the more computational work can be done in advance. The successive transformational techniques to be examined here correspond to increasing levels of commitment, as follows:

(i)   nothing beyond the *PiE* model itself
          —no assumptions about i;
(ii)   an additional model (e.g., state transition machine)
          —restricts possible i;
(iii)   a particular application
          —reflected in a definition for i.

7.5.1   *Transforming the model alone*

Even before any details of the interpretation function i are known there
is scope for improving the **pie** definition by transformation. This transformation of **pie** may be compared to that of **folds** in §7.2, although
things are more complicated in at least two respects: **pie** is non-strict in
its second argument, the natural choice for instantiation, so a *maximal
strict auxiliary* must be extracted; then an immediate attept at promotion proves unsatisfactory because the promotion lemma introduces
an expensive auxiliary, so a *preparatory generalisation* is necessary. (If
these forewarnings of complication are discouraging, keep in mind that
all this is *prefabrication*—it is done only once for a whole class of specifications and prototypes.)

Maximal strict auxiliary

Recall the sole defining clause for **pie**:

```
pie i p -> map (i o reverse) (prefixes p)
```

Since we are assuming nothing about the function i, the conventional
strategy of transformation suggests considering instances of p. But for
this to be valid, **pie** must be strict in that argument, whereas in fact
it is non-strict:

```
pie i ⊥
= map (i o reverse) (prefixes ⊥)
= map (i o reverse) ([] : prefixes' ⊥)
= (i o reverse) [] : map (i o reverse) (prefixes' ⊥)
```

There is no need to go any further in this evaluation to show non-
strictness, since x:y can never be ⊥ whatever x and y may be. The final
expression obtained also indicates the form of the required maximal
strict auxiliary [164], which we shall call **pie2**. The definition of **pie**
can be recast in terms of it as follows:

$$\text{pie i p -> i [] : pie2 i p} \tag{14}$$

$$\text{pie2 i p -> map (i o reverse) (prefixes' p)} \tag{15}$$

This auxiliary `pie2` represents the bulk of the `pie` computation, and it is strict in p since `prefixes'` is strict and `map` is strict in its second argument. So, `pie2` becomes the subject of transformation.

Weak promotion of `pie2`

Beginning with the simple case of an empty command sequence, the appropriate instance of (15) can be fully evaluated by appealing to the defining clauses of functions involved:

```
pie2 i []
= map (i o reverse) (prefixes' [])
= map (i o reverse) []
= []
```

For the non-empty case, transformation can begin similarly with symbolic evaluation:

```
pie2 i (c:cs)
= map (i o reverse) (prefixes' (c:cs))
= map (i o reverse) (map (c:) (prefixes cs))
= map (i o reverse) (map (c:) ([] : prefixes' cs))
= map (i o reverse) ([c] : map (c:) (prefixes' cs))
= (i o reverse) [c] :
  map (i o reverse) (map (c:) (prefixes' cs))
= i [c] : map (i o reverse) (map (c:) (prefixes' cs))
```

Now, as earlier for `folds`, we may appeal to law *M1* (see appendix) to obtain an expression in which the tail is similar to the *RHS* of the original defining clause for `pie2`:

$$\text{= i [c] : map (i o reverse o (c:)) (prefixes' cs)} \tag{16}$$

To reach a direct recursive definition for `pie2` by promotion we should like a functional *expr* such that:

```
i o reverse o (c:) = expr o i o reverse
```

but this equation cannot be solved without further information about i, whereas our present aim is a transformational refinement that does not depend on i. Hence, we consider a weaker promotion based on an *expr* such that:

$$\text{i o reverse o (c:)} = expr \text{ o reverse}$$

Note, the omission of i from the *RHS*. A solution to this equation not depending on the choice of i can be formed from a solution to the equation:

$$\text{reverse o (c:)} = expr' \text{ o reverse}$$

by putting *expr* = i o *expr'*.

Lemma (pie2 *promotion)*
> reverse o (c:) = (::[c]) o reverse

Proof
> (reverse o (c:)) x
> = reverse (c:x)
> = reverse x :: [c]
> = ((::[c]) o reverse) x

□

Hence, the transformation of the recursive case of pie2 can be resumed from (16) as follows:

> pie2 i (c:cs)
> = i [c] : map (i o reverse o (c:)) (prefixes' cs)
> = i [c] : map (i o (::[c]) o reverse) (prefixes' cs)
> = i [c] : pie2 (i o (::[c])) cs

Here promotion has been achieved at the cost of a *quadratic* functional argument to pie2, since after n commands have been interpreted this argument will have the form:

$$\text{i o (::[}c_1\text{]) o (::[}c_2\text{]) o ... o (::[}c_n\text{])}$$

The cost of :: is linear in the length of its first argument.

Generalisation

When promotion is difficult, Bird [20] suggests generalising the function under transformation to incorporate an additional argument, adding that this is an *essentially creative step* for which no fixed derivation rules can be given. In the present context, however, the dominant argument of the function we wish to transform is a single list, so the creative step can be assisted by the following heuristic: consider how the result of applying the function to the entire list is related to the results of applying it to an arbitrary prefix and to the corresponding suffix. For the `pie2` function the relationship is something like this:

$$\text{pie2 i (cs :: cs') =} \tag{17}$$
$$\text{pie2 i cs :: pie2 (i o (:: reverse cs)) cs'}$$

We could, if we wished, try to prove this. However, it is worth stressing that the correctness of subsequent transformations will *not* depend on the validity of (17). The equation simply formalises a source of inspiration for a transformational idea. It suggests certain steps to take. The steps may or may not be productive, but they cannot be incorrect.

The technique for extracting a generalisation from (17) is to consider the application of `pie2` with `cs'` as argument. In the expression for this application, replace the maximal complete application containing `cs`, that is (`reverse cs`), by a new argument. The intuition is that this argument represents all the computation over the sequence prefix that will be needed for the computation over the suffix. The resulting generalised form of `pie2`, which we shall call `pie3`, should therefore be defined as follows:

$$\text{pie3 i r p -> pie2 (i o (::r)) p} \tag{18}$$

To obtain a `pie2` computation, `pie3` can be applied with [] as the additional argument `r`. For by definition:

$$\text{pie3 i [] p = pie2 (i o (::[])) p} \tag{19}$$

and (`::[]`) is an identity function over lists. Moreover (`o id`) is an identity over functions, so the composite function in the *RHS* of (19) simplifies to just `i` as required. A refined version of `pie3` could therefore be used to provide a refined version of `pie2`:

$$\text{pie2 i p -> pie3 i [] p} \tag{20}$$

Promotion of pie3

Just as our original aim of transforming pie was deflected a little to that of transforming pie2, so now it is further deflected to the transformation of pie3. Consider once again the case p=[], evaluating the corresponding instance of (18):

```
pie3 i r []
= pie2 (i o (::r)) []
= map (i o (::r) o reverse) (prefixes' [])
= map (i o (::r) o reverse) []
= []
```

And now the case p=(c:cs):

```
pie3 i r (c:cs)
= pie2 (i o (::r)) (c:cs)
= map (i o (::r) o reverse) (prefixes' (c:cs))
= map (i o (::r) o reverse) (map (c:) (prefixes cs))
= map (i o (::r) o reverse)
(map (c:) ([] : prefixes' cs))
= map (i o (::r) o reverse)
([c] : map (c:) (prefixes' cs))
= i (c:r) :
  map (i o (::r) o reverse) (map (c:) (prefixes' cs))
= i (c:r) :
  map (i o (::r) o reverse o (c:)) (prefixes' cs) (21)
```

Once more, a promotion lemma is needed. This time, we may argue as follows:

Lemma (pie3 *promotion)*
```
        (::r) o reverse o (c:) = (::c:r) o reverse
```
Proof
```
        ((::r) o reverse o (c:))  x
        = reverse (c:x) :: r
        = (reverse x :: [c]) :: r
        = reverse x :: ([c] :: r)
        = reverse x :: (c:r)
        = ((::c:r) o reverse) x
```
□

Resuming the transformation of `pie3` from (21), application of this lemma leads to a new directly recursive definition by appeal to the original definitions of `pie2` (15) and `pie3` (18):

```
  i (c:r) : map (i o (::r) o reverse o (c:))
                                   (prefixes' cs)
= i (c:r) : map (i o (::c:r) o reverse)
                                   (prefixes' cs)
= i (c:r) : pie2 (i o (::c:r)) cs
= i (c:r) : pie3 i (c:r) cs
```

Eliminating `pie2`

Collecting defining clauses together, we now have the following transformed definition of `pie`, in terms of the auxiliary functions `pie2` and `pie3`:

$$\text{pie i p -> i [] : pie2 i p} \tag{14}$$

$$\text{pie2 i p -> pie3 i [] p} \tag{20}$$

$$\text{pie3 i r [] -> []} \tag{22}$$
$$\text{pie3 i r (c:cs) -> i (c:r) : pie3 i (c:r) cs} \tag{23}$$

The auxiliary `pie2` was originally introduced with the expectation that it would be transformed to a directly recursive form. This expectation was transferred to `pie3`, and fulfilled. Consequently, the sole application of `pie2` occurs in (14), the definition of `pie` itself. It is a simple matter to evaluate this application symbolically. This means that (20) can be discarded as redundant:

$$\text{pie i p -> i [] : pie3 i [] p} \tag{24}$$

The defining clauses (22), (23) & (24) will be used as the basis of further derivation in §7.5.2.

Finishing touches

Since the argument `i` is invariant, it can be eliminated in `pie3` by making this auxiliary function local to the definition of `pie`:

```
pie i p -> ( i [] : pie3 [] p
              where
              pie3 r [] -> []
              pie3 r (c:cs) -> i (c:r) : pie3 (c:r) cs )
```

Yet another generalising auxiliary, `pie4`, can be used to share construction work, assuming an implementation based on *graph reduction* [201, 152]:

```
pie i p -> ( pie4 [] p
              where
              pie3 r [] -> []
              pie3 r (c:cs) -> pie4 (c:r) cs
              pie4 r p -> i r : pie3 r p )
```

(These finishing touches are not carried forward into subsequent sections because they would complicate later reasoning.)

7.5.2   *Model shifting and state-machine specialisation*

Although the above transformation of the `pie` definition eliminates the heavy computation of `prefixes`, it still leaves in place recurrent computations of `i` over (at worst) complete command sequences. There are various ways in which this might be avoided. The general idea to be illustrated here is that of a *model shift*. A new model higher order function `m` is defined and applications `pie i` are replaced by applications of `m` to arguments precisely derived from `i`.

A state machine model

A *state transition machine* `stm t s` applied to a sequence of inputs:

$$c_0, c_1, \ldots$$

should compute the sequence of states:

$$s_0, s_1, \ldots$$

where $s_0 = s$ and $s_{i+1} = t\ c_i\ s_i$. This is reminiscent of the natural numbers, but with s_0 for 0 and with $t\ c_i$ for $(+1)$. Recalling the definition of the naturals:

```
nat -> 0 : map (+1) nat
```

inspires the following initial definition for stm:

```
stm t s p -> s : map2 t p (stm t s p)

map2 f (x:xs) (y:ys) -> f x y : map2 f xs ys
map2 f [] ys -> []
map2 f xs [] -> []
```

Here map2 applies a binary function to all corresponding elements in two given sequences to obtain a new sequence. Applying a similar transformational procedure to stm as was used for pie, map2 can be eliminated in favour of a maximal strict auxiliary stm2:

$$\text{stm t s p -> s : stm2 t s p} \tag{25}$$

$$\text{stm2 t s [] -> []} \tag{26}$$
$$\text{stm2 t s (c:cs) -> stm t (t c s) cs} \tag{27}$$

Here also, as for pie, the auxiliary has an invariant argument: t could be eliminated in stm2 making its definition local. For the purposes of further derivation, the above form is more convenient.

Basic pie—stm equivalence

Shifting from the pie model to the stm model can always be accomplished by making the degenerate choice of entire command histories as states. A more worthwhile choice, and the one to be explored here, makes stm states correspond exactly to pie effects. This will be possible only when the pie interpretation function i is such that we can solve the following *characteristic equation* to obtain a suitable initial state s0 and transition function t for the state machine:

$$\text{stm t s0 p = pie i p} \tag{28}$$

One way to go about solving (28) is to proceed as though trying to prove it as an equivalence. The solution is obtained from the properties of s0 and t that such a proof is found to require. Let's begin by applying the definitions of stm and pie in (28):

LHS
```
= stm t s0 p
= s0 : stm2 t s0 p
```

RHS
```
= pie i p
= i [] : pie3 i [] p
```

Equating heads yields the solution for s0, the initial state: it must be i [], the effect obtained by interpreting an empty command sequence. Equating tails yields a new equation for t:

$$s0 = i \; [] \tag{29}$$

$$stm2 \; t \; (i \; []) \; p = pie3 \; i \; [] \; p \tag{30}$$

Consider a proof of (30) by induction over p. When p=⊥ or p=[] both sides evaluate to p regardless of what t is. This leaves only the case p=(c:cs), assuming inductively that (30) holds when p=cs:

LHS
```
= stm2 t (i []) (c:cs)
= stm t (t c (i [])) cs
= t c (i []) : stm2 t (t c (i [])) cs
```

RHS
```
= pie3 i [] (c:cs)
= i [c] : pie3 i [c] cs
```

Equating heads and tails as before:

$$t \; c \; (i \; []) = i \; [c] \tag{31}$$

$$stm2 \; t \; (t \; c \; (i \; [])) \; cs = pie3 \; i \; [c] \; cs \tag{32}$$

Once again, progress is blocked for want of generality. In (31), t is defined, but only for the case where the state argument is initial. In (32), the inductive hypothesis cannot be applied in the *LHS* because the state is not initial, and it cannot be applied in the *RHS* because the command history is not empty.

Generalised pie—stm *equivalence*

We need to formulate a more general equivalence than (28) between pie and stm. Imagine a change-over from pie to stm in *mid computation*, with the latest pie effect being inherited as the stm state, no difference should be observed in comparison with continued operation of pie. The following equation formalises this stronger idea of equivalence:

$$\begin{aligned} \texttt{body (pie i p) :: stm t (foot (pie i p)) p' =} \qquad (33) \\ \texttt{pie i (p :: p')} \end{aligned}$$

Putting p=[] and simplifying, we can see that (28) is a special case of (33):

```
LHS
= body (pie i []) :: stm t (foot (pie i [])) p'
= body [i []] :: stm t (foot [i []]) p'
= [] :: stm t (i []) p'
= stm t (i []) p'
```

```
RHS
= pie i ([] :: p')
= pie i p'
```

So let's analyse the more general equivalence (33), considering the different cases for p':

Case p' = []

```
LHS
= body (pie i p) :: stm t (foot (pie i p)) []
= body (pie i p) :: [foot (pie i p)]
```

```
RHS
= pie i (p :: [])
= pie i p
```

The equivalence concluded in this case is an instance of law *B1*. It would be true for any finite list, not just pie i p. It therefore says nothing about i, and nothing about t:

Case p' = ⊥

LHS
```
= body (pie i p) :: stm t (foot (pie i p)) ⊥
= body (pie i p) :: (foot (pie i p) : ⊥ )
= body (pie i p) :: [foot (pie i p)] :: ⊥
= pie i p :: ⊥
```

RHS
```
= pie i (p :: ⊥ )
```

Note that the final forms of *LHS* and *RHS* here are not *identical*, but they are *equivalent*, as recorded in law *P2*. So consideration of the base cases in a proof of (33) has not revealed anything to prevent, or even restrict, the formulation of a pie-equivalent application of stm. But we have yet to derive anything about the state transition function t. Let's now proceed to the inductive case:

Case p' = (c:cs)

LHS
```
= body (pie i p) :: stm t (foot (pie i p)) (c:cs)
= body (pie i p) :: [foot (pie i p)] ::
  stm t (t c (foot (pie i p))) cs
= pie i p :: stm t (t c (foot (pie i p))) t cs
```

RHS
```
= pie i (p :: c:cs)
= pie i (p :: [c] :: cs)
```
which by inductive hypothesis
```
= body (pie i (p :: [c])) ::
  stm t (foot (pie i (p :: [c]))) cs
= pie i p :: stm t (foot (pie i (p :: [c]))) cs
```

Hence, we obtain the following equation:

$$\text{stm t (t c (foot (pie i p))) cs} = \tag{34}$$
$$\text{stm t (foot (pie i (p :: [c]))) cs}$$

Equating the second argument of stm in the *LHS* with that in the *RHS* would plainly be *sufficient* to ensure that (34) holds since given equal arguments stm must yield equal results. It is also *necessary*, as may be seen by putting cs = r []. So we may legitimately simplify (34) to the following equation:

$$t \ c \ (\texttt{foot} \ (\texttt{pie} \ i \ p)) = \texttt{foot} \ (\texttt{pie} \ i \ (p \ :: \ [c])) \qquad (35)$$

We now appeal to laws *P1*, *R1* and *R2*.

> *LHS*
> = t c (foot (pie i p))
> = t c (i (reverse p))
>
>
> *RHS*
> = foot (pie i (p :: [c]))
> = i (reverse (p :: [c]))
> = i (c : reverse p)

Hence we obtain, in addition to the earlier rule:

$$s0 = i \ [] \qquad\qquad\qquad (29)$$

which defines the initial state, a simple rule stating the requirements for the state machine transition function t in terms of the interpretation function i:

$$t \ c \ (i \ p) = i \ (c \ : \ p) \qquad\qquad (36)$$

Rules (29) and (36) together constitute a prefabricated transformation scheme for shifting from one model to the other.

Examples revisited

To illustrate the use of rules (29) and (36) to derive state machines, let's return to the ghosts and wordcount examples for which we have already seen pie-based definitions in (12) and (13):

> ghostspie
> = pie i
>   *where* i = id
> = stm t s0
>   *where* t c (id p) = id (c : p)
>   *and* s0 = id []
> = stm t []
>   *where* t c p = c : p
> = stm (:) []

```
wordcountpie
= pie i
  where i = map wordsin
= stm t s0
  where t c (map wordsin p) = map wordsin (c : p)
  and s0 = map wordsin []
= stm t []
  where t c (map wordsin p) =
  wordsin c : map wordsin p
generalising to
  stm t []
  where t c ws = wordsin c : ws
= stm ((:) o wordsin) []
```

7.5.3   *Application-specific transformation*

Once the interpretation function i is known, changing the model to something like a state machine is only one possibility. It is also possible to transform away the higher order functions of the general purpose model altogether. An independent and specialised version of the model (call it ipie) can be derived. This has the property that:

```
ipie p = pie i p
```

for all command sequences p. Transforming a general function to a more specialised one, because some but not all arguments are known at *transformation time*, is called *partial evaluation* [171]. The specialised function can be more efficient than the general purpose function from which it is derived because some (and possibly much) of the computational work has been done during the transformation process. Partial evaluation is not to be confused with *partial application*, which is the *run time* application of a function to less than its full quota of arguments.

Partial evaluation of wordcount

For example, the stm model could be specialised for wordcount by partial evaluation starting from the following specification:

```
wcstm p -> stm ((:) o wordsin) [] p
```

Since this transformation involves much the same techniques as have
been illustrated in preceding sections, details are omitted. The end
result could be the following definition of the specialised state machine:

```
wcstm p -> wcstm3 [] p

wcstm3 s p -> s : wcstm4 s p

wcstm4 s [] -> []
wcstm4 s (c:cs) -> wcstm3 (wordsin c : s) cs
```

Referring back to the original presentation of wordcount, the wcstm
function must itself be supplied as an argument to the higher order
function red handling result and display:

```
wordcount -> red wcstm head sum

red pie d r -> pair (map d) (r o foot) o pie
```

We might therefore consider symbolic (partial) evaluation of the red
function also—an exercise left for the reader. And, hence, the transformational refinement can continue, just as far as we please.

7.6   Summary and conclusion

In this chapter I have sought to demonstrate two things. First, an abstract model of interaction, such as the *PiE*, can be expressed quite directly as a higher order function in a functional programming language
with non-strict semantics. Particular applications correspond to particular arguments to which these higher order functions can be applied.
Enrichments of the model do not require the original programmed form
to be redefined; rather they can be expressed as higher order functions
to which the original simple model is passed as argument. Secondly,
some transformational refinements of the programmed models, to make
them more efficient and hence more useful as prototypes, can be prefabricated. This prefabrication is worthwhile precisely because all the
programs to be refined share a common model. The effort required
to apply such a prefabricated transformation is far less than the effort
required for transformation from scratch.

Appendix: laws used in transformations

A1   `x :: [] = x`
A2   `(x :: y) :: z = x :: (y :: z)`

B1   `body x :: [foot x] = x` for finite x

M1   `map f (map g x) = map (f o g) x`

P1   `foot (pie i p) = i (reverse p)` for finite p
P2   `pie i p :: ⊥ = pie i (p :: ⊥)`

R1   `reverse (reverse x) = x` for finite x
R2   `reverse (x :: [a]) = a : reverse x` for finite x

CHAPTER EIGHT

DESIGNING ABSTRACTIONS FOR COMMUNICATION CONTROL

GILBERT COCKTON

8.1 The need for specialised software tools.

Programming is a difficult task. It involves the transformation of design representations into the constructs of a programming language. This transformation bridges a gap between human ways of representing designs on the one hand, and computer representations of executable programs on the other.

Formal methods addresses this transformation in a number of ways. On the one hand, the gap between design and implementation is narrowed, whilst on the other, the transformation process is given a rigorous structure. Narrowing the gap takes the form of changing either the designer's, or the computer's, representations. In the former case, formal specification techniques try to encourage designers to settle on a formal representation of a design at an early stage. In the latter case, more mathematical constructs, such as functions and higher-order operations on functions, replace the machine constructs of assignment, branching, iteration and procedure calls. This brings the computer representation closer to formal design representations.

Ideally, narrowing the gap and providing a rigorous method for its traversal should go hand in hand, but the two tactics are separable in practice.

The mathematical focus of mainstream formal methods at once subscribes to generality and uniqueness. The mathematical forms proposed for specification and programming are intended to be general, and suitable for any part of any computer application. At the same time, the combination and instantiation of forms to produce a specification or implementation tends to be regarded as an isolated event. Typically, little attention is paid to those specialised, composite and synthesised forms which are designed for only certain components of specific types of computer applications.

User interfaces are such components, and interactive systems are such applications. There are design traditions in these areas which will favour one higher level form over another. If the structures used for specification and implementation are specialised to support user interfaces, then the gap between design and implementation has been further narrowed by this specialisation of formal abstractions.

Just as general forms such as functions and operations on them can be encapsulated in a formal specification technique or a functional programming language, so can specific forms be packaged in paper or code based tools. Since William Newman's Reaction Handler [136] and David Parnas' informal use of network specifications [145] there has been a tradition in interactive systems research and development of developing specialised abstractions for user interface design.

The most potentially usable code based abstractions occur in *software tools*. These tools bring the computer closer to the designer by providing an interface to specialised abstractions. This interface is generally a textual notation, although recent tools use a combination of text and graphics for design configuration [105, 65]. Early software tools were text-processing languages [24], compiler-compilers [108] and data base management systems [51]. These tools used abstractions such as regular expressions, attribute grammars and relations, and provided designers with a notation for configuring designs structured by these abstractions.

Software tools provide both higher level abstractions and a notation which gives a direct interface to these abstractions. This approach should be contrasted with the subroutine, module or procedure library, and its object-oriented replacement, the class hierarchy [47]. This approach does allow classes or modules to encapsulate abstractions, but provides no isomorphic interface to these abstractions. The result is that designers and programmers must configure high level abstractions *via* the low level interface of procedure calls or message passing. One notation is used for every abstraction, and usually a distracting, fiddly imperative programming notation at that. The structure of any underlying abstraction can quickly be lost in the code of the program.

8.2   Architecture and abstraction

Good abstractions and notations simplify the programming task. Software architectures can provide further simplifications.

A software architecture provides a set of components and a way of joining these components together. Software architectures provide a generic decomposition for classes of applications. A well known architecture is the compiler, providing a lexical analysis component, a parsing component and a code-generating component. This last component may be divided into machine-independent and machine-dependent subcomponents. These subcomponents may further sub-divide, allowing different optimisers to be placed within each. Components can be linked in a pipeline, so interconnection is simple—components are designed to work with the output of others, so lexical analysers pass tokens to parsers, which pass parse-trees to code-generators.

The architecture for compilers simplifies implementation by providing a re-usable decomposition of the design task. For compilers, design can be seen as the separate design of lexical analysers, parsers and code-generators. Data bases are another example, where logical data models can be designed separately from physical ones. In both compilers and data bases specialised abstractions structure the configuration of individual components.

The design of software tools for User Interface Management Systems (abbreviated UIMS [153, 142]) should also begin with the derivation of a software architecture. This architecture will be a set of components and the means of integrating them into a functioning whole.

Appearance, behaviour, interpretations and functionality can be argued to be the necessary components of an interactive system. First, input and output objects must be represented in some medium to the user, giving rise to the appearance or *media* component. Secondly, temporal relationships between user and system events must be defined, giving rise to the behavioural or *session* component. Thirdly, many user actions must be interpreted as requests for functionality, and the outcomes of the functionality of the system must be interpreted as requiring representation to the user; this gives rise to the interpretative or *linkage* component. Finally, an interactive system must do something, and something is required to do this; this gives rise to the functionality or *application* component.

There is nothing more to an interactive system than its appearance, behaviour, interpretations and functionality, just as there is nothing more to a compiler than lexical analysis, parsing and code-generation! The argument is that anything which an interactive system does, can be decomposed into these four aspects, at most. All other decompositions, say into error handling, help, semantic feedback or support, widgets, interaction techniques, undoing, history mechanisms or dialogue styles, can either be further decomposed into or are already subcomponents.

A software architecture for interactive systems will thus have four components.

The **media component** covers all appearance, regardless of the medium involved, for both output and input (controls). As controls are commonly simulated in a computer medium (e.g., physical sliders simulated as mouse-controlled display objects), these too are configured as media, so physical input devices such as joysticks and keyboards might just as well be considered as instances of a medium, just as are physical output devices. The media component only determines the presentation of controls and displays at a *specific moment in time*. Input device simulation apart, the media component only changes its configuration in response to events created at session level.

The *session component* covers all behaviour, except the context-free behaviour of (simulated) input devices. Behaviour is to be understood as all the (temporal) connections between media and linkage events, as well as the manipulation of an independent session state. Thus an input media event can give rise to output media events (feedback) and linkage events (interpretation as request for functionality). This behaviour is defined, once and for all in the design, but the actual behaviour will vary from one interactive *session* to the next, hence the naming of this

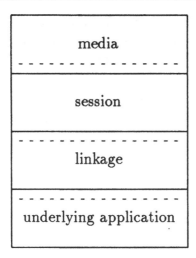

Figure 8.1: An architecture for interactive systems

component. The session component determines the possible variations
between sessions.

The **linkage component** interprets activity at the session level and
in the underlying application. It is a translation component which
maximises separability in interactive systems. It does this by acting as
an enhancer for user requests and application responses. Enhancement
takes the form of adding information which would reduce separability
were it included in the specification of the user interface (media and
session) or in the underlying application. The linkage works out the
functionality required to carry out a user request (or reject this request
in a way which the user interface can handle). The linkage also anno-
tates results and other messages from the underlying application so that
the user interface can communicate the information without recourse
to further information about the underlying application. Finally, the
linkage supports semantic feedback, thus incorporating the *semantic
support component* of recent UIMSs [50].

The fourth component is the **underlying application**, which provides the functionality of an interactive system. Figure 8.1 illustrates
the architecture. Listing components does not result in a complete
architecture: ways of integrating components are required. This normally depends on the abstractions used to structure each component,
as these define the domains which can be handled by the architecture.
Thus abstractions for input and output media could define the domains
for the interface between the media and session layer. This is not the

only possibility, as it is possible for the session component to define
how the media will exchange information with it. Thus the integration
of components is not wholly determined by the domains of each component's abstraction. There is some choice as to which component will
dominate, and this is an architectural decision.

The architecture in Figure 8.1 is completed by subordinating the
session component, and allowing the underlying application to use any
abstractions as required. This is indicated by the dashed lines which
represent the interface between two components. Containment within
a component's box signifies 'ownership' of the interface by that component.

The session component is subordinated for the simple reason that
otherwise it would determine the interfaces for two components, the
media and the linkage. Finding a session level abstraction which can
act as a domain for all possible types of media and interpretation is a
challenging task which can only maximise the chance of unsatisfactory
compromises. Rather than make both media and the linkage fit into a
session view of the world, both the media and the linkage components
are free to define their own interfaces. The session level abstractions
will then be modified to use these interfaces. Furthermore, letting the
linkage fix its interface with the session level results in integration tactics which maximise the stability of the linkage under changes to the
user interface [39].

The vast range of possible functionalities means that there is no sense,
and much hazard, in forcing a common abstraction onto even the surface level of an underlying application [44]. Thus linkages must be able
to interface with whatever abstractions are best for the functionality of
an interactive system.

Thus the architecture allows the extremes of an interactive system,
the media and the underlying application, to dictate the terms of their
integration, and makes the session level subordinate to both its neigh-
bours.

8.3   Tooling the user interface

Tooling the user interface within the above architecture involves selecting abstractions, not necessarily one per level, for each of the three
generic levels (media, session and linkage). Abstractions can only be

selected rationally if the requirements for each component are clearly identified. This is where an interdisciplinary approach is essential. The *exclusive reliance* on mathematical reasoning in some formal methods work is utterly unacceptable in an HCI context. Requirements for each component are derived from knowledge of user interface design and knowledge of how people use computers.

Once a suitable abstraction has been identified *via* proof of properties, further issues which are not mathematical still remain, such as the design and evaluation of the notation which will be used to configure designs. Efficient computer handling of the notation and the abstraction also require careful attention in order to produce viable software tools.

8.3.1   *Communication control*

This chapter focuses on a specific function of the session level: the control of the activities through which user-system communication is effected. This can be regarded as an event structure, where events are related to each other in time, or possibly in separate processes.

The actual *content* of an event can be kept separate from the *structure* which relates events together. These structures are instances of *communication control abstractions*. The content of an event, and its recognition, is handled by a family of abstractions which are called *Session Support Objects*, **SSOs**, abstractions which provide operations for event classification and generation. Events can have quite complex internal structures (e.g., display updates, results from underlying application), so SSOs may require arbitrary computation in order to generate or spot events.

Other functions include session monitoring and session recording, both of which can add considerably to the supportiveness of a user interface. The distinction between communication control and session support is similar to that achieved by *eventCSP* and *eventISL* in *SPI* [3], see also Chapter 9. The crucial difference is that *eventISL* handles all media and linkage management, and thus fails to differentiate between radically different components of a user interface. Without a proper architectural distinction, the focussed selection or creation of appropriate abstractions is unlikely.

8.4   Requirements for communication control

Communication control has been isolated as a function of the session
level, indeed, as the function that gives the session level its session feel.
It has been defined as involving event sequences and parallel sequential
activities. This may seem reasonable, and should be so to thoughtful
interactive systems designers, yet the definition of communication control, and the need for it are not some part of nature, to be accepted
uncritically.

The concept of communication control must be sufficiently well motivated for any potential user of an interactive system to understand
what it should involve and why it is important. It should also be clear
enough for technophile followers of fashions such as modelessness to understand why the latest universal design solutions are narrow-minded
and inadequate! As communication control is being treated as a key
function of a universal component of interactive systems, a convincing
argument for its necessity and function must be expected. Such an
argument must address the ways in which people interact with computers.

8.4.1   *User requirements for communication control*

A user commences interaction at some terminal or workstation. Before
the user lifts a finger, or mouths a word, we can ask:

1. Is the user experienced in the use of computers?

2. Is the user experienced in the task domain of the application?

3. How regularly does/will the user use the application?

4. How long has the user been using the application?

If the answer to the first two questions is "no", then a supportive user
interface is required. The user is unlikely to understand the controls,
all the displayed information or the significance of all the activity. The
common solution to the support problem is a sequence of orientations,
making clear the purpose of questions, the possible answers and the
significance of questions and answers. The most common example is the
automatic cash dispenser. For this type of task, sequential interaction
is often the best design solution.

If the first two questions were answered in the negative, then the chances are that the answer to the fourth question will be something like "not long". However, the user may be expected to become a regular user (third question), which means that in time the answers to the first two questions will change. The user will develop some understanding of both computers and the application tasks. Rigid supportive interaction will begin to feel inflexible and over-constrained. The user will begin to want to skip steps, combine steps or change the order of steps. The user will have grown from a passive novice to an active problem solving learner.

Users will not become experts immediately, and they will have to pass through a phase of conscious problem solving before parts of their interaction settle down into automatic, unconscious, skilled behaviour. The need at this point is for good signposting in the interaction, that is some means of *suggesting* the next possible steps in an interaction, rather than *enforcing* them. The interaction may still be sequential, but modeless direct manipulation can be just as supportive for this stage of user growth. Prompting signposts are replaced by timely feedback which allows users to evaluate their problem solving and backtrack to try another plan if necessary.

Many users may *never* leave this problem solving phase, as interaction may offer sufficient cues, feedback or user-requested help to reduce the user's need to progress to fully accurate and optimal skilled interaction [62, 121]. Thus even when the answer to the fourth question is "years" and the answer to the third is "every day", users may not fit the stereotype of the infallible omnicompetent expert. Often the realisation of this fact is masked behind designers' and system commissioners' complaints that most users are only using a fraction of a system's capabilities. Users may even be blamed for their lazy under use of such expensive, and painstakingly designed, technology. However, it could be the designers and commissioners who are to blame for developing a system for a stereotypical user, who may not exist.

Expert behaviour does develop but it involves far more than experience [163]. Computer experts are invariably computing professionals or technophiles who either have come to understand the importance of reading the documentation and exploring the system, or may just find this learning experience an intrinsically satisfying conquest. The need here is flexibility, just as is required when the answer to the second question is "yes." If users are already skilled in the task domain, this means (by the definition of skill), that they will be coming to the system with preset ways of achieving task goals. They will know (or more likely, be able to demonstrate) how to get from wherever they are to where they want to be. The chances are that no technical specialist will be able to capture an adequate description of all the practices of a system's intended users. Another fact about expertise is that skilled performance varies from one individual to another. One expert's way of doing something may be no more acceptable to another expert than a designer's way.

The above account is a simple view of how psychological phenomena like learning, problem solving, planning and skill interact. However, this does not reveal all the relevant issues, since computer technology constrains the problem solving tactics and skills which may be developed.

If all interaction is constrained to a single process, however flexible or modeless, then capabilities for parallel planning are not going to be seen. Where interleaving of interaction is allowed, parallel *activity structures* [17] emerge. Outside human-computer interaction, there is evidence of people solving problems by advancing several subplans in parallel [213]. There are also obvious examples of parallel interaction with physical controls, such as driving a car, or playing a musical instrument. Despite this human capability for interleaved activity from motor skills up to problem-solving, few interactive systems allow users to exploit these capabilities [132]. To the requirements for sequence, flexibility, signposting and safe, profitable exploration, we must add the need for interleaved activities. Note that the level of interleaving is significant. Actually, all degrees of interleaving are covered, from the complete intromission of single step tasks (e.g., panning, zooming, changing drawing or paint tools, seeking help) to comprehensive cycling through a number of uncompleted interactions (e.g., window-based workstation, group and co-operative work).

8.4.2   *Designer requirements for communication control*

All the requirements identified above arise because of human behaviour. They address what users need, but it is designers who must be able to meet these needs. No abstraction for communication control should get in the way of the designer's obligation to produce usable systems, at least not without an explicit and intentional recognition that constraints are imposed. It may well be that what is constrained is not needed for a specific design, thus making a restrictive abstraction more suitable than a more general one.

Good control abstractions are ones which let designers design well and meet user requirements—these are not the only requirements however. The designer's requirements must be met. Most important is the design notation, which can use media other than text. (Many algebras are amenable to graphical representation, allowing designs to be configured by a direct manipulation user interface.) The designer is also helped considerably if manual transformation of a specification into an implementation is unnecessary. The notation or configuration must be supported by a software tool which can transform the notation into some executable form. The need for executable specifications places further constraints on abstractions. They must be efficiently executable, so notations which require use slow algorithms (e.g., Shaw [172]) are unsuitable.

The quality of a notation and the possibility of efficient implementation are thus important *designer* rather than *user* centred requirements for communication control. Other designers' requirements are related to these dimensions of software tooling. An important influence on the usability of a notation is straightforward modularisation, with parameterisation of modules.

Parameterised modules are an essential element of system software construction, whether or not they are gathered around a data object in the object-oriented style. Indeed, they are such an obvious requirement to most software professionals that their mention here may seem unnecessary. Unfortunately, many UIMSs use control abstractions which may not be modular nor parameterised [38]. This brings out the observation that the synthesis of requirements for software tools is not an analytic, *a priori* exercise, but an ongoing process.

Once a notation is supported by computer-based tools, automatic analysis becomes possible. Programming language compilers have long checked code for certain problems. Similar checking is also possible for notations, creating the opportunity for machine checking of computable properties for user interfaces.

Finally, the execution of notations should bring no surprises. Designers should be able to know in principle what their configurations will do. The meaning of a notation should be clear and unambiguous. Neither complexity nor the resolution of anomalies should require designers to run a design in order to find out whether what they have specified is what they want.

To summarise, designers need good, effective and efficient notations. Part of this effectiveness derives from modularisation facilities. Good notations need to be supported by good software tools. The quality of such software tools is partly determined by the efficiency of the execution of specifications, the extent of useful and valid automated metrics, and the lack of surprises in the behaviour of a specification.

8.4.3   *Satisfying requirements*

In formal methods, satisfaction of requirements is taken to mean proved properties. Requirements are to be cast as predicates which a specification can be proved to satisfy. Thus for a communication control abstraction to satisfy the above requirements, it must be possible to state the requirements as predicates and then prove that the abstraction satisfies them.

All user requirements are easily expressed as very simple predicates *once they are argued to be equivalent to certain mathematical constructs*.

Satisfaction of properties is not enough: *how* properties are satisfied is also very important. For example, parallel activities at every level of action from motor control to creative exploration can be argued to be equivalent to a need for processes, or at least interleaving or permutation of event sequences. But an *ability* to permute events or to group them into processes is not the only concern. The *complexity* of satisfaction is just as important. Most notations for context-free grammars make permutation difficult to express, but extending context-free grammars to handle permuted right hand sides of rules is straightforward, so a permutation construct (similar to the familiar alternation construct) is a simple addition. Showing that permutation is hard in Backus-Naur form is irrelevant if a simple extension to the notation can produce acceptable analytical or experimental results.

Learning, skill and user growth underpin many of the user requirements for communication control. Supporting growth at all levels requires smooth transitions from one user interface to another [14]. Adapting user interfaces to different users' skilled behaviour requires flexibility in the communication control abstraction. Of these two requirements, flexibility is easier to satisfy than smooth transitions, since flexibility is easy to formalise, but the 'smoothness' of a skill transition is not.

Flexibility can only be satisfied by the most general communication control abstractions. It is not a basic requirement, but a second order one which is satisfied when *all* the basic requirements are. An abstraction which is restricted, in that it does not satisfy some properties, cannot be configured to produce a design which requires these properties. Thus simple transition networks are not flexible enough to support designs which require any interleaving property which can only be satisfied by production rules which can fire 'simultaneously'. If total flexibility is the dominant user requirement, only general and unrestrictive control abstractions can be used. There are also some technical issues concerning the timing and the agent of adaptation [40].

Flexibility is a property which designers can exploit to provide user interfaces which are either tailored to different skilled behaviours, or designed for different stages of user growth [144]. However, a single user's knowledge and skills at a particular moment are not fully addressed. This problem-solving aspect of human-computer interaction also needs to be supported by the communication control abstraction.

Requirements for active and successful problem solving involve techniques such as signposting, direct manipulation and explorability. In all cases, the designer has to imagine what users may wish to do *at some points* in the interaction. The focus is very local, either in time, or in both time and space for direct manipulation interfaces. Ideally, designers are trying to make safe exploration easy for the user, so the requirement for the control abstraction is to make it easy for the designer to make this easy for the user. Many interactive designers feel that a *point construct* is a vital aid to this design activity [115]. This consensus holds for direct manipulation, where some might think that the spatial focus of a display object is enough. However, there is considerable moded behaviour *within* an object; many tools recognise this and allow transition networks to be associated with display objects [107, 46, 65]. This is a specific solution.

The general requirement here is for *named points* in the interaction. The designer can step out from such a point and think through possible scenarios. Formally, the need is for a set of named points as an element in the abstraction's definition *which is distinct from the events element(s) in the abstraction.* Additionally, there must be mappings between named points and events which map to the events immediately before and after a named point. Such mappings give some indication of the constraints in an interactive session, since one or a few events before and after each point suggests a very constrained, system-driven application, whereas large sets of immediate successor and predecessor events suggest a modeless, user-driven application.

The need for named points appears controversial. For readers who are sceptical: both survey and experience suggest that the branching points of syntax diagrams [104] and the nodes of recursive transition networks [79] substantially improve the designer's ability to step through a design. The argument is thus not mathematical, but psychological. The world of axioms, theories and theorems may not need this paraphernalia, but the world of human designers does.

Requirements for parameterised modularity and 'no surprise' implementations are easily formalised but not without some controversy. The semantics of parameterisation have long been studied in programming language research; as for no surprise implementation, the requirement becomes one of giving appropriate denotations for the syntax of the notation. Accidents have happened, notably in the concrete syntax for subnetwork traversal in the RAPID user interface management system: preventing the same subnetwork being called more than once by some other network [36].

Other designer requirements can be formalised so that analytic proof of properties is possible. Efficiency, for example, is a major concern in computer science. Time and space complexity can be analysed. However, there are also empirical techniques which are usually essential for realistic estimates of actual performance.

Automated analysis is always possible. Mathematicians have never been long in following up a new structure with further properties, subsets and partitions. Many such properties are important to the integrity of a design configuration. They can be used to trap *specification* errors, but not design errors where human factors are concerned. Transition networks can be checked for graph properties [5]. Grammars, indeed, have no end of properties [2]. However, the properties and metrics reported by automated analysis have to be meaningful. Thus few obvious grammar metrics relate to user performance [148, 157]. The issue is that of so-called *construct validity* in psychometrics. It is one thing to measure something, but the real problem is deciding upon the legimate interpretation of the measurement, especially with regard to how it relates to the problem at hand. It should be clear that automated analysis of user interface designs is not a mathematical problem, but a psychological problem involving mathematics. See Kirakowski and Corbett [114] for an example of relating affective measures to performance measures in HCI. Similar relationships must be shown for formal metrics.

8.5   A new communication control abstraction

At this point, the argument is suspended to describe a new communication control abstraction, the *Generative Transition Network*. Its structure is very similar to that of an Augmented Transition Network [210]. It is called a *generative* network because it *generates* arcs which designers would otherwise have to *enumerate*. This generation is achieved by new constructs for arc definition.

8.5.1   *Generative transition networks: fundamentals*
The key contribution of *Generative Transition Networks* (GTNs) is to simplify the specification of responses to globally enabled events within a sequential network formalism. Without GTNs, the designer is forced to choose between abstractions which are good at sequence, but not interleaving, or vice-versa. With GTNs, designers can have both. This is because GTNs encapsulate regularity rather than enumerate it. The generative property of a GTN is reflected in descriptions which *generate* arcs rather than describe each of them individually.

GTNs are equivalent in power to Augmented Transition Networks (ATNs), but superior in their economy. They are actually extensions of *Dialogue ATNs* (DATNs [36]) and will be described first.

DATNs are parametrised ATNs for recursively traversable (sub) networks. A number of scoping strategies are possible for local and global variables. As network traversal can be regarded as procedure execution with input/output and other side effects, networks call other networks as part of a transition action and thus the initiation of DATN subnet traversal is restricted to arc actions. The registers of ATNs are generalised to a set of **SSO**s (session support objects; see §8.3.1) which may be media-independent (e.g., intelligent help object) or media-dependent (e.g., graphical display computation). It is the SSOs which access media and the linkage for the communication controller. This provides a useful logical separation of control from object manipulation.

Formally, a DATN is a 7-tuple $\langle l, n_0, N, F, A, p, v \rangle$. Where:

l is the name (label) of the network;

$n_0 \in N$ is the start node of the network;

N is the set of nodes for the network;

$F \subseteq N$ is the set of terminating nodes for the network;

$A \subseteq seq(\langle N \times N \times E \times seq(R) \rangle$ is the arc list for the network;

p is a vector of session object names used to parameterise the DATN;

v is the vector of names of returned session object values.

$seq(\langle N \times N \times E \times seq(R) \rangle)$ is a list of tuples, each with elements of type N, N, E and $seq(R)$. E and R are the domains of events and responses, they are propositions and procedures defined outside the DATN as operations on SSOs, media managers and linkage. p is a vector of SSO names; the named SSOs will be set to values from a parameter vector passed to the DATN traversal function. SSOs named in v are returned together as the value of a DATN on termination. (The initialisation element of [41] has been dropped.) SSOs should now be initialised with a procedure after the start node. The issue of SSOs local to networks and scoping issues have not been addressed. One network based UIMS which does have a scoping mechanism is RAPID [205].

An arc or edge is a 4-tuple $\langle i, o, e, r \rangle$ where:

$i \in N$ is the start of the arc (its initial endpoint);

$o \in N$ is the end of the arc (its terminal endpoint);

$e \in E$ is the transition condition of the arc. It is typically the name of
       a proposition;

$r \in seq(R)$ is the transition actions of the arc. It is a sequence of
       procedure names.

DATNs implement user interfaces *via* arc conditions and actions, which are defined separately as operations on SSOs.[1] A DATN traverser begins at node n_0 with SSOs set from p. It looks for an arc $\langle n_0, o, e, r \rangle$ in A where e is true. When it finds this arc, the procedures named in r are executed and the traverser moves to a new node o. If o is not in F, the traverser looks for a new arc $\langle o, o', e', r' \rangle$ in A and the process continues until a node in F is reached. The values in v are then returned as the value of the traversed network. Traversers thus operate like procedures which return values, but they search their arcs (clauses) in a fixed order; A is thus a list.

The problem with DATNs is that they can only respond to events matched on arcs from the current node. Globally active options must be specified using event matching propositions *at every node*. This is tedious. Generative Transition Networks avoid this verbosity.

Formally, a **GTN** is an 8-tuple $\langle l, n_0, N, F, G, p, v, t \rangle$ where $l, n_0,$ $N, F, p,$ and v are as for DATNs. The differences are that G replaces A, and t is new. The types of these new elements are:

$G \subseteq seq(\langle \mathcal{P}(N) \times seq(N) \mapsto N \times E \times R \rangle)$ is the list of *arc generators*.

$\quad \mathcal{P}(N) = \{S \mid S \subseteq N\}$ is the *power set* of N.

$t \in seq(N)$ is the GTN traverser's node trace.

A **GTN arc generator** is a 4-tuple $\langle S, f, e, r \rangle$ where:

$S \subseteq \mathcal{P}(N)$ is the set of the starts of the generated arcs (their initial endpoints);

$f \in seq(N) \mapsto N$ computes the ends of the generated arcs (their terminal endpoints);

$e \in E$ and $r \in R$ are as for DATN arcs.

A GTN traverser behaves almost like a DATN interpreter. One difference is its *node trace* which is maintained during network traversal. The other is its behaviour when looking for arcs with true propositions.

---

[1] This is the main difference between the 1985 DATNs and the DATNs described here on which GTNs are based. Conditions in the 1985 DATNs, and early GTNs [42], were restricted sentences of first order logic. Actions were blocks of operations on abstract data types. This detail is hidden behind the proposition and procedure name interface. This results in more readable specifications [41].

The node trace is a list of all the nodes which the traverser has visited in the course of the current interaction. The GTN traverser maintains this list, rather like a pushdown automata's traverser maintains the pushdown stack. The current interaction starts when the network is called (to start a session, or by another network) and ends when the network reaches a terminal state.

The trace type has two simple constructors: newTrace :: $seq(N)$ and addToTrace :: $N \times seq(N) \mapsto seq(N)$. The initial value of the trace at the start of the traversal is newTrace; addToTrace is applied to the current trace on each transition. The transition function returns both a new node and a new trace. The node added to the trace is computed when an arc with a true proposition is found.

An arc with a true proposition is found by looking for an arc generator $\langle S, f, e, r \rangle$ such that the current node is a member of S and e is true. The procedures named in r are then called. Finally, the next node is computed by applying f to the node trace t. f is usually one of the following operations on traces:

bar: an application of the function
  bar :: $\alpha \times \beta \mapsto \alpha$ to a node $n \in N$, $\text{bar}(a, b) \equiv a$.

same: an observer on traces,
  $\text{same}(\text{addToTrace}(n, t)) \equiv n$.

back: another observer,
  $\text{back}(\text{addToTrace}(n, \text{addToTrace}(p, t))) \equiv p$.

The use of a partially applied bar function is equivalent to the static specification of terminal endpoints in ATNs (and less powerful networks). It supports transitions which effectively ignore the current trace, since they are completely determined at specification. same supports arcs which loop at nodes, since the computed endpoint will be the current node (the head of the trace). Such endpoints are also effectively determined at specification time. back is the first real computed endpoint, since the value of the endpoint is completely determined during the session by the current trace.

Most GTN specifications only use bar, same and back operations, and even back is very rare. Most of the economy and effectiveness is due to the combination of these few endpoint operations with subsets of initial endpoints.

GTN arc generators have set and function endpoints, whereas DATN arcs have node endpoints. Simple alteration of two elements in arc definition vectors $(\langle i, o, e, r\rangle \mapsto \langle S, f, e, r\rangle)$, allows economical expression of multi-threaded dialogues without losing the sequential and mode capabilities of transition networks. The simplest arc generators, with $S = N$ as the initial endpoints (so the *starts* are the set of all the networks nodes) and *same* as the terminal endpoint function, are really production rules which are activated at each node. They bring production system capabilities to a network formalism.

The development of GTNs was inspired by Zisman's demonstration of the equivalence between labelled production systems and ATNs ([214] pp49ff), and by Jacob's use of lists of initial nodes and the **SAME** end node in his network-based specification technique ([105], p.232). Knowledge of the equivalence of ATNs and labelled production systems inspired the idea of extending Jacob's syntactic shortcuts into a generalised automaton.

8.5.2   *A notation for GTNs*

The design of notations requires as much testing as the design of good interactive user interfaces. This research has now reached the stage where designing alternative notations for testing is possible. A visual representation is essential. Concepts developed in Harel's *Statecharts* [82] may be transferable to representations of GTNs. The use of Venn diagrams to surround state subsets in Statecharts transfers easily to the subset initial endpoints of GTN arc generators. However, the visual representation of GTNs is still under study.

A GTN has a name, formal parameters, a return vector, an initial node and final nodes. These are declared:

```
GTN: aName(param₁, ...,paramₙ) @ start
-> <return₁, ..., returnₙ> @ { end₁, ..., endₙ}
```

Here aName is the name of the GTN. The formal parameters follow in parentheses, with the initial name **start** declared after the @ symbol. The return vector is declared after the right arrow, within angle brackets, with the set of final nodes $\{end_1, \ldots, end_N\}$ after another @ symbol. A GTN ends with the corresponding construct:

```
End GTN: aName
```

Between these constructs, the arc generators are listed thus:

```
starts:  aSentence => procedure₁;
  ⋮
procedureₙ ;
-> endpoint
```

A GTN arc generator specified with the above syntax would be read:
"At all nodes in **starts**, if the **aSentence** is true, then call **procedure**$_1$
, ... , **procedure**$_N$ and then go to the node computed by **endpoint**".
The *starts* of a generator are declared as a set expression. The notation
predefines the set of all nodes in a network as **all**. Other node subsets
are defined after the declaration of call and return parameters and start
and final nodes, using the syntax:

```
subset:  name = set expression
```

Standard set notation is used for set construction, union, difference,
intersection and complement.

Any name can be used for propositions and procedures (an empty
procedure list is written ';'). Full sentences of propositional calculus use
familiar syntax, which will be described as it appears in examples. Most
transition conditions are simple propositions, including the Boolean
constant **true**.

Node names can be used as endpoints and produce a proper end
point function.

Examples of arc generators illustrate the use of the notation. The
first example declares that at all nodes, if the **hit_help** proposition is
true, the response is the **dohelp** procedure. The traverser is to stay at
the same node:

```
all:  hit_help => dohelp;
-> same
```

The next example declares that at all nodes, if the **hit_quit** proposition is true, the response is the **traverse_safe_quit** procedure. This
procedure can be assumed to call a traverser for a different network and
then return control to the current network. The traverser is to stay at
the same node:

```
all:  hit_quit => traverse_safe_quit;
-> same
```

This next arc generator declares that for all nodes, *except* a, b and c, if the hit_quit proposition is true, the response traverse_safe_quit is true. The traverser is to stay at the same node:

```
all - {a, b, c}:  hit_quit => traverse_safe_quit;
-> same
```

The fourth example generator states that at all nodes, if the quitflag proposition is true, the traverser should go to the quit node, executing no procedures:

```
all:  quitflag => ;
-> quit
```

The sort of internal event defined for the quitflag proposition would use SSOs rather than media queries (as for user events). The traversal of some other network from within the traverse_safe_quit response would have to reset objects referenced in this test if the the attempt to quit is aborted.

The next example uses subsets, which would be declared after the GTN's interface. It states that at all nodes except any in subsets irreversibles and no_changes, if undo_event proposition is true, the response is to invoke undo_last_action. The traverser is to stay at the same node:

```
all - (irreversibles ∪ no_changes):
undo_event => undo_last_action;
-> same
```

The last example states that at layout node, if add_symbol_event is true, the response is addmode. The traverser is to go to the add_symbol node:

```
{layout}:  add_symbol_event => addmode;
-> add_symbol
```

This concludes the presentation of the notation. In the remainder of this chapter, only arc generator and subset definition syntax is required, as no families of disjoint networks are defined or initialised.

8.5.3   *Example GTN specifications*

With no usage data, the power, economy and capabilities of GTNs can be demonstrated by re-expressing three published specifications as GTNs. An example from a user interface developed by the author and others at the Scottish HCI Centre also demonstrates the economy of GTNs over DATNs.

Straightforward comparisons between communication control abstractions in UIMSs are not possible, since these abstractions are generally closely integrated with the other components of the interactive system architecture. The propositions in transition conditions reference input media managers, SSOs and the linkage. The response procedures affect all of these originators, as well as the output media managers.

The control manager can thus delegate much *via* propositions and procedures to SSOs (which in turn can delegate much to media managers and the linkage). The extent of this delegation depends on the capabilities of the SSOs which interface with the other system components. UIMSs with fixed SSOs will have to compensate for limitations by performing session support functions *via* the communication control abstraction. Synchronisation with the underlying application (*via* the linkage) is one such function. Various expressions of the third published specification demonstrate that the capabilities of other system components (or their absence) directly determine the complexity of control specifications. UIMS control abstractions can thus only be compared in the context of complete interactive system architectures. Direct comparison which ignores the embracing architecture would be misleading.

Foley and van Dam's room layout program is specified as a simple (i.e., unaugmented, not recursive) transition network [70]. There are 37 arcs in the diagram. Only 17 GTN arc generators are required, a 54% reduction. 12 of these are DATN arcs, and they can be expressed using only 9 syntactic groupings, as transitions with the same endpoints can be clustered together. The published network specification gives no details of most actions, so few can be suggested here by response names.

First, a subset of nodes is defined to simplify specification:
```
subset:  MainCmds = {add_symbol, delete_symbol, change_view}
```

The five non-DATN arc generator skeletons are:

```
MainCmds:  {new_title}:cancel => ?;
-> LastNonHelp

MainCmds:  {new_title}:done => ?;
-> LastNonHelp

MainCmds :  {place_symbol, zoom_in}:
time_out => ?;
-> same

MainCmds :  {zoom_in}:  help -> ?;
-> help_user

MainCmds :  {dohelp, new_title}:
carriage_return -> ?;
-> back
```

These 5 generators replace 25 arcs in the simple network. They encapsulate all the regularity about dones, carriage-returns, cancels, timeouts and help. A special trace function, *lastNonHelp*, is needed to backup over the help node if this was visited before a done or cancel event. The semantics of this trace function are:

```
lastNonHelp::  seq(N) -> N
lastNonHelp(addToTrace(n,r))
            = lastNonHelp(r) if n = dohelp
              n               otherwise
```

There is no way of specifying such additional functions in the notation at the moment. They are specified separately, using any convenient function notation.

An implementation of this very moded network in ERL (Event Response Language) was reported as cumbersome [90]. This is because the multi-threading economy of ERL is gained at the expense of sequence and mode economy. This trade-off does not exist for GTNs, making them a more general purpose abstraction.

For completeness, the DATN arcs required to complete the specification are:

```
{layout}: exit => ?;
-> exit_layout
```

```
{layout}:  add_symbol => ?;
-> add_symbol

{layout}:  change_view => ?;
-> change_view

{layout}:  delete_symbol => ?;
-> delete_symbol

{change_view}:  reset => ?;
-> layout

{change_view}:  zoom => ?;
-> zoom_in

{zoom_in} -> zoom_in:
    valuator => set_window_size;
    locator => set_window_position;

{add_symbol}:  symbol(i) => ?;
-> place_symbol

{place_symbol} -> place_symbol:
    place => ?;
    valuator => rotate_symbol;
    locator => place_symbol;
```

The **RAPID restaurant review user interface**[205] can be specified as 11 arc generators and 6 nodes. The RAPID specification requires 11 arc statements and 8 nodes. However, arc statements represent *all* the arcs from a node, so there are actually 18 arcs in the specification. The GTN specification reduces nodes by 25% and arcs by 39%. The arc generators are:

```
{setup}:  setup => menu_display;
-> start

{setup}:  true => no_database_error_message;
-> finish

{start}:  key_A => traverse_addnew; menu_display;
-> start
```

```
{start}:   key_M => traverse_modify; menu_display;
-> start

{start}:   key_G => traverse_giverev; menu_display;
-> start

{start}:   key_R => traverse_readrev; menu_display;
-> start

{start}:   key_L => traverse_listall; menu_display;
-> start

{start}:   key_Q => quit_message;
-> finish

{start}:   key_H => help_display;
-> help

{start}:   true => error_message;
-> error

{help,error}:  anykey => menu_display;
-> start
```

Alternative inputs are hidden in event propositions. Response procedures hide details of actions, mostly node displays in RAPID. The total
avoidance of conditional side-effects advocated elsewhere [36] is relaxed
here, although certain proofs of properties will become exceptionally
difficult because of this. Where they are used, there should be only two
(generated) arcs sharing the initial endpoint. The proposition for the
second must be the boolean constant **true**. This arc will be traversed
if the event test fails.

RAPID's idiosyncratic handling of subnetworks is responsible for
most superfluous arc statements, and has other more serious drawbacks [36]. If RAPID allowed net traversal as a transition action, and
also allowed events which tested the results of an operation (e.g., the
setup event above) then only 4 arc statements, rather than 11, would
be required. However, RAPID's use of nodes for display handling does
simplify things. Several GTN responses redisplay the menu. The simple
solution in GTNs is to introduce a new node between **setup** and **start**,

to which all command, help and error arcs connect without redisplay of the menu. An arc with `true` as its 'proposition', from the new node to `start` node, could centralise menu display management in a single response.

The ERL command interpreter example is a command interpreter which takes the command and single argument in any order [91]. Five ERL rules are required. The three equivalent GTN arc generators are:

```
all:  arg_event => set_arg;
-> same

all:  cmd_event => set_cmd;
-> same

all:  got_arg & got_cmd
=> call_linkage; unset_arg_and_cmd;
-> same
```

The `call_linkage` procedure would be defined to pass the command and argument values to a linkage and wait for the processing to complete before returning control to the GTN traverser, which would then call the `unset_cmd_and_cmd` procedure. This results in one ERL rule needing no equivalent GTN arc generator. Asynchronous communication with a linkage component [39], is also possible in responses, and would require an extra generator to respond to an end of processing event, as in the ERL specification. This illustrates how other parts of the user interface architecture can simplify control in the session level. It is not clear how much control should be delegated by the session level, as it can result in distributed control specifications, and these are harder to analyse.

The GTN specification allows the user more freedom than the ERL one, as the first input can be re-entered many times, allowing correction before processing. This is not possible in the ERL example. However, this arbitrary inconsistency between revision of the first and second inputs can be corrected by changing the third generator:

```
all:  got_arg & got_cmd & got_ok
=> call_linkage; unset_arg_and_cmd;
-> same
```

This generator requires the user to give an explicit 'ok' input (noted by the definition of **got_ok**) up to which point, both command and argument can be re-entered. There is no automatic processing on the second input. A specification closer to the ERL behaviour requires:

```
all:  not (got_arg) & arg_event => set_arg;
-> same

all:  not (got_cmd) & cmd_event => set_cmd;
-> same

all:  got_cmd & got_arg => call_linkage;
unset_arg_and_cmd;
-> same

all:  got_cmd or got_arg => repeated_input_error;
-> same
```

This specification relies on sequential testing of the four arc generators. Note though that the published ERL specification has no error rules, so this GTN specification is 'more than' equivalent with only four generators rather than five rules. However, by changing the events in which the GTN traverser is interested in, we can have complete freedom of revision until a final 'ok' event. This can be described using only *two* generators:

```
all:  ok_event_but_incomplete
=> not_all_there_message;
dequeue_ok;
-> same

all:  ok_event_and_complete => get_events;
pass_to_linkage;
-> same
```

The first generator traps early entry of 'ok' events when other inputs are missing, informs the user and removes any record of 'ok' events. The second generator uses a proposition defined as the presence of all three inputs in the queue. In response, a procedure removes events from the queue and calls the linkage with the values of the last command and argument events. These operations show how sophistication

in other components of an architecture reduces the control specification. The ability to search input media event queues and to dequeue
arbitrary events transforms the control specification. The generalisation of event *queues* to event *lists* will reduce event management in the
propositions and procedures at session level, and result in less complex
control specifications.

Finally, control of closure could be left to the linkage, with a single
generator passing values from a command, argument and 'ok' events
straight to it. However, other generators would be required to respond
to the different error tokens which the linkage could pass back. The
point is that there is a considerable interaction between a control abstraction, input management abstractions and the linkage abstraction.
Thus crude comparisons of specification size may be misleading. The
SSO types used to define events and responses can greatly reduce the
size of the control specification. Despite these object-type sleights of
hand in this section, GTNs are at least as economical as ERL for multi-
threaded dialogues, and considerably more economical for sequential
and moded ones.

Reduction in menu hierarchy specification. At the Scottish
HCI Centre, the author was involved in the design and prototyping of
a report processing system which used a hierarchical menu structure.
In the most complex case, there were five levels, with two types of
objects at the lower two levels. These levels are named **level1** etc. in
the examples. This created seven nodes in a DATN. Each odd level
node's menu allowed a retreat to the higher levels. Even level node
menus were selections from dynamic lists, and retreat from here was
handled differently. The ten resulting arcs, plus one from a higher level
to a lower one, can be represented by three GTN arc generators:

```
{level3,level5a,level5b}:  level1 =>
to_level_1; -> level1

all - {level2,level4a,level4b}:  level2 =>
to_level_2; -> level2

all - {level1,level2,level3}:  level3 =>
to_level_3; -> level3
```

A single arc generator can describe retreat from even level nodes:

```
{level2,level4a,level4b}:  escape => to_level_3;
-> back
```

Three arcs can be abbreviated as they share the same conditions and actions:

```
{level2}  -> level3
{level4a} -> level5a
{level4b} -> level5b:  select => set_select;
```

Two arcs describe the remainder of the menu structure:

```
{level3}:  level4a => to_level_4a;
-> level4a

{level3}:  level4b => to_level_4b;
-> level4b
```

This is evidence of the practical applicability of GTNs to *post hoc* specification of an implemented commercial prototype. Many other specification reductions over the DATN version are possible, due to the designed regularity of the dialogue. Consistency is expensive in DATNs, due to tedious repetition, but is economically encapsulated in GTNs. The use of constants such as `subset:   level5 = {level5a,level5b}` would enhance the salience of dialogue consistency—indeed exposing inconsistencies between retreats at different levels.

The exposure of inconsistency in human-computer communication is only possible because of the use of nodes as named points. As a requirement, the status of named points may be controversial. The argument for the need for named points is not particularly strong. However, weaknesses here are compensated for by the *benefits* of named points as a basis for generative specifications. This hints at limitations to any approach which concentrates wholly on requirements, to the exclusion of benefits.

8.5.4   *Remarks on the examples*

The GTN is the first communication control abstraction to combine economy of expressiveness for both unmoded and moded user interfaces. It captures both sequence and interleaving by replacing arc enumeration with arc generation. It can generate arcs from all nodes, and thus bring production system capabilities to a sequential network abstraction.

Existing specifications translate readily into GTNs, although assumptions about other UIMS components results in considerable freedom. This makes direct comparison difficult, unless we assume that other parts of the architecture are fixed to match those in use for the example specifications. This was not done here, since the 'feel' of a specification is influenced by all the abstractions in use. I chose to make assumptions about better components for input and linkage management, first to show that such choice exists, and secondly to drive home the interdependence of user interface abstractions. Control specification cannot be independent of controlled objects, and thus the rigid logical separation of syntax is an ideal which cannot be realised in the multi-party dialogues of human-computer communication.

8.6   GTNs as communication control abstractions

The combination of freedom and supportiveness in GTN control specifications is an advantage for the design of interactive systems. The following requirements are satisfied by GTNs: sequence; interleaving; named points; modularity. The need for sequence is properly satisfied, as arcs are 'happens-after' relations. Production rule style interleaving is possible since arc generators of the form:

> `all:` *sentence* `->` *procedure*$_1$; ...; *procedure*$_N$
> `-> same`

are production rules. Such generators will be called *global*, as they apply globally to every node in a GTN. However, if complex processes are interleaved, this results in 'write-only' specifications. On reading a specification, it may not be obvious what is being interleaved with what. Logical processes are not easily re-constituted in production rule interleaving, and this must count against both production systems and GTNs for interleaving of complex processes.

If processes are required, processes should be provided. As the possible 'length' of processes increases, their multiplexing into one specification becomes less and less desirable. Conversely, as the 'length' of processes decreases, the ability to multiplex several virtual processes into one is particularly useful.

GTNs are a single process formalism, and thus do not satisfy the need for a process construct. Only the most courageous (or foolish) designer would attempt to simulate complex simultaneously active processes *via* interleaving.

The nodes of GTNs are the *named points* elements which are distinct from events (the sentence element of the arc generators element). For any node, the events on immediately incoming and outgoing arcs are easily computed, indeed, the definitions of the arc generators are the basis for the mapping.

The need for permutation is poorly satisfied. Permutation is possible, as is shown in the examples. However propositions and procedures have to monitor and manage the setting and unsetting of flags for each permuted event. By contrast, control models such as *petri nets* [151], or BNF extended with a permutation construct, allow *direct* specification of permutations of events, as do interleaved single event processes. However, it is arguable that the latter construct requires 'more work' than the first two.

GTNs are obviously modular, and *could* be efficient. However, no serious study of theoretical complexity or efficient implementations is yet available, so the honest judgement here is one of some uncertainty. A GTN interpreter has been implemented in the programming language 'C' as part of the UIMS in the Glasgow-Bell Northern Research AURORA project. This very small interpreter is linked in with a C data structure which is generated by the GTN compiler. No performance problems have yet been experienced, although the current restriction of trace functions to nodes, *same* and *back* has been exploited to compile a structure very similar to a DATN data structure, the only differences being the use of stack references for *same* and *back*.

Two designers' requirements, for a friendly notation and automated analysis could not be formalised. Empirical study is required to improve both our knowledge of these requirements and to establish when they are satisfied. Only guesses can currently be offered here for GTNs; my guess is that GTNs are fairly easy to use—but I cannot back this up as yet. §8.5.3 did offer crude numerical comparisons of specification size. The figures are of some interest, but their proper interpretation is in no way straightforward. Note that any ATN can be reduced to a single arc! A reasonable interpretation is that GTNs reduce specification size *without* reducing clarity. Indeed by encapsulating consistency, GTNs can *increase* clarity. Still, there is more to ease of use than this, so to accept this argument as the final word would trivialise usability.

As for automated analyses, nothing of consequence can really be said. Properties of graphs and production systems are *applicable*, but not necessarily *relevant*. Much more work is required before meaningful links can be forged between properties of mathematical structures and human performance.

A user requirement, for smoothness of transitions between skill levels, was also not formalised. As no interactive system with multiple user interfaces has yet been specified or implemented with GTNs, no comment can be made on the adequacy of GTNs for this design need.

GTNs thus do reasonably well when evaluated with references to the identified requirements. They do better than either ATNs or production systems (increasingly known as *event-response systems*). ATNs are very poor at interleaving, and have poor modularisation and parameterisation. Production systems are poor on sequence, named points and modularity.[2]

The only control formalism which satisfies as many, but not the same, requirements as GTNs is CSP (as used in [3] and the following Chapter). This provides process constructs, but not named points. It is also arguable that its extra complexity makes it harder to use, even in the restricted form used for *eventCSP* [3]. GTNs, like production systems, have an advantage over CSP for local and small scale interleaving, since this can be done in one network or module, whereas in CSP several processes must be declared. In operating systems, the need for *lightweight processes* is well understood. The same is true of specification. Designers should only have to use heavyweight processes (*à la* CSP) when they are interleaving several complex event sequences. Lightweight constructs are essential for more trivial interleaving, which CSP does not offer. There are also doubts about efficient execution of CSP-based specifications on normal sequential architectures [90]. Finally, the addition of process constructs, perhaps based on CSP, would remove the final disadvantages of GTNs as control abstractions for user interface management.

GTNs are only matched by CSP in the degree to which different requirements are satisfied. The different advantages and disadvantages

---

[2] Hill's SASSAFRAS UIMS gathers event-response rules into modules which are linked together using a *Local Event Broadcast Mechanism*, LEBM. This provides modularity, processes and two levels of interleaving within and between modules. This is not a production system though it is a UIMS. Papers cited in this chapter do not describe LEBM in great detail, although Hill's thesis, cited in [91], may do.

of each can be argued to balance in any comparison unless process constructs are added to GTNs, resulting in a most suitable abstraction for communication control in user interface management. Only then will GTNs satisfy the requirement for maximum flexibility, as only then will they be fully general.

8.7   The casting requirements

Formalisation of requirements is vital to the ultimate usefulness of the abstraction. Rather than just pull properties off the shelf, we should derive properties from accounts of requirements. We argued that many of the identified requirements were equivalent to needs for certain mathematical constructs. Explicit argument here is again a vital part of the design method for software abstractions. This is not because we can all always produce certain arguments, but rather because others are good at spotting flawed ones. An essential part of any formal method is a group of able and critical colleagues. By laying each argument bare, inadequacies become obvious to others, if not also to the person advancing the argument.

The current presentation of requirements and their formalisation has itself gained much from public presentations. The value of any review process depends on the structure of the material under review. The more explicit the arguments, the more chance there is of others improving them. When the arguments address such important abstractions as communication control in user interface management, then it is well worth spending a considerable amount of time and effort on this process.

For the satisfaction of requirements to be evaluated, clear targets for the evaluation are essential. Arguing the equivalence of requirements and mathematical constructs is one way to produce such targets. This is not always possible; but satisfaction of requirements can be evaluated by observing human performance. Actually, far more than observable performance is relevant, there just isn't space to address so-called 'soft' measures here. Attitudes and feelings are vital, and seem to tie up well with performance too [114]. Here again, the dynamics of the design process depend on argument.

Evaluation activities must be designed. Decisions must be taken in advance on what data to collect, how to collect it, and how to interpret it. All these decisions rest on argument, and if they are invalid, then so is the evaluation exercise. Once again, making explicit arguments for empirical processes increases the chances of flaws being detected and corrected. Successful evaluation must be designed along with the artefact under test [89].

Our requirements call for empirical evaluation. No experimental designs were presented however. The intention was to make clear what should happen when, even though it has not yet happened in the case of this work.

To conclude these comments: argument is the main dynamic for proceeding from accounts of requirements to testable empirical and mathematical hypotheses. System quality rests on the quality of the arguments advanced. No amount of rigour in the conduct of an experiment or a proof can rescue a design which has been advanced by poor arguments at this stage.

8.7.1   *Choice of abstraction and notation*

Applied mathematics addresses the applicability of mathematical structures by looking for situations which can be seen as instances of a formal structure. The structure precedes its application. But the reverse situation makes more sense. Rather than having the applied mathematics of solutions looking for problems, it is better to select or create structures *after* a thorough analysis of the problem, based on a survey of requirements for an identified subcomponent of an interactive systems architecture. The design of computing systems requires such selection and invention on a regular basis.

This stage is fairly simple, initially. A survey of candidate abstractions is required. Most such candidates have been mentioned in this chapter: recursive and augmented transition networks, statecharts, (extended) context-free grammars, production systems, event-response systems, petri-nets, and (restricted) CSP. One abstraction should be chosen on the basis of a rapid evaluation. If a notation exists, it can be used; otherwise one should be designed.

8.7.2   *Evaluation of abstraction and notation*

An important part of the development of abstractions is the study of their behaviour. To a mathematician, such study would normally mean proof of properties. No such proofs have been presented in this chapter, largely because less formal arguments sufficed. Nevertheless, rigorous proofs should have been attempted, as this can reveal flaws in the arguments.

Empirical evaluation has been even poorer! The current notation for GTNs was a response to comments from colleagues on the illogical reading order of the previous notation [41]. This could count as iterative design, but I admit that a little more punishing testing is required for the notation. More information on the usability of the current notation is essential. As for early evaluation metrics, no work is currently planned for GTNs, but the notation should be of interest to psychologists working in this area.

The evaluation stage traps those software designers with a 'suck it and see' mentality. 'Just trying something out' is not a basis for rigorous research. User interface designers are discovering that debugging event-response user interfaces is difficult. Also, the poor sequential capabilities of event-response systems are being noted—a decade after labelled production systems were developed to get around this problem. Some evaluation criteria must be developed before work on abstractions begins. Otherwise, any design can be argued to be successful, merely by describing what it turns out to do. Its behaviour retrospectively becomes the requirements.

8.7.3   *Iterate or terminate?*

Deficiencies will likely appear in the abstraction or the notation during evaluation. This forces a decision on what to do.

If problems lie in the abstraction, the first step is to decide how much this matters. In many practical contexts, it may not, although that cannot be guaranteed to be true for the next project.

Researchers should not have this luxury of writing-off problems in order to complete projects. To improve knowledge of software abstractions, research itself must iterate and return to one of the earlier stages.

The shortest retreat is to choose another abstraction for development. However, existing abstractions have already been exhausted, so most UIMS research will involve the design of new ones.

All the best work on abstractions for UIMS design has been based on extending existing abstractions. Context-free grammars, production systems, transition networks and petri nets have all been extended to satisy more requirements. GTNs are such an extension, adding production system capabilities to transition networks. GTNs are still not adequate for many design tasks, and now must have process constructs added in order to improve their acceptability.

Returning to the stage of choosing, creating or extending abstractions is the simplest form of iteration in the formal method for abstraction design. More backtracking is required if errors of argument at the third stage of hypothesis formation reveal themselves during the evaluation process. Experiments may have to be re-designed, or new mathematical associations established. The choice stage can be skipped and experiments or proofs can be carried out again as part of a new evaluation. Oversights will cause further iteration if the new evaluation results in a less favourable judgement on the abstraction or notation under review. The abstraction or notation may have to be extended or replaced with another one, and this will be evaluated in turn.

The most common iterations are caused by the discovery of new requirements. Where the early stages of design have been poorly addressed, this is very common. Workshops on UIMSs [198, 153, 142] reveal that designers often only realise requirements when an abstraction (or architecture) has been in use for some time. Some of these oversights are avoidable, but in all fairness, the quality of the requirements stage will never be adequate. We do not have enough competence, either in psychology or interactive system design, to be able to produce the final survey. This should not, however, be used as an argument for not doing a survey at all, or for not taking one seriously.

Use of an abstraction or notation can thus quickly expose unidentified requirements. Designing with abstractions creates a context for bumping into new potential properties. Often a new structure will lead to the discovery that new properties are important design considerations. Impulsive acceptance of such occurrences, however, is inadvisable. In exploratory studies, the significance of some created behaviour must be argued.

The architectural context of the abstraction may prove to be wrong, forcing design right back up to the first stage of the formal method. UIMS research recently passed through such a revelation. Semantic feedback proved to be difficult in existing input syntax centred architectures [50]. The need for a *semantic support component* similar to the linkage [39] became clear. This is hardly surprising, as the attempt to interface the communication control directly to the underlying application was bound to result in poor separation of the user interface and the underlying application.

The cost of arguing for the wrong architecture is high, yet attention to detail in the published literature is still disappointing. Problems are regularly attributed to the Seeheim model [74] which cannot rationally be derived from the minimal account of it which was developed at Seeheim. The Seeheim model is similar to the architecture presented in section 8.2. The major differences lie in the interfaces. The Seeheim model pipelines tokens through the first three components, and the suggestion is that procedure calls would be used as the interface with the underlying application. The only disagreement is that in the architecture developed here, each component has an internal feedback loop, and the linkage fixes its interface with the session level, and not vice-versa. Also, a wide range of interfaces between the linkage and the underlying application is to be expected, as different applications will impose different interfaces. Linkages have to be sufficiently general to accommodate this. It is as capable of semantic feedback as the so-called new architectures. The problem of UIMSs at the time of the Seeheim model was that none of them followed it, in that none had a recognisable *application interface model* to manage semantic support, and furthermore abstractions at session level couldn't have done anything with this feedback even if it was made available to them. The distinction between architecture and abstraction is crucial. Most Seeheim style architectures used very poor abstractions.

The architectural stage of software tooling for interactive system has to be taken more seriously and lifted above the casual conversations and delayed reporting of research workshops. Otherwise, this design process will never approach termination, but will thrash around as one half-baked architecture steps aside for this year's model. Something as stable as the lexer, parser and code-generator architecture for compilers is urgently needed to provide a better focus for UIMS research.

These increasingly expensive iterations are due to problems with the architecture or the abstraction. If the notation proves inadequate, such drastic iterations are less likely unless the problems are traced to the abstraction. Refining notations should thus be less expensive, and the common interactive system design cycle of prototyping and user testing is to be expected here.

Design should only stop because it has to (e.g., production pressures) or because the research goals have been met. The latter has not yet occured, and the current work is liable to require further attention at all levels, that is: architecture; user and designer requirements; abstraction and notation design; and evaluation. This framework should improve the management of the research process.

8.8   Summary

Communication control covers the *session level* of user interface design. It involves design of the operation sequences and concurrent activities. These constrain the course of events during an interactive session. Communication control abstractions are re-usable structures which can be configured to produce sequences and parallel activities for a system's users. They are one of a family of abstractions for user interface management. Such abstractions need to be designed to fit requirements, rather than just be imported from another area of computing. This chapter placed formal abstractions in a user interface management context, presenting a new abstraction for communication control, the *Generative Transition Network*. It was argued that *structured* and *formal* methods need to be combined in order to properly exploit mathematical descriptions and techniques. The role of the structured method is to draw in non-mathematical knowledge and techniques which are essential to the proper *application* of mathematics in a user interface management context.

User interface management research is attempting to raise the standard of software tools beyond the pre-coded components of user interface *toolkits* by specialising the formal methods in use in computing. This specialisation can only be guided by a user- and designer-centred approach to requirements and evaluation. Any other method could not be an application of mathematics to the specific problems of human-computer interaction.

Software tools, by providing an appropriate notational or graphical interface to specialised high-level abstractions, can considerably narrow the gap between design and implementation for *some* components of *some* computer systems. Mainstream formal methods, by contrast, narrow the gap less, but perhaps for all computer systems, and they provide methods for structuring the transformation over the remaining gap. However, they require a formal statement of the design problem before they can be used.

Structured methods encourage designers to draw on all relevant knowledge sources and elicitation techniques *before* firming up on a formal statement. This broad approach to requirements was applied to the problem of designing a high-level abstraction for a single user interface management component. A structured and less mathematically formal approach was found to be essential for proper evaluation of the designed abstraction.

It should be clear that formal descriptions, and formal methods for manipulating such descriptions, are essential in the design of *any* software abstractions. At the same time, the limits of this brand of formalism need to be noted. Fortunately for the designer, there are many other sources of knowledge and techniques which neatly complement the mathematical contribution to the design of high-level abstractions.

Acknowledgements

This work began while I was working at the Scottish HCI Centre [42, 41], and has continued since I joined the AURORA project at Glasgow University, funded by Bell Northern Research. I am grateful to John Patterson, the director of this project and for his support in completing this work.

Members of Glasgow University's Graphics and HCI group have listened to several presentations of this work. Their comments have been most helpful in the development of GTNs. In particular, Philip Gray and Stephen Draper have drawn my attention to deficiencies in the requirements and their formulation. Kieran Clenaghan made some useful comments on an earlier notation.

CHAPTER NINE

STRUCTURING DIALOGUES USING CSP

HEATHER ALEXANDER

9.1   Introduction

In designing the interaction between a system and its users, there are
clearly many aspects to be considered. The organisational context, the
kinds of users, the communication devices, the style of interaction, the
influence of the underlying system, the details of how information is
presented to users these are all legitimate concerns for the designers of
human-computer interaction.

One important aspect which was identified early in the history of interactive systems is that of the dialogue structure; that is, the description of what each partner in the interaction is allowed to say and when.
In the days when textual command languages (such as IBM's OS/JCL
or ICL's SCL) were the primary means of user communication with a
system, the dialogue structure was simply the syntax of the command
language concerned. The user issued a command, conforming to the
language syntax, and the system responded. As menu-based interaction
became more common, there came the need to express the hierarchy
of menus and the valid choices at each stage. This too can be seen as
the structure of the dialogue—it is still concerned with who says what

when, only now the syntax includes such concepts as menu selection
and navigation. With the advent of more complex styles of interaction, notably direct manipulation, has come an attendant requirement
to allow designers to express complex and often highly concurrent dialogue structures. Before looking at notations for describing interaction,
though, we consider the architecture of interactive systems since this
has influenced the development of these notations.

For a number of reasons, it is useful to separate modules handling
the user interface and its dialogue from those concerned solely with the
application. Taking this a step further, user interfaces can be described
separately and supplied to a generic user interface manager which then
provides the user interface described in the supplied specification. An
analogy is with database management systems, where data storage, organisation and retrieval are delegated to a single back-end subsystem,
the DBMS. There are cases where such a separation of dialogue from
application is not easy or even possible [37]. Even where it is possible,
the point where the line between the two is drawn is often an arbitrary choice. Nevertheless, the benefits of separation are sufficiently
high to encourage designers to adopt this approach wherever possible.
An interactive system following this model has the architecture shown
below:

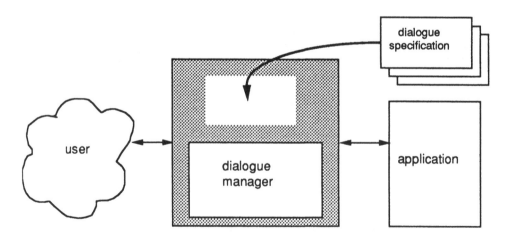

This chapter traces the development of notations for describing dialogues and shows how a mathematical language called CSP [93] allows
designers to specify formally the structure of complex and concurrent

user-system dialogues. Moreover, the language is executable and so can be supplied to a dialogue manager, which in this case consists of a set of tools which enable designers to experiment with the interfaces they create.

9.2   Specifying user interfaces

When the primary means of interaction with a system is using a textual command language, it is relatively straightforward to devise ways of describing that interaction. The structure of possible dialogues with the system is defined by the structure of the command language. Since command languages are, in essence, little different from any other programming languages, they can be defined by existing programming language description techniques, such as BNF (Backus-Naur Form) and state-transition diagrams [145]. Enhancements to command language interfaces, such as parameter prompting or prompted conversations can also be handled by such notations, although some language extensions have appeared, for example, to enable more modular descriptions [52] or to allow for the increasingly interactive nature of communication with the system.

It becomes more difficult to use these notations with more elaborate use of the screen in user interfaces, however, since the notations have no way of describing the spatial layout of the screen. This is not particularly surprising since the notations were never intended to handle such concepts. Extending the notations still further, for example by allowing a node in a state transition diagram to describe its screen representation, has allowed the specification of some menu-based and simple graphical systems [158, 28, 204].

There is another significant reason for extending these specification notations, namely to allow descriptions written in them to be executed in order to provide a working version of the user-system interface immediately. There are no doubt several motives behind this development, but one is certainly the recognition that it is difficult for designers to visualise a dialogue from a static description alone [118]. Moreover, this executability is a step towards providing a rudimentary user interface manager, initially consisting of the interpreter for the dialogue specifications.

However, the continued development of user interface technology, with the introduction of direct manipulation, sophisticated graphics capabilities, concurrent input devices and so on, has stretched these programming language techniques to their limits. For example, in one direct manipulation system [107], the overall description now uses object-oriented techniques, with state-transition diagrams relegated to specifying individual interactions with each object. In particular, we can distinguish two aspects of user interface technology that have proved difficult for existing notations to handle satisfactorily, namely screen presentation and concurrency in the structure of the dialogue.

Considering the latter first, there are notations available now which have been intentionally designed for expressing concurrent activities and which could therefore be applied to modern user-system interfaces. Examples of these are CCS [125], CSP [93] and Petri nets [191], each of which is a formal notation with well-defined semantics. This chapter investigates the use of one of these notations, CSP, for describing dialogue structure. CSP was chosen, amongst other reasons, because it lends itself better to execution than CCS and because it is more succinct than most Petri net notations.

To return to the other area of specifying screen presentation, it should be noted that CSP by itself does not offer a means of describing the spatial layout or presentation characteristics of interaction. Like the earlier notations, some extension is required to deal with these. However, this chapter shows how they can be described in a way which is separate from, yet linked to, the CSP specification and which does not compromise the formality of the CSP specification.

9.3   Introduction to CSP

The language of Communicating Sequential Processes has evolved over the years [92, 93]. Originally intended as an extension for Algol-like languages, it has developed into a succinct and powerful mathematically-based notation for describing the behaviour of systems when seen as groups of communicating processes set in some environment. A system is described by one or more processes. Each process represents the behaviour pattern of some object in the system. A process is made up of events, where events are atomic and represent some incident or activity in the system. A system specified in CSP can encompass activities attributable to either the system or its users. CSP makes no distinction between events caused by a user and events caused by the system. They are all simply events in which the overall system participates, regardless of their origin. To use Hoare's example, a simple vending machine may only be aware of two events: `coin` and `choc`. The fact that the user supplies the coin and the machine dispenses the chocolate is irrelevant to the process describing the behaviour of the machine. Such a process can be written as:

VEND = (coin -> (choc -> VEND))

which says that the vending machine repeatedly accepts a coin and then dispenses a chocolate. It cannot dispense a chocolate without first receiving a coin, nor can it accept two coins without yielding a chocolate. In this chapter, we use a subset of the full language described in [93]. Firstly, as shown above, a process is defined by a statement of the form:

<Process Name> = <Process Expression>

If P and Q are process expressions and e is some event, then the following are also process expressions:

(e -> P) "prefix" : do event e, then behave like P;

P [] Q "choice" : behave like process P or behave like process Q;

P ; Q "sequence" : behave like P then behave like Q;

P || Q "parallel" : behave like P and behave like Q, synchronising on common events;

SKIP "termination" : the process which indicates successful completion.

Where a choice exists, as in P [] Q, the decision about which process is selected is based on the events offered by the processes. Of those which are offered, the event which occurs first determines the choice of process. In this chapter, all process names are shown in upper case and all event names are shown in lower case—this is not a requirement in CSP but a notational convention adopted in [93].

9.4   Examples

This section presents two examples to illustrate the use of the notation.

9.4.1   *Example: a menu-based system*

Consider the following example in which we wish to describe the behaviour of a simple menu package. First, the top-level process:

```
MENU = ( choose-menu -> M )
```

This specifies that the event `choose-menu` occurs before the system goes on to behave as described by the process M.

```
M = ( display -> selection ->
                ( OK [] NOT-OK [] END ) )
```

Note first that we can drop the nested bracketing around the prefix construct, as illustrated here. The package displays the current menu (the display event) then allows the user to make a selection from it (the selection event). After this, it has a choice between the three processes:

```
OK = ( valid -> MENU )
NOT-OK = ( invalid -> error -> M )
END = ( quit -> bye -> SKIP )
```

In order to choose between these processes, the system examines them all to see what events can happen next; in this case valid, invalid and quit are possible. The choice of process then depends on the selection made by the user. If the quit event occurs, the END process is selected and the system stops after some final message. If a valid selection is made (event `valid`), the process OK will be chosen and the system will go on to behave as MENU again, i.e. choosing a new menu and repeating the selection activity by the user. If the user has not made a valid choice, the package behaves as described by NOT-OK instead, so that some form of error indication is given (event `error`) and the system carries on behaving as given by the process M, i.e. it will redisplay the current menu and ask for a user selection. The menu package could simply involve information retrieval, displaying screens and offering further menus for the user, as in teletext systems, for example. Alternatively, it might act as the front-end to some application, giving the user access to its underlying functionality. We can describe the behaviour of the application by the process:

```
APPLIC = ( choose-menu ->
                ( valid -> action -> APPLIC
                [] quit -> SKIP ) )
```

This application considers that users never make mistakes and that valid selections will always be made. Once a menu has been chosen for display, the application is only interested in valid selections and termination requests. If valid occurs, the application undertakes the appropriate action for the selection made and goes back to choose a new menu. The joint behaviour of the application and the menu package is given by:

```
APPLIC || MENU
```

The above is synchronised on the common events `choose-menu`, `valid`, and `quit`. Run together, the first event is still `choose-menu`. The application then waits for a `valid` event or a `quit` event Q, it can do no more until one of them occurs. Meanwhile, the menu package displays the menu and acquires a selection from the user. Any invalid selections are fielded by the menu package, as described above. On quitting, the application stops immediately, while the menu package stops after bidding farewell to the user (event **bye**). On making a valid selection, the menu package has to wait for the application to perform whatever processing is required (event **action**), before the two processes synchronise again on choose-menu. The full specification can be given more succinctly as:

```
SYSTEM = APPLIC || MENU

APPLIC = ( choose-menu ->
                ( valid -> action -> APPLIC
                [] quit -> SKIP ) )

MENU = ( choose-menu -> M )

M = ( display -> selection ->
                ( valid -> MENU
                [] invalid -> error -> M
                [] quit -> bye -> SKIP ) )
```

The example above has illustrated most of the notation as well as the style of describing systems in CSP. In particular, the parallel operator has allowed us to modularise a system description and to run processes in parallel, synchronising where appropriate.

Writing interface descriptions in a mathematically formal language, like CSP, opens up the prospect of being able to prove that the description possesses or avoids specified properties. For example, in this case, we can prove that the application is not capable of undertaking an action after an invalid menu selection. That is, we can prove that the sequence of events <invalid,action> is not a valid subsequence of any of the possible sequences of events in SYSTEM. The proof is omitted here as it relies on a more detailed knowledge of CSP and its laws than is possible to give here.

It is also possible to specify a process representing the behaviour pattern of the *user* of the system and then to analyse their joint activity. For example, a user may be described by:

SIMPLE-USER = (selection -> SIMPLE-USER)

This type of user repeatedly makes selections from the menu and takes no other action. If their joint behaviour is:

SIMPLE-USER || SYSTEM

then the user has the opportunity to make a choice whenever the process indicates that a selection is possible. The system suspends until that choice is made. A different user may be characterised by the process:

BORED-USER = (selection -> BORED-USER
               [] read-book -> BORED-USER
               [] go-home -> SKIP)

This user has the option of making a selection when offered the opportunity to do so, but may choose to otherwise occupy himself, or may choose to leave altogether. Run in parallel with the SYSTEM process, all is well unless the user goes home without having quit the system (this interpretation of the user's selection is decided by the MENU process), in which case it will suspend waiting for a non-forthcoming selection. These have been trivial examples of this technique—later we will see how it can be used to discover deficiencies in the interaction described by a CSP specification.

9.4.2   *Example: concurrent dialogues*

The parallel operator also permits the description of concurrent and direct-manipulation user interfaces, where the events relevant to the interface are unordered or only partially ordered. Consider a small part of the interaction possible with a direct manipulation word-processing package: namely, text selection. The general mechanism is that pressing the mouse button causes the text cursor to be placed where the mouse cursor is pointing. Text can then be typed at the position given by the text cursor. Alternatively, if the mouse button is held down and the mouse cursor dragged across the screen, a larger piece of text can be selected, up to the point where the mouse button is released. There are two processes to describe the relevant activities of the mouse:

```
MOUSE = ( press -> get-position -> send-position ->
                            TRACK-MOUSE ; MOUSE )

TRACK-MOUSE = (release -> SKIP)
              [] (get-position -> send-position2 ->
                            TRACK-MOUSE)
```

In this, the **press** and **release** events represent depressing and releasing the mouse button. When the button is pressed, the mouse position is noted and sent to some other process which has still to be defined. Until the button is released, the mouse position is repeatedly sent to the other process. If the button was not released immediately, a second event, **send-position2**, is used for this communication in order to show that it is a longer selection which is to be made. Now we specify a process to describe the activity of the text cursor:

```
TEXT-CURSOR = ( send-position -> mark-start ->
                            TEXT-CURSOR
                [] send-position2 -> mark-end ->
                            TEXT-CURSOR )
```

The action of this process depends on whether it is sent an initial or subsequent position, indicated by the type of event that happens (**send-position** or **send-position2**). For an initial position, the process places the text cursor at that position (**mark-start**) and then goes back to behaving like TEXT-CURSOR again, waiting for a new mouse position to be sent. If the mouse was dragged, the current end of the selection is marked before the process begins again. This process does not have to concern itself with checking the details of what happens to the mouse but simply synchronises on the events in which it is interested. The required behaviour, that is, positioning the text cursor as controlled by the mouse, is specified by:

```
TEXT-POSITION = MOUSE || TEXT-CURSOR
```

This is synchronised on **send-position** and **send-position2**, the events of interest to both processes. Of course, it is likely that the mouse will be used for other activities as well. For example, when the mouse cursor is within a displayed menu, pressing the button highlights the indicated menu entry while releasing it selects the entry. If the mouse cursor is dragged while the button is pressed, any entries to which it points are highlighted in turn until the button is released and an entry selected. A separate process can specify this activity:

```
MENU-CURSOR = ( send-position -> SKIP
            [] send-position2 -> SKIP ) ;
                (highlight -> MENU-CURSOR)
```

This process is only concerned with the effect on the displayed menu. Irrespective of the type of position given to it, the entry at that position is highlighted. The overall effect is given by the process:

```
MOUSE || MENU-CURSOR
```

As before, this is synchronised on **send-position** and **send-position** as before. On the other hand, a process concerned with selecting the indicated entry is only interested in when the button is released:

```
MENU-ACTION = (release -> select -> MENU-ACTION)
```

The menu activity can be specified as:

```
MENU = MOUSE || MENU-CURSOR || MENU-ACTION
```

This is synchronised on the appropriate events. This example has illustrated how direct-manipulation interfaces can be specified. Each object on a screen is represented by a separate process, and the entire display is specified as the parallel operation of the processes for all the objects it contains. The user is then free to interact with objects in any order, or to leave interactions with objects incomplete while pursuing some other activity in the system.

9.5   Executing CSP specifications

From the argument and examples above, we can conclude that CSP is potentially useful as a notation for describing the overall structure of dialogues as well as more general systems. Further, its formal basis gives us scope for analysing and asserting properties of dialogues specified in CSP. However, recall that another desirable characteristic of dialogue specifications is the ability to use them to produce a working demonstration. An issue for CSP dialogue specifications, then, is whether or not such specifications can be executed. One approach would be to treat the CSP as a programming language and find ways to execute its more novel constructs. This can be seen in "squeak" [34] for example, in functional implementations of CSP [134] and in the occam programming language [120]. But we have not used all the language constructs of CSP and can be content with a less ambitious method of executing the subset we have chosen. (In order to distinguish this subset from CSP proper, in the rest of this chapter it will be referred to as "eventCSP"). Rather than directly executing eventCSP as if it were a programming language, we provide a simulator which takes an eventCSP specification and simulates the behaviour of the system that was specified. In executing the specification, some mechanism external to the simulator determines which events happen when offered a choice. Thus, in the example above, the event `choose-menu` would be offered by the process (and automatically selected since it is the only event offered), followed by `display` and `selection`. The simulator then offers a choice between `valid`, `invalid` and `quit`, so that one of these events has to be selected for the simulation to continue. This eventCSP simulator is the central component of the dialogue design tools described in this chapter. In its original form, it was first specified by Professor

Peter Henderson, then at the University of Stirling, as part of research concerning formal specification languages and rapid prototyping.

9.6   A family of dialogue design tools

Simulation of the behaviour of systems specified in eventCSP has been made the basis of several tools which allow designers to examine the activity in a dialogue. These tools differ primarily in the amount of detail given in the design and hence range from a 'bare-bones' simulation through to a prototyping system covering most aspects of the interaction. This section describes the tools, collectively known as SPI (Specifying and Prototyping Interaction), and illustrates their use by means of an example. In this example, a bank acquires a simple automated teller system for which it plans to design its own user interface. The system allows a customer to:

- withdraw cash;

- order a statement;

- order a new cheque book;

- check an account balance.

Each customer has a numbered card issued for their account and with each card there is an associated secret personal identification number (PIN). Access to the system is granted in the usual way by inserting the card and typing the PIN.

9.6.1   *Dialogue outlines*

The examples in the previous section were given in outline only, illustrating the way in which designers can "sketch" a plan of a proposed dialogue. The simplest tool in the SPI family allows these outlines, written in eventCSP, to be executed on the simulator. The user interface for the atm, then, might begin as a simple outline:

```
ATM = ( put-in-card -> enter-pin ->
            ( pin-ok? -> ATM1
            [] pin-not-ok? -> error -> ATM ) )
```

```
ATM1 = ( menu -> ( cbook -> SKIP
            [] withdraw -> amount -> money ->
                                              SKIP
            [] statement -> SKIP
            [] balance -> SKIP ) ;
              (eject-card -> take-card -> ATM) )
```

Executing this on the simulator, we are first informed that the following events occur in order:

- put-in-card;

- enter-pin.

This process specification allows no other alternatives. It also indicates that a card has been inserted and that the customer has been requested to supply their PIN. The simulator then offers a menu of events that could happen next:

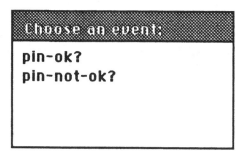

This represents the possibilities that the customer might or might not supply the correct PIN. The designer selects one of these events, and the subsequent behaviour of the simulator will depend on the choice made. For example, if pin-not-ok? is chosen, the designer is informed that the following events occur next:

- error;

- put-in-card;

- enter-pin.

That is, the customer has been informed of their error, and a new transaction has been started (presumably with a new card and customer).

Note that the card has not been returned to the customer, who is being regarded as a potential thief. The simulator then presents the same menu as above, for the new transaction.

If pin-ok? is selected, the event menu occurs, indicating that the customer has been presented with a list of the various services offered by the atm. The designer is then offered the following choice:

```
Choose an event:

cbook
withdraw
statement
balance
```

This represents the services available to the customer. Only one of these, withdraw, involves further events (amount and money). In all cases, the event eject-card happens and the simulator returns to behaving as ATM again. As noted above, the existence of a specific event for returning a card to its owner indicates, by its absence, that customers who give an invalid PIN do not receive their cards back. Now we consider the behaviour of atm users. A user who always checks the balance of their account before deciding how much to withdraw, for example, wants to behave as follows:

```
EFFICIENT-USER = PRELIM ; CASH ;
                    (quit -> take-card -> SKIP)
```

where

```
PRELIM = (find-an-atm -> put-in-card ->
                            enter-pin -> SKIP)

CASH = (balance -> decide -> withdraw ->
            amount -> money -> SKIP)
```

If we attempt to put this user together with our atm, we find that there is a problem. They co-operate successfully until the user has decided how much to withdraw. However, the next desired action of the user is to request a withdrawal, whereas the atm will not permit that but ejects the card and insists on a new transaction before it will part with any money. Since this user is not prepared to take their card, the two processes deadlock, no doubt leaving this customer unhappy with the facilities of the system.

After this and other experimentation with this outline, we decide that it is not elaborate enough. Customers should be offered more than one attempt at supplying a correct PIN, for example. If a customer wishes to check their account balance before deciding how much cash to withdraw, the current outline (as with many existing atm systems in real use) insists that the customer performs two separate transactions, much of which is both tedious and redundant. And what if a card is presented that cannot be processed by the banking group operating the atm?

With these issues in mind, a more realistic dialogue is specified:

```
ATM = ( put-in-card ->
            ( read-card -> ATM1
            [] cant-read -> eject-card ->
                                take-card -> ATM
            [] stop-atm -> SKIP ) )


ATM1 = ( enter-pin ->
            (  pin-ok? -> TRANSACTION
            [] pin-not-ok? ->
                    ( try-again? -> ATM1
                    [] thief? -> ATM ) ) )


TRANSACTION = ( menu ->
            (  cbook -> TRANSACTION
            [] withdraw -> WITHDRAWAL
            [] statement -> TRANSACTION
            [] balance -> TRANSACTION
            [] quit -> eject-card -> take-card -> ATM
            [] error -> TRANSACTION ) )


WITHDRAWAL = ( amount ->
                ( ok? -> money -> TRANSACTION
                [] too-much? -> WITHDRAWAL
                [] over-50? -> WITHDRAWAL
```

```
[] quit -> TRANSACTION ) )
```

Will our efficient user succeed in their intended transaction now?—the answer is yes. We can either use the proof theory of CSP to demonstrate the absence of deadlock or we can demonstrate it in practice using the SPI Outliner.

Our final experiment involves tackling another known characteristic of users, namely their tendency to forget to remove their card from the atm:

```
FORGETFUL-USER = PRELIM ; CASH
```

What happens in the system FORGETFUL-USER || ATM? The atm is left displaying the menu of its facilities and any passerby is at liberty to withdraw cash from the account of our forgetful user. This is not usually regarded as a desirable characteristic of an atm, so we modify the WITHDRAW process to insist that withdrawal necessarily ends the interaction with the atm and that the card is removed before the cash is made available:

```
WITHDRAWAL = ( amount ->
                  ( ok? -> eject-card -> take-card
                       -> money -> ATM
                  [] too-much? -> WITHDRAWAL
                  [] over-50? -> WITHDRAWAL
                  [] quit -> TRANSACTION ) )
```

Now that we are satisfied with this specification, we can begin to consider other aspects of the dialogue using other tools.

9.6.2   *Dialogue scenarios*

With an eventCSP specification, it has to be admitted that the intended meaning behind a dialogue is conveyed only by a judicious choice of event names. The intent behind the following process is far from clear:

```
X = ( a -> X [] (b -> SKIP) )
```

while

```
VEND = ( coin -> choc -> VEND )
```

The process **VEND** could equally well be describing an automatic franking system which is given a letter and then franks it, or indeed any other system that repeatedly executes two distinct steps in sequence.

Such limitations are acceptable during dialogue 'sketching', but sooner or later the effects of the events have to be made more explicit. There are two aspects of an event to consider: the effect it has on the screen; and the activity it represents. In this section, we deal with the presentation of an event of the screen. The approach taken is to create 'scenarios' [35], which can be thought of as a 'slide show' of what the screen will look like to a user of the system. At this stage, there is no need to link the dialogue or screen layout to the application. All that is required is that a picture of the screen be associated with each event in the eventCSP specification. Adding these screen descriptions to the specification does not change the CSP part of the specification or its properties.

In the present Lisp-based version of SPI, the association between screen and event is achieved by defining a parameter-less screen display function for each event, using the name of the event as the function name. For example, the function for **put-in-card** is:

```
(defun put-in-card ()
    (draw-atm)
    (set-cursor 9 13)
    (print "Welcome to Caledonia Bank")
    (set-cursor 11 14)
    (print "Please insert your card") )
```

In the above **draw-atm** is a function which draws a screen representation of the atm screen, key pad, cash and card slots. The result of executing this event, then, is that the following screen is displayed:

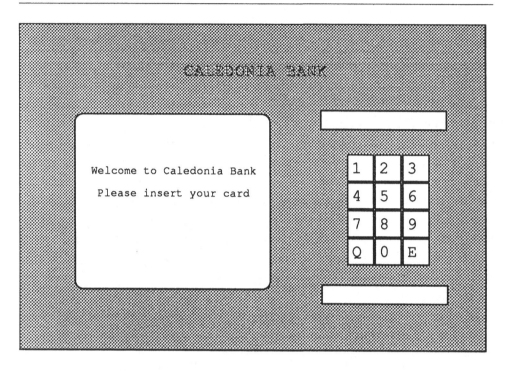

As further examples, other events have display functions:

```
(defun read-card ()
    (draw-atm)
    (set-cursor 5 55) (print"Card In"))

(defun thief? ()
    (draw-atm)
    (set-cursor 5 55) (print "Card In")
    (set-cursor 10 12)
    (print "Your card has been kept")
    (set-cursor 12 12)
    (print "Please see the manager") )
```

while the **menu** event results in the screen:

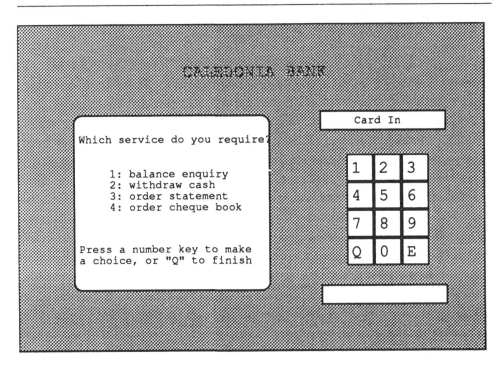

Once these display functions have been written, the designer can execute an eventCSP specification using the SPI Scenarios tool. This tool is also based on the simulator but, unlike the SPI Outliner, it does not trace the event names. Instead, it calls the display functions to draw the screen representation of each event. Where the specification indicates a choice of events, the designer is offered a menu from which to select one. After a screen has been viewed, it is dismissed by pressing any key.

In this way, a designer can add presentation detail to the dialogue outline. The resulting animation of the design is suitable for user trials at an early stage of product design, particularly since the technique does not depend on the existence of application code to present the screen information. Unlike many scenario tools, SPI allows conditional branching in the sequence of screens shown to the user.

At some point, though, the limitations of scenarios mean that the dialogue has to be linked to the functionality with which the eventual users are to communicate. This step from scenarios to prototypes is described in the next section.

9.7   Dialogue prototypes

Moving to a full prototype means that three issues have to be addressed. Firstly, where there is a choice of events offered by the underlying eventCSP simulator, it is no longer appropriate to present that choice to the user in a menu. Instead, some means of determining which event happens has to be found—for example, has a correct PIN been entered or not? Secondly, when an event is selected, it is not sufficient simply to display a screen. Instead, the activity caused by that event (which may or may not affect changes to the screen) has to be executed. Thirdly, some form of description of the system's functionality is required, be it in program code or executable specification. Note that if the functionality is specified, rather than coded, the specification must be executable if the dialogue specification is also to be executable. At present, the SPI tools require that the functionality be expressed in a Lisp-based executable formal specification language called *me too* [87] or in the programming language 'C'.

In order to meet the first two requirements, we introduce a *dialogue state* (which, as the name suggests, records the current state of the dialogue, maintaining any data objects required by the dialogue and acting as a buffer for input and output) and a language for describing events. At this stage too, it is necessary to impose a restriction on events, each event may at most describe *one* interaction between the system and its user. An interaction may include one input from the user and one output from the system. Given an eventCSP specification, then, we need some means of describing when each of its events can occur and what is to happen when it does. Event descriptions are written in eventISL, the Interaction Specification Language for events. An event description consists of the name of the event and a number of optional attributes, as given in the outline below:

```
event <event-name> =
    when <boolean>
    out <output value>
    prompt <boolean>
    set <state-change>
```

Note that these attributes need not be given in the order listed. The *when* attribute defines the conditions under which the event can be selected. For example, for `read-card`, it might be:

```
when is-known ( card-number,atm)
```

or for **thief?** it might be:

```
when attempts-at-pin > 3
```

If omitted, the attribute defaults to **true**, that is, the event can occur
at any time. These *when* conditions are only examined when the SPI
dialogue manager finds it has a choice of possible events to happen
next; their presence removes the need to present a menu of choices to
the designer.

The above definitions have accessed data objects in the dialogue
state: **card-number**, **atm** and **attempts-at-pin**. Equally, events can
create or update information held in the state:

```
event pin-not-ok? =
     when input = pin
     set attempts-at-pin = attempts-at-pin + 1
```

When an incorrect PIN is supplied, the count of attempts made is
incremented (which will then be monitored by the **thief?** event as
shown above).

Interaction between user and system is controlled by two attributes:
out and *prompt*. The value given for the out attribute should be a
display function, writing to the screen. At its simplest, this may just
print a text string, or it may be a more elaborate presentation. In some
cases, it may be possible to re-use display functions created for the SPI
Scenarios tool. For example:

```
event put-in-card =
     out put-in-card()
     prompt true
```

This event also requests, by the boolean-valued attribute prompt,
that the user supply some input (in this case, the number of the card).
Although the value **true** is given here, the attribute may, as for *when*,
be given any condition or function returning a boolean value. Whenever
input is requested, the user reply is held in the input object in the
dialogue state, available to any subsequent events wishing to access it,
as in:

```
event too-much? =
    out too-much?()
    when input > balance
```

Thus, by conditions, access to the dialogue state and calls on underlying functionality, the events can provide a prototype of the system
under development. All of these can be formally specified in *me too* or
implemented in C.

9.8   Discussion and conclusions

The chapter has concentrated on two reasons for using CSP—it is a
formal language for communicating the design of a dialogue and it is an
executable language allowing prototyping of the interaction. What are
the drawbacks associated with this approach? A concern for those who
are interested primarily in the formal aspects of the use of CSP is that
there is no mechanism for ensuring that scenarios or event specifications
are consistent with their associated CSP specification. For those more
interested in using CSP for prototyping, its inability to express the
screen presentation may be a significant flaw.

These problems arise from the compromise that has been sought in
bringing together the techniques of formal specification and prototyping. Not all has been lost, however. Many of the benefits of formality
are retained in the CSP part of the specification, so that proofs of
properties of a dialogue specification are one method of analysing its
behaviour. At the same time, the CSP specification is the basis of the
prototyping tools, offering a complementary method of exploring the
dialogue design.

Another area of potential difficulty for designers lies in choosing the
level of abstraction for a specification. An event can represent anything
from a single keystroke or button press to a highly complex set of
activities in the underlying application. The examples in this chapter,
for instance, are at different levels of abstraction: **release** represents
a single mouse button action, **display** represents the display of an
entire menu while **put-in-card** abstracts from the physical reality of
inserting a plastic card into a teller machine. Moreover, in CSP an
event is atomic, that is, it cannot be decomposed into "smaller" events.
It is therefore the task of the designer to consider what aspects of the

system are to be specified and decide what kinds of events are going to be appropriate and of interest.

It is worth noting too that experience with the notation shows that it may be appropriate to include more constructs from the original CSP language, such as parameterised processes, in order to reduce the number of processes in a specification.

In summary, then, the techniques presented in this chapter recognise that there are two significant aspects to dialogue design: the events which make up the dialogue structure and the effects of those events. Moreover, these two aspects impose different requirements on any language used to specify them. The structure of a dialogue is composed from primitive units called events, allowing both sequential and concurrent combination. The effects of these events are more concerned with state changes, for the dialogue and for the application. Consequently SPI separates the sequences of events in a dialogue from the state-transformational nature of the events, and offers two linked notations to describe these two aspects.

The dialogue structure for communicating with the system is specified using eventCSP in terms of individual events, each of which defines an interaction and/or activity in the dialogue. This specification can be exercised simply as a sketch of the dialogue or it can be used to control more detailed visualisations of the dialogue. For scenarios, each event requires a display function, capable of drawing a screen image corresponding to the event. For prototyping, each event has to be specified in eventISL, stating any output to be given, any input required and any state transformations to be made along with the conditions under which the event can happen.

Despite the difficulties mentioned above, it has been found in practice that the subset of CSP described in this chapter offers a formal, expressive and powerful language for dialogue structure, capable of specifying the concurrent dialogues which are increasingly a part of modern user interfaces. The languages, the tools and their implementations are described in more detail in [4].

BIBLIOGRAPHY

[1] ISO 8807. Information processing systems—open systems interconnection— LOTOS—a formal technique based on the temporal ordering of observational behaviour. Technical report, ISO Standards Authority, 1988.

[2] A. V. Aho, R. Sethi, and J. D. Ullman. *Compilers: Principles, Techniques and Tools.* Addison-Wesley, 1985.

[3] H. Alexander. Executable specifications as an aid to dialogue design. In H. J. Bullinger and B. Shackel, editors, *Human-Computer Interaction — INTERACT'87*, pages 739–744. North Holland, 1987.

[4] H. Alexander. *Formally-Based Tools and Techniques for Human-Computer Dialogues.* Ellis Horwood Ltd., 1987.

[5] J. L. Alty. Path algebras: a useful CAI/CAL analysis technique. *Computers and Education*, 8(1), 1984.

[6] S. O. Anderson. Proving properties of interactive systems. In M. D. Harrison and A. F. Monk, editors, *People and Computers: Designing for usability*, pages 402–416. Cambridge University Press, 1986.

[7] Anon. ASPECT: Specification of the public tool interface. Technical report, System Designers PLC. Camberley, U.K., 1987.

[8] Anon. *NeWS Manual*. Sun Microsystems, Mountain View, CA, USA, 1987.

[9] Anon. Assessment report for the Aspect HCI. Technical Report BAe-WSD-R-ASP-SWE-1563, British Aerospace PLC, Preston, UK., 1988.

[10] Anon. *MIT X Window System Manual Set Version 11, Release 2*. IXI Ltd., Wellington Court, Cambridge, U.K., 1988.

[11] E. Anson. The device model of interaction. *ACM Computer Graphics*, 16(3):107–114, 1982.

[12] W. Appelt, R. Carr, and G. Richter. The formal specification of the document structures of the ODA standard. In J. C. van Vliet, editor, *Document Manipulation and Typography*, pages 95–108. Cambridge University Press, 1988.

[13] J. Backus. Can programming be liberated from the Von Neumann style? A functional style and its algebra of programs. *Communications of the ACM*, 21(8):613–641, 1978.

[14] A. N. Badre. Designing transitionality into the user-computer interface. In G. Salvendy, editor, *Human-Computer Interaction*, pages 27–34. Elsevier, 1984.

[15] R. Baecker. Towards an effective characterisation of graphical interaction. In R. A. Geudj, P. J. W. ten Hagen, F. R. A. Hopgood, H. A. Tucker, and D. A. Duce., editors, *Methodology of Interaction*, pages 127–147. North-Holland, 1980.

[16] W. A. Bailey, S. T. Knox, and E. F. Lynch. Effects of interface design upon user productivity. In E. Solloway, D. Frye, and S. B. Sheppard, editors, *Proceedings ACM CHI'88*, pages 207–212. Addison Wesley, 1988.

[17] L. Bannon, A. Cypher, S. Greenspan, and M. L. Monty. Evaluation and analysis of user's activity structures. In *Proceedings CHI'83 Conf. on Human Factors in Computing Systems*, pages 54–57, 1983.

[18] W. Bartussek and D. L. Parnas. Using assertions about traces to write abstract specifications for software modules. In N. Gehani and A. D. McGettrick, editors, *Software Specification Techniques*, pages 111–130. Addison-Wesley, 1986.

[19] D. Benyon. Monitor: A self-adaptive user interface. In B. Shackel, editor, *Human-Computer Interaction — INTERACT'84*, volume 1, pages 307–313, 1984.

[20] R. S. Bird. The promotion and accumulation strategies in transformational programming. *ACM Transactions on Programming Languages and Systems*, 6(4):487–504, 1984.

[21] D. Bjorner and C. B. Jones. *Formal Specification and Software Development*. Prentice Hall International, 1982.

[22] A. Borgida. Features of languages for the development of information systems at the conceptual level. *IEEE Software*, 2(1):63–73, 1985.

[23] J. Van Den Bos. Whither device independence in interactive graphics? *International Journal Man-Machine Studies*, 18:89, 1983.

[24] S. R. Bourne. *The UNIX System*. Addison-Wesley, 1983.

[25] J. Bowen. Formal specification of window systems. Technical report, Oxford University Computing Laboratory, Programming Research Group, 1987.

[26] P. Briggs. What we know and what we need to know: the user model versus the user's model in human-computer interaction. *Behaviour and Information Technology*, 7(4):431–442, 1988.

[27] M. L. Brodie, J. Mylopoulos, and J. W. Schmidt. *On Conceptual Modelling: Perspectives from Artificial Intelligence, Databases and Programming Languages*. Springer Verlag, 1984.

[28] J. W. Brown. Controlling the complexity of menu networks. *Communications of the ACM*, 25(7):412–418, 1982.

[29] J. S. Bruner, J. Goodnow, and G. Austin. *A Study of Thinking*. John Wiley, 1956.

[30] S. Burbeck. *Applications Programming in Smalltalk-80: How to Use Model-View-Controller (MVC)*. Softsmarts Inc., 1987.

[31] R. M. Burstall. Proving properties of programs by structural induction. *Computer Journal*, 12(1):41–47, 1969.

[32] R. M. Burstall and J. Darlington. A transformation system for developing recursive programs. *Journal of the ACM*, 24(1):44–67, 1977.

[33] S. K. Card, T. P. Moran, and A. Newell. *The Psychology of Human Computer Interaction*. Lawrence Erlbaum, 1983.

[34] L. Cardelli and R. Pike. Squeak — a language for communicating with mice. *ACM Computer Graphics*, 19(3):199–204, 1985.

[35] T. T. Carey and R. E. A. Mason. Informations systems prototyping: techniques, tools and methodologies. *INFOR*, 21(3):177–191, 1983.

[36] G. Cockton. Three transition network dialogue management systems. In P. Johnson and S. Cook, editors, *People and Computers: Designing the Interface*, pages 135–144. Cambridge University Press, 1985.

[37] G. Cockton. Where do we draw the line? — derivation and evaluation of user interface software separation rules. In M. D. Harrison and A. F. Monk, editors, *People and Computers: Designing for Usability*, pages 417–432. Cambridge University Press, 1986.

[38] G. Cockton. Interaction ergonomics, control and separation: Open problems in user interface management. *Information and Software Technology*, 29(4):176–191, 1987.

[39] G. Cockton. A new model for separable interactive systems. In H. J. Bullinger and B. Shackel, editors, *Human-Computer Interaction — INTERACT'87*, pages 1033–1038. North Holland, 1987.

[40] G. Cockton. Some critical remarks on abstractions for adaptable dialogue managers. In D. Diaper and R. Winder, editors, *People*

and Computers III, pages 325–344. Cambridge University Press, 1987.

[41] G. Cockton. Generative transition networks: A new communication control abstraction. In D. M. Jones and R. Winder, editors, *People and Computers IV*, pages 509–528. Cambridge University Press, 1988.

[42] G. Cockton. Generative transition networks: A new communication control abstraction. Technical Report 30, Scottish HCI Centre, 1988.

[43] B. Cohen, W. J. Harwood, and M. I. Jackson. *The Specification of Complex Systems*. Addison-Wesley, 1986.

[44] J. Coutaz. Abstractions for user interface design. *IEEE Computer*, 18(9):21–34, 1985.

[45] J. Coutaz. Abstractions for user interface toolkits. In K. Hopper and I. A. Newman, editors, *Foundation for Human-Computer Communication*, pages 335–354. North-Holland, 1986.

[46] J. Coutaz. PAC, an object oriented model for dialog design. In H. J. Bullinger and B. Shackel, editors, *Human-Computer Interaction — INTERACT'87*, pages 431–436. North-Holland, 1987.

[47] B. Cox. *Object-Oriented Programming: An Evolutionary Approach*. Addison-Wesley, 1986.

[48] M. Cramer. Structure and mnemonics in command languages. *International Journal of Man-Machine Studies*. in press.

[49] C. Crampton. A portable object-oriented toolkit. In *Proceedings Eurographics Workshop on Higher Level Tools for Window Managers*, Amsterdam, 1987.

[50] J. R. Dance, T. E. Granor, R. D. Hill, S. E. Hudson, J. Meads, B. A. Myers, and A. Schulert. The run-time structure of UIMS-supported applications. *ACM Computer Graphics*, 21(2), 1987.

[51] C. J. Date. *An Introduction to Data Base Systems*. Addison-Wesley, 1983.

[52] E. Denert. Specification and design of dialogue systems with state diagrams. In *Proceedings International Computing Symposium*, pages 417–424. North Holland, 1977.

[53] E. W. Dijkstra. *A Discipline of Programming*. Prentice-Hall, 1976.

[54] A. J. Dix. *Formal methods and interactive systems: Principles and Practice.* PhD thesis, University of York, 1987.

[55] A. J. Dix. Giving control back to the user. In H. J. Bullinger and B. Shackel, editors, *Human-Computer Interaction — INTERACT'87*, pages 377–382. North Holland, 1987.

[56] A. J. Dix. The myth of the infinitely fast machine. In D. Diaper and R. Winder, editors, *People and Computers III - Proceedings HCI'87*, pages 215–228. Cambridge University Press, 1987.

[57] A. J. Dix and M. D. Harrison. Principles and interaction models for window managers. In M. D. Harrison and A. F. Monk, editors, *People and Computers: Designing for usability*, pages 352–366. Cambridge University Press, 1986.

[58] A. J. Dix and M. D. Harrison. Formalising models of interaction in the design of a display editor. In H. J. Bullinger and B. Shackel, editors, *Human-Computer Interaction — INTERACT'87*, pages 409–414. North Holland, 1987.

[59] A. J. Dix, M. D. Harrison, and E. E. Miranda. Using principles to design features of a small programming environment. In I. Sommerville, editor, *Software Engineering Environments*, pages 135–150. Peter Peregrinus, 1986.

[60] A. J. Dix, M. D. Harrison, C. Runciman, and H. W. Thimbleby. Interaction models and the principled design of interactive systems. In H. Nichols and D. S. Simpson, editors, *European Software Engineering Conference*, pages 127–135. Springer Lecture Notes, 1987.

[61] A. J. Dix and C. Runciman. Abstract models of interactive systems. In P. Johnson and S. Cook, editors, *People and Comput-*

ers: Designing the interface, pages 13–22. Cambridge University Press, 1985.

[62] S. W. Draper. The nature of expertise in UNIX. In B. Shackel, editor, *Human-Computer Interaction — INTERACT'84*, pages 182–186. North-Holland, 1985.

[63] D. A. Duce and E. V. C. Fielding. Towards a formal specification of the GKS output primitives. In A. A. G. Requicha, editor, *Proceedings Eurographics '86*, pages 307–324, 1986.

[64] H. Ehrig and B. Mahr. *Fundamentals of Algebraic Specification 1*. Springer, 1985.

[65] D. England. Graphical prototyping of graphical tools. In D. M. Jones and R. Winder, editors, *People and Computers IV*, pages 407–420. Cambridge University Press, 1988.

[66] M. U. Farooq and W. D. Dominick. A survey of formal tools and models for developing user interfaces. *International Journal Man-Machine Studies*, 29:479–496, 1988.

[67] G. Fischer. Human-computer interaction software: Lessons learned, challenges ahead. *IEEE Software*, 6(1):44–52, 1989.

[68] G. Fischer, A. Lemke, and T. Schwab. Knowledge-based help systems. In *Proceedings CHI'85 Human Factors in Computing Systems*, pages 161–167, 1985.

[69] J. D. Foley. The structure of interactive command languages. In R. A. Geudj, P. J. W. ten Hagen, F. R. A. Hopgood, H. A. Tucker, and D. A. Duce., editors, *Methodology of Interaction*, pages 227–234. North-Holland, 1980.

[70] J. D. Foley and A. van Dam. *Fundamentals of Interactive Computer Graphics*. Addison-Wesley, 1982.

[71] J. D. Foley and V. L. Wallace. The art of natural graphic man-machine conversation. *Proceedings IEEE*, 62(4):462–471, 1974.

[72] G. Gazdar, E. Klein, G. K. Pullum, and I. A. Sag. *Generalized Phrase Structure Grammar*. Basil Blackwell, 1985.

[73] N. Gehani and A. D. McGettrick, editors. *Software Specification Techniques*. Addison-Wesley, 1986.

[74] M. Green. Report on dialogue specification tools. In G. E. Pfaff, editor, *User Interface Management Systems*, pages 9–20. Springer-Verlag, Berlin, 1985.

[75] M. Green. A survey of three dialogue models. *ACM Trans. on Graphics*, 5(3):244–275, 1986.

[76] T. R. G. Green. Limited theories as a framework for human-computer interaction. In D. Ackermann and M. J. Tauber, editors, *Mental Models and Human-Computer Interaction*. North Holland, 1989.

[77] T. R. G. Green, F. Schiele, and S. J. Payne. Formalisable models of user knowledge in human-computer interaction. In G. C. van de Veer, T. R. G. Green, J. M. Hoc, and D. Murray, editors, *Working with Computers: Theory versus Outcome*, pages 3–46. Academic Press, 1988.

[78] J. G. Greeno. Conceptual entities. In D. Gentner and A. Stevens, editors, *Mental Models*. Erlbaum, 1983.

[79] S. P. Guest. The use of software tools for dialogue design. *International Journal of Man Machine Systems*, 16:237–262, 1982.

[80] J. V. Guttag and J. J. Horning. The algebraic specification of abstract data types. *Acta Informatica*, 10:27–52, 1978.

[81] J. V. Guttag and J. J. Horning. Formal specification as a design tool. In *Proceedings 7th Symp. Principles of Programming Lang.*, pages 251–261. ACM, 1980.

[82] D. Harel. Statecharts: A visual formalism for complex systems. *Science of Computer Programming*, 8:231–274, 1987.

[83] M. D. Harrison, C. R. Roast, and P. C. Wright. Complementary methods for the iterative design of interactive systems. In G. Salvendy and M.J. Smith, editors, *Designing and Using Human-Computer Interfaces and Knowledge Based Systems*, pages 651–658. Elsevier Scientific, 1989.

[84] M. D. Harrison and H. W. Thimbleby. Formalising guidelines for the design of interactive systems. In P. Johnson and S. Cook, editors, *People and Computers: Designing the Interface*, pages 161–171. Cambridge University Press, 1985.

[85] I. J. Hayes. Applying formal specification to software development in industry. *IEEE Trans. Software Engineering*, SE-11(2):169–178, 1985.

[86] S. Hekmatpour and M. Woodman. Formal specification of graphical notations and graphical software tools. Technical report, Open University, 1987.

[87] P. Henderson. Functional programming, formal specification and rapid prototyping. *IEEE Transactions on Software Engineering*, SE-12(2):241–250, 1986.

[88] P. Henderson and C. Minkowitz. Software design using executable formal specifications — a consideration of two approaches. Technical report, STC Technology Ltd., 1986.

[89] T. T. Hewett. The role of iterative evaluation in designing systems for usability. In M. D. Harrison and A. F. Monk, editors, *People and Computers: Designing for Usability*, pages 196–214. Cambridge University Press, 1986.

[90] R. D. Hill. Supporting concurrency, communication and synchronisation in human-computer interaction — the Sassafras UIMS. *ACM Transactions on Graphics*, 5(3):179–210, 1986.

[91] R. D. Hill. Event-response systems — a technique for specifying multi-threaded dialogues. In *Proceedings SIGCHI+GI '87: Human Factors in Computing Systems*, pages 241–248, Toronto, Canada, 1987.

[92] C. A. R. Hoare. Communicating sequential processes. *Communications of the ACM*, 21(8):666–677, 1978.

[93] C. A. R. Hoare. *Communicating Sequential Processes*. Prentice Hall International, 1985.

[94] T. Hoeber. Open look design goals. *Sun Technology*, pages 63–75, 1988.

[95] J. D. Hollan, E. L. Hutchins, and L. M. Weitzman. Steamer: An interactive inspectable simulation-based training system. *AI Magazine*, 5(2):15–28, 1984.

[96] S. Holmes. User manual for doubleview. Technical report, University of York, 1988.

[97] J. Honeywell. Publication systems at TODAY. In R. A. Earnshaw, editor, *Workstations and Publication Systems*, pages 65–72. Springer-Verlag, 1987.

[98] H. U. Hoppe. Task-oriented parsing: a diagnostic method to be used by adaptive systems. In *Proceedings CHI'88 Human Factors in Computing Systems*, pages 241–247, 1988.

[99] A. Howes and S. J. Payne. Display-based competence: towards user models for menu-driven interfaces. University of Lancaster.

[100] S. E. Hudson. UIMS support for direct manipulation interfaces. *ACM Computer Graphics*, 21(2):120–124, 1987.

[101] R. J. M. Hughes. Why functional programming matters. Technical Report PMG-40, Chalmers Institute, Goteborg, Sweden, 1984.

[102] E. L. Hutchins, J. D. Hollan, and D. A. Norman. Direct manipulation interfaces. *Human-Computer Interaction*, 1:331–338, 1985.

[103] R. Jackendoff. *Cognition and Semantics*. MIT Press, 1983.

[104] R. J. K. Jacob. Using formal specifications in the design of a human-computer interface. *Communications ACM*, 26(4):259–264, 1983.

[105] R. J. K. Jacob. A state transition diagram language for visual programming. *IEEE Computer*, 18(8):51–59, 1985.

[106] R. J. K. Jacob. Direct manipulation. In *Proceedings IEEE Conf. on Systems, Man and Cybernetics*, 1986.

[107] R. J. K. Jacob. A specification language for direct manipulation user interfaces. *ACM Transactions on Graphics*, 5(4):238–317, 1986.

[108] S. C. Johnson. Yacc: Yet another compiler-compiler. Technical report, Bell Laboratories, 1979.

[109] C. B. Jones. *Software Development, a Rigorous Approach*. Prentice Hall International, 1980.

[110] A. Kamran and M. B. Feldman. Graphics programming independent of interaction techniques and styles. *ACM Computer Graphics*, 17(1):58–66, 1983.

[111] D. Kapur and M. Srivas. Computability and implementability issues in abstract data types. *Science of Computer Programming*, 10(1):33–63, 1988.

[112] W. A. Kellogg. Conceptual consistency in the user interface: effects on performance. In H. J. Bullinger and B. Shackel, editors, *Human-Computer Interaction — INTERACT'87*, pages 389–394. North Holland, 1987.

[113] D. E. Kieras and P. G. Polson. An approach to the formal analysis of user complexity. *International Journal of Man-Machine Studies*, 22:365–394, 1985.

[114] J. Kirakowski and A. M. Corbett. Measuring user satisfaction. In D. M. Jones and R. Winder, editors, *People and Computers IV: Proceedings HCI'88*, pages 329–338. Cambridge University Press, 1988.

[115] J. Kirakowski and A. J. Good. Human-computer interaction — a framework for analysis. In H. J. Bullinger and B. Shackel, editors, *Human-Computer Interaction — INTERACT'87*, pages 535–540. North Holland, 1987.

[116] K. A. Lantz. On user interface reference models. In J. M. Carroll P. P. Tanner, editor, *Proc CHI+GI'87*, volume 18, pages 36–42, 1987.

[117] K. A. Lantz et al. Reference models, window systems, and concurrency. *ACM Computer Graphics*, 21(2):87–97, 1987.

[118] H. Lieberman. Designing interactive systems from the user's viewpoint. In P. Delgano and E. Sandewall, editors, *Integrated Interactive Computing Systems*, pages 45–59. North Holland, 1983.

[119] B. H. Liskov and V. Berzins. An appraisal of program specifications. In N. Gehani and A. D. McGettrick, editors, *Software Specification Techniques*, pages 3–23. Addison-Wesley, 1986.

[120] Inmos Ltd. *occam Programming Manual*. Prentice-Hall International, 1984.

[121] J. T. Mayes, S. W. Draper, A. M. McGregor, and K. Oatley. Information flow in a user interface: the effect of experience and context on the recall of MacWrite screens. In D. M. Jones and R. Winder, editors, *People and Computers IV: Proceedings HCI'88*, pages 275–290. Cambridge, 1988.

[122] D. L. Medin and M. M. Schaffer. A context theory of classification learning. *Psychological Review*, 85:207–238, 1978.

[123] L. G. L. T. Meertens, editor. *Program Specification and Transformation*. North-Holland, 1987.

[124] S. L. Meira. The Kent Recursive Calculator (KRC): Syntax and Semantics. Technical report, Computing Laboratory, University of Kent, 1984.

[125] R. Milner. Using algebra for concurrency: some approaches. In B. T. Denvir, W. T. Harwood, M. I. Jackson, and M. J. Wray, editors, *The Analysis of Concurrent Systems*, pages 7–25. Springer-Verlag LNCS 207, 1985.

[126] A. F. Monk. Mode errors: a user-centred analysis and some preventative measures using keying contingent sound. *International Journal of Man-Machine Studies*, 24:313–327, 1986.

[127] A. F. Monk, P. Walsh, and A. J. Dix. A comparison of hypertext, scrolling and folding. In D. M. Jones and R. Winder, editors, *Proceedings HCI'88*, pages 421–435, 1988.

[128] C. C. Morgan. *Programming from Specifications.* Prentice-Hall International, 1989.

[129] C. C. Morgan and B. A. Sufrin. Specification of the UNIX filing system. *IEEE Transactions on Software Engineering,* 10(2):128–142, 1984.

[130] B. Myers. Issues in window management design and implementation. In F. R. A. Hopgood, D. A. Duce, E. V. C. Fielding, K. Robinson, and A. S. Williams, editors, *Methodology of Window Management,* pages 59–69. Springer-Verlag, Berlin, 1986.

[131] B. A. Myers. Tools for creating user interfaces: An introduction and survey. Technical Report CMU-CS-88-107, CMU, 1988.

[132] B. A. Myers and W. Buxton. Creating highly-interactive and graphical user interfaces by demonstration. In *ACM Computer Graphics SIGGRAPH'86,* pages 249–258, 1986.

[133] P. Naur. Intuition in software development. In H. Ehrig, C. Floyd, M. Nivat, and J. Thatcher, editors, *Formal Methods and Software Development Vol. 2,* pages 60–79. Springer-Verlag LNCS 186, 1985.

[134] R. Neely. A protocol simulation tool. MSc. Thesis, 1983.

[135] A. Newell and S. Card. Prospects for psychological science in human computer interaction. *Human Computer Interaction,* 1:209–242, 1985.

[136] W. M. Newman. A system for interactive graphical programming. In *AFIPS Spring Joint Computer Conference,* pages 47–54, 1968.

[137] W. M. Newman and R. F. Sproull. *Principles of Interactive computer graphics.* McGraw-Hill, 1979.

[138] D. A. Norman. Categorization of action slips. *Psychological Review,* 88(1):1–15, 1981.

[139] D. A. Norman. Cognitive engineering. In *User-Centered System Design,* pages 31–62. Erlbaum, 1986.

[140] D. R. Olsen. Pushdown automata for user interface management. *ACM Trans. Graphics*, 3(3):177–203, 1984.

[141] D. R. Olsen. Mike: The Menu Interaction Kontrol Environment. *ACM Trans. Graphics*, 5(4):318–344, 1986.

[142] D. R. Olsen. Larger issues in user interface management. *ACM Computer Graphics*, 21:134–137, 1987.

[143] A. J. Palay et al. The Andrew toolkit — an overview. In *Proceedings USENIX Conference*, pages 9–21, 1988.

[144] J. Palme. A human-computer interface encouraging user growth. In M. E. Sime and M. J. Coombs, editors, *Designing for Human-Computer Communication*, pages 139–156. Academic Press, 1983.

[145] D. L. Parnas. On the use of transition diagrams in the design of a user interface for an interactive computer system. In *Proceedings 24th National ACM Conference*, pages 379–385, 1969.

[146] D. L. Parnas. On the criteria to be used in decomposing systems into modules. *Communications ACM*, 15(12):1053–1058, 1972.

[147] S. J. Payne. Task-action grammars. In B. Shackel, editor, *Human-Computer Interaction — INTERACT'84*, pages 527–532. North-Holland, 1985.

[148] S. J. Payne and T. R. G. Green. The user's perception of the interaction language: a two-level model. In *Proceedings CHI'83 Human Factors in Computer Systems*, pages 202–206, 1983.

[149] S. J. Payne and T. R. G. Green. Task-action grammars: a model of mental representation of task languages. *Human-Computer Interaction*, 2(2):93–133, 1986.

[150] S. J. Payne and T. R. G. Green. The structure of command languages: an experiment on task-action grammar. *International Journal of Man-Machine Studies*, 30:213–234, 1989.

[151] J. L. Peterson. *Petri Net Theory and the Modeling of Systems*. Prentice Hall, 1981.

[152] S. L. Peyton-Jones. *The implementation of functional programming languages*. Prentice Hall International, 1987.

[153] G. E. Pfaff, editor. *User Interface Management Systems*. Springer, 1985.

[154] P. G. Polson and D. E. Kieras. A quantitative model of the learning and performance of text editing knowledge. In *Proceedings CHI'85 Human Factors in Computing Systems*, pages 207–212, 1985.

[155] P. G. Polson, E. Muncher, and G. Engelbeck. A test of a common elements theory of transfer. In *Proceedings CHI'86 Human Factors in Computing Systems*, pages 78–83, 1986.

[156] R. Rao and S. Wallace. The X toolkit — the standard toolkit for X version 11. In *Proc USENIX Conference*, pages 117–129, 1987.

[157] P. Reisner. Formal grammar and human factors design of an interactive graphics system. *IEEE Transactions on Software Engineering*, SE-7(2):229–240, 1981.

[158] P. Reisner. Formal grammar as a tool for analysing ease of use: some fundamental concepts. In J. C. Thomas and M. L. Schneider, editors, *Human Factors in Computer Systems*, pages 53–78. Ablex, 1983.

[159] J. M Robert. An approach for verifying the consistency of user interfaces. In *Proceedings of the International Scientific Conference on Work with Display Units*, pages 516–521, 1986.

[160] J. M. Robert. A formal method for designing the interface of interactive systems. In *Proceedings 2nd IFAC/IFIP/IFORS/IEA Conference on Analysis, Design and Evaluation of Man-Machine Systems (Varese, Italy, Sept 10-12, 1985)*, pages 255–260. Pergamon, 1986.

[161] E. Rosch and C. B. Mervis. Family resemblance: studies in the internal structure of categories. *Cognitive Psychology*, 7:573–605, 1975.

[162] D. S. H. Rosenthal, J. C. Michener, G. Pfaff, R. Kessener, and M. Sabin. The detailed semantics of graphics input devices. *ACM Computer Graphics*, 16(3):33–38, 1982.

[163] M. B. Rosson. The role of experience in editing. In B. Shackel, editor, *Human-Computer Interaction — INTERACT'84*, pages 225–230. North-Holland, 1985.

[164] C. Runciman, M. Firth, and N. Jagger. Preserving interactive behaviour through transformation. Technical report, Department of Computer Science, University of York, 1988.

[165] C. Runciman and I. Toyn. Notes for Glide users (4th edition). Technical report, Department of Computer Science, University of York, 1989.

[166] R. W. Scheifler and J. Gettys. The X window system. *ACM Trans. Graphics*, 5(2):79–109, 1986.

[167] W. L. Scherlis and D. S. Scott. First steps towards inferential programming. In *Information Processing'83*, pages 199–212. North Holland, 1983.

[168] D. A. Schmidt. *Denotational semantics: A methodology for language development*. Allyn and Bacon, 1986.

[169] D. S. Scott. Data types as lattices. *SIAM Journal on Computing*, 5:522–587, 1976.

[170] M. L. Scott and S. K. Yap. A grammar-based approach to the automatic generation of user interface dialogues. In E. Solloway, D. Frye, and S. B. Sheppard, editors, *Proceedings CHI'88*, pages 73–78. Addison-Wesley, 1988.

[171] P. Sestoft and H. Sondergaard. A bibliography on partial evaluation. *ACM SIGPLAN Notices*, 23(2):19–27, 1988.

[172] A. C. Shaw. On the specification of graphics command languages and their processors. In R. A. Guedj et al., editors, *Methodology of Interaction*, pages 160–171. North-Holland, 1980.

[173] M. Shaw, E. Borison, M. Horowitz, T. Lane, D. Nichols, and R. Pausch. Descartes: A programming-language approach to interactive display interfaces. *ACM Sigplan Notices*, 18(6):100–111, 1983.

[174] B. Shneiderman. The future of interactive systems and the emergence of direct manipulation. *Behaviour and Information Technology*, 1(3):237–256, 1982.

[175] J. L. Sibert, W. D. Hurley, and T. W. Bleser. An object-oriented user interface management system. *ACM Computer Graphics*, 20(4):259–268, 1986.

[176] E. E. Smith and D. L. Medin. *Categories and Concepts*. Harvard University Press, 1981.

[177] R. B. Smith. The alternate reality kit—an animated environment for creating interactive simulations. In *Proceedings IEEE Workshop on Visual Languages*, pages 99–106, Dallas, Texas, 1986. IEEE.

[178] J. M. Spivey. *The Z Notation: A Reference Manual*. Prentice Hall International, 1988.

[179] J. M. Spivey. *Understanding Z., a Specification Language and its Semantics*. Cambridge University Press, 1989.

[180] B. Stroustrup. What is "Object-Oriented Programming"? In *Proceedings USENIX C++ Workshop*, pages 159–180, Santa Fe, NM, 1987.

[181] B. Sufrin. Formal specification of a display editor. *Science of Computer Programming*, 1:157–202, 1982.

[182] B. Sufrin. The Z Handbook. Technical report, Oxford University Programming Research Group, 1986.

[183] B. Sufrin. A formal framework for classifying interactive information systems. In *IEE Colloquium—Formal Methods and Human Computer Interaction*, 1987.

[184] W. Swartout and R. Balzer. The inevitable intertwining of specification and implementation. *Communications ACM*, 25(7):438–440, 1982.

[185] R. R. Swick and M. S. Ackerman. The X toolkit: More bricks for building user-interfaces or widgets for hire. In *Proceedings USENIX Conf.*, pages 221–228, 1988.

[186] P. Szekely. *Separating the User Interface from the Functionality of Application Programs*. PhD thesis, CMU, 1988.

[187] P. P. Tanner. Multi-thread input. *ACM Computer Graphics*, 21(2):142–145, 1987.

[188] P. P. Tanner, S. A. MacKay, D. A. Stewart, and M. Wein. A multitasking switchboard approach to user interface management. *ACM Computer Graphics*, 20(4):241–248, 1986.

[189] M. J. Tauber. On mental models and the user interface. In G. C. van de Veer, T. R. G. Green, J. M. Hoc, and D. Murray, editors, *Working with Computers: Theory versus Outcome*, pages 89–119. Academic Press, 1988.

[190] R. D. Tennent. *Principles of Programming Languages*. Prentice Hall International, 1981.

[191] P. S. Thiagarajan. Some aspects of net theory. In B. T. Denvir, W. T. Harwood, M. I. Jackson, and M. J. Wray, editors, *The Analysis of Concurrent Systems*, pages 26–54. Springer-Verlag LNCS 207, 1985.

[192] H. W. Thimbleby. Dialogue determination. *International Journal of Man Machine Systems*, 13:295–304, 1980.

[193] H. W. Thimbleby. Character level ambiguity: consequences for user interface design. *International Journal of Man-Machine Studies*, 16:211–225, 1982.

[194] H. W. Thimbleby. Generative user-engineering principles for user interface design. In B. Shackel, editor, *Human-Computer Interaction — INTERACT'84*, pages 661–666. North-Holland, 1985.

[195] H. W. Thimbleby. The design of two innovative user interfaces. In M. D. Harrison and A. F. Monk, editors, *People and Computers: Designing for usability*, pages 336–351. Cambridge University Press, 1986.

[196] H. W. Thimbleby. Ease of use—the ultimate deception. In M. D. Harrison and A. F. Monk, editors, *People and Computers: Designing for usability*, pages 78–94. Cambridge University Press, 1986.

[197] H. W. Thimbleby. Delaying commitment. Technical Report YCS 90, University of York, Computer Science Dept., 1987.

[198] J. J. Thomas and G. Hamlin. Graphical input interaction technique workshop summary. *ACM Computer Graphics*, 17(1):5–30, 1983.

[199] R. K. Took. Constructs for interface generation and management. In A. Williams, editor, *Proceedings Eurographics Workshop on Higher Level Tools for Window Managers*, Amsterdam, 1987. Springer-Verlag.

[200] R. K. Took. *Surface Interaction: A Formal Model for the Presentation Level of Applications and Documents*. PhD thesis, University of York, 1989. in preparation.

[201] D. A. Turner. A new implementation technique for applicative languages. *Software—Practice and Experience*, 9(1):31–49, 1979.

[202] D. A. Turner. The semantic elegance of applicative languages. In *ACM Conference on Functional Programming Languages and Computer Architecture*, pages 85–98, 1981.

[203] D. A. Turner. Functional programming and proofs of program correctness. In D. Neel, editor, *Tools and Notions for Program Construction*. Cambridge University Press, 1982.

[204] A. I. Wasserman. Extending state transition diagrams for the specification of human-computer interaction. *IEEE Transactions on Software Engineering*, SE-11(8):699–713, 1985.

[205] A. I. Wasserman, P. A. Pircher, and D. T. Shewmake. A RAPID/USE tutorial. Technical report, Medical Information Science, University of California, San Francisco, 1985. Release 1.3.

[206] L. K. Welbourn and R. J. Whitrow. A gesture based text editor. In D. M. Jones and R. Winder, editors, *People and Computers IV: Proceedings HCI'88*, pages 363–371. Cambridge University Press, 1988.

[207] K. Whiteley, M. J. Birch, and A. Parker. A Mascot 3 paintbox for Aspect. In *Proceedings Software Engineering 88*, Liverpool, 1988.

[208] M. D. Wilson, P. J. Barnard, T. R. G. Green, and A. Maclean. Knowledge-based task analysis for human-computer systems. In G. C. van de Veer, T. R. G. Green, J. M. Hoc, and D. Murray, editors, *Working with Computers: Theory versus Outcome*, pages 47–87. Academic Press, 1988.

[209] T. Winograd. *Language as a Cognitive Process. Volume 1: Syntax.* Addison-Wesley, 1983.

[210] W. A. Woods. Transition network grammars for natural language analysis. *Communications ACM*, 13(10), 1970.

[211] M. Young, R. N. Taylor, D. B. Troup, and C. D. Kelly. Design principles behind Chiron: A UIMS for software environments. *Proceedings 10th Intl. Conf. Software Engineering*, pages 367–376, 1988.

[212] R .M. Young, T. R. G. Green, and T. Simon. Programmable user models for predictive evaluation of interface designs. In *Proceedings CHI'89 Conference on Computer-Human Interaction*, pages 15–19, 1989.

[213] R. M. Young and T. Simon. Planning in the context of human-computer interaction. In D. Diaper and R. Winder, editors, *People and Computers III — Proceedings HCI'87*, pages 363–370. Cambridge University Press, 1987.

[214] M. D. Zisman. *Representation, Specification and Automation of Office Procedures.* PhD thesis, University of Pennsylvania, 1977.

INDEX

Z